I0168644

Modern-Day Pentecostalism

Curtis Carr and Max Dawson

ONE STONE
BIBLICAL RESOURCES

© 2024 One Stone Press — All rights reserved.

All rights reserved. No part of this book may be reproduced in any form without written permission of the publisher.

Published by:
One Stone Press
979 Lovers Lane
Bowling Green, KY 42103

Printed in the United States of America

ISBN 13: 978-1-941422-93-9

Cover design and interior design by Hinds Design (hindsdesign.com)

ONE STONE
BIBLICAL RESOURCES

This book is dedicated to those faithful saints who love the word of God and whose passion is to teach others the gospel of Christ. To those hard-working soldiers of the Lord who do battle in the trenches, we encourage you to keep up the fight of faith, to stand up for Jesus and for His truth against all the enemies of His word. May you have success in rescuing lost souls from error. And may you give great glory to God as you do so.

Contents

List of Figures

Preface

When we first discussed the idea of writing this book in the early part of 2023, we both agreed that this very important topic is one that is not widely understood by most Bible students or by people in general. And, unfortunately, it is a topic that few are qualified to write on. We felt uniquely qualified due to the large number of cases over the years where we visited Pentecostal services and so-called healing revivals. We both spent many hours visiting not only with members of the various kinds of Pentecostal churches, but in some cases even with their pastors and preachers, some even claiming to be Apostles and Prophets. Many of those visits involved lengthy Bible studies where we delved into why the Pentecostal people believe the way that they do. An important part of our exchanges with them was to ask, what Bible passages do they appeal to in defending their beliefs and practices? We believe that our extensive interaction with them qualifies us to speak on the topic at hand.

In addition to those studies that were generated by visiting numerous churches, it is important that we also talk about our radio work that was a key factor in making contact with Pentecostals and setting up studies with them. In 1978, I (Max) began my work with the Pinecrest Church of Christ in Beaumont, Texas as an evangelist. One of my primary tasks was to host a radio program with a call-in format. I began the radio work in the fall of 1978 with a Sunday evening broadcast. I, along with the Evangelist Larry Dickens, hosted that call-in program for six months. In 1979, our program moved to another station where I was on the air for two days every week, Thursdays and Fridays. The hour-long broadcast, entitled "Prove All Things," stirred up a lot of interest. After one year, the station manager wanted us to do a daily call-in broadcast, Monday through Friday. The church accepted the offer. That broadcast, entitled "Searching the Scriptures" aired on station KDVE from 1980–1987. It averaged ten calls per day in a one-hour format. In 1983, according to the Arbitron rating services, the broadcast had an audience of as many as 10,000 listeners per day, which was considered to be a large number at that time.

But the broadcast came to an end in 1987. The station manager came to us and told us that KDVE could no longer continue as a gospel station. It was starving for money. The Jim Bakker and Jimmy Swaggart scandals had cast a pall over gospel radio and TV. Nearly all of the programming on our station depended on the donations of listeners. The donations to the programs had dried up. Listeners did not know who to trust. They stopped sending money to the radio preachers. It is important to note that our broadcast did not depend on listener donations, as it was solely supported by the Pinecrest Church of Christ. The station manager told us that nearly every account on the station was six months behind in paying their bills. Our account was the only one that was current. So, the station manager said that he was changing the station from gospel radio to an easy listening format.

While our congregation later purchased time on other stations, religious radio was changing. And media itself was changing. In 1980, when we began our five-day a week broadcast format, we were the only talk show of any kind heard regularly in Southeast Texas. Cable TV had only nine channels, and the only talk show on TV was Donahue. Today, AM radio is nearly all talk, and on cable TV, there is every kind of talk show imaginable. Religious radio today is nearly all nationally syndicated. The opportunity that was afforded to us in the 1980s was unique and our program was very successful. We had a steady stream of callers, set up lots of Bible studies, and converted a substantial number of souls. We thank God for that.

Our broadcast was controversial, to be sure. But it never sought controversy just for the sake of controversy. The broadcast opened every day with about ten minutes of plain Bible teaching, often from the book of Acts, or from one of the gospels. Most of the controversy came from people who opposed the straightforward Bible teaching that was presented. Baptists, Pentecostals, Catholics, and even atheists were regular listeners and callers. It was the Pentecostals who stirred up much of the controversy through those years. Whether the topic was miraculous spiritual gifts, the baptism of the Holy Spirit, or speaking in tongues, there were people who wanted to know what the Bible actually taught on those topics—rather than them just taking some preacher's word on the topic. Much of what we learned about Pentecostals came from interacting with them and their preachers on the radio.

As noted earlier, we also learned a lot about Pentecostalism from attending their revival services. Pentecostal churches used to do a lot of newspaper advertising. We would see a church advertising a "miracle healing revival" in our area and we would attend it. It was that simple. In some of those services we would bring someone with us who had a readily visible ailment to let the "healer" attempt a healing. We were always courteous in our conduct when we attended those services. The radio broadcast also prompted a number of visits to those churches. People would call in to the program and tell us about their services, promising us that if we came, we would see real miracles. They invited us. We attended. We saw a lot of things, but never any miracles, not even one time. As noted earlier, we were always courteous in our conduct and treated our hosts with respect. We always tried to avoid being disruptive, yet our very presence and our asking questions often stirred up the anger of their preachers. On a few occasions, the preachers wanted us to leave and did not want us talking to their people.

By contrast, a few of the Pentecostal preachers were willing to engage in public discussions. Max did participate in several debates with Pentecostal preachers, though public religious debates have fallen out of favor with a lot of people today. In fact, they were falling out of favor even in the mid-1980s when a debate with Pentecostal preacher, Billy Stanley was held. After we held two or three debates with Pentecostals during that time, they were unwilling to hold any more. They were clearly losing the debates. One of their preachers said to me, "Debates aren't very popular among our people right now." And he knew why they were not popular. Among some people in churches of Christ there is sometimes also seen distaste for public discussion. The reason is related to a belief that controversy hurts the Lord's cause. That is something we disagree with. Controversy causes people to look at the issues. It can open eyes and open hearts.

In the midst of controversy, we were able to set up Bible studies with some of the people we met at the Pentecostal meetings and debates. Many of those Bible studies led to their abandoning of false doctrines and to laying hold of the truth. Some of the studies conducted by Max and Curtis were done together, but mostly they were done independent of each other, though with members of the same groups.

Much of what you will find in this book are simple examinations of the various topics related to the Pentecostal and charismatic teachings. We have done our best to honestly examine those teachings in the light of the scriptures. You will also find a variety of stories in this book about some of our experiences we have had with the people who claim to have miraculous spiritual gifts today.

We have spent a lot of time "in the trenches." By that, we mean we have spent a lot of time and energy interacting with people from a variety of different kinds of Pentecostal churches. One of the reasons so many people (even preachers) today do not know how to answer Pentecostalism is that they don't even know what the Pentecostal arguments are. That leaves them open to deception and vulnerable to the false doctrines that Pentecostals teach. Gospel preachers need to engage with those who profess to have miraculous spiritual gifts. Get in the trenches! Sit down with them. Open your Bible and study with them. If you have the truth, you have nothing to fear.

You do not need to be intimidated by claims of the Pentecostals. And, if you are a preacher, the people in your congregation do not need to be intimidated—but you need to prepare them to stand against the false claims that are made by Pentecostal people. The most common claim is, "We have the Holy Ghost, and you do not!" Someone may ask one of your members, "Do you have the Holy Ghost, with the evidence of speaking in tongues?" (By the way, they like to say, "Holy Ghost"

[KJV] instead of "Holy Spirit." The word "Ghost" provides a mystical element to their faith, which is something they like.)

In any case, what will you do when someone challenges you with respect to the Holy Spirit? By knowing their doctrines and knowing the scriptures, you can answer their claims and challenges. But you need to be prepared, as Peter said in 1 Peter 3:15:

> But sanctify the Lord God in your hearts, and always be ready to give a defense to everyone who asks you a reason for the hope that is in you, with meekness and fear.

We need to be ready to answer and to defend God's truth. It is hoped that after examining this book and carefully pondering the Bible truths presented, the reader will come to a fuller understanding of the subjects contained under the heading of "Pentecostalism" and will be better equipped to study with anyone affiliated with one of those groups.

—*Curtis Carr and Max Dawson*

1

Introduction

One of the fastest growing religious movements in America and in the world today is Pentecostalism. Pentecostalism goes by a variety of names and is found in a number of different sects. Some elements of it call themselves the "Full Gospel Movement" or the "Charismatic Movement." And some just call themselves "Pentecostals." Whatever it may be called, it has affected nearly every denomination and non-denominational group in some respect, many of whom are losing a large number of their members to that movement. There are many factions within this large grouping of churches, each teaching variations of the same basic doctrines. Some of these groups do not refer to themselves as "Pentecostals," as they try to differentiate themselves from the other groups who use that name. However, this seems to be among the relatively newer groups to the movement.

This movement borrows its name from Acts chapter two, where the events that took place on the day of Pentecost are recorded. (By the way, Pentecost was the name of a Jewish feast day that took place fifty days after the Passover. It was also known as the Feast of Weeks. See Leviticus 23:15-19.) The claim is made that the miraculous events of that day in Acts chapter two are replicated in Pentecostal churches today. The people who were present on that day in Acts chapter two witnessed a miraculous outpouring of the Holy Spirit. The twelve apostles who received this outpouring were "overwhelmed" or "immersed" in the power of the Holy Spirit; this is referred to as the "baptism of the Holy Spirit." They spoke "in tongues," which meant they were miraculously empowered to speak in foreign languages that they had never learned. Immediately following that day, other miraculous events took place, such as the healing of the sick, prophesying, and raising the dead. Since such events began on the day of Pentecost, the term Pentecostal simply refers to those churches today that claim to have those same miraculous manifestations of the Holy Spirit that took place in Acts chapter two. The largest of these groups is the Assembly of God Church. Other smaller groups include the United Pentecostal Church, the Apostolic Church, the Gospel Assembly Church and the Church of God in Christ. There are also some non-traditional groups such as the Mormons which are not usually grouped in with Pentecostals but who claim to also have the same miraculous spiritual gifts in their church.

An important point to note, is that virtually all of the various groups that fall under the heading of Pentecostalism have doctrinal disagreements among themselves. As an example, some teach that everybody who is saved must speak in tongues as a sign of salvation. But others teach that not everyone who is saved will speak in tongues, but only some. So, we know that they cannot both be right; and it is possible that they are both wrong. Some of these churches teach that the Father, Son, and Holy Spirit are one person, while other churches teach that they are three separate and distinct persons. Who is right? If you were to ask a preacher in one of these churches, he or she will tell you that they know that they are right because God is working miracles in their church as confirmation of their doctrine. And yet, there may be a different type of Pentecostal church right across the street that teaches an opposing view; that church makes the exact same claim that they know they are correct because God is working miracles in their church as confirmation of their doctrine. As outsiders, listening to both groups, we know that God is not using miracles to confirm conflicting doctrines in different churches. So, it is up to us to try to figure out what exactly is going on in these churches by examining their claims to miraculous powers. Ultimately, we want to study the Bible with them in order that we might all come to a common understanding of God's will. To that end, this book has been written. The authors have produced this work to help Christians understand what various Pentecostals believe and how to study with them.

What follows in this book will be a careful examination of the basic doctrines set forth by these groups. This is important because most Bible students today, regardless of the religious group that they are affiliated with, seem to have a very limited understanding of Pentecostal doctrines. This applies even to Pastors and Preachers. And, as a result they are unable to scripturally answer questions related to Pentecostalism.

So, how did the modern-day Pentecostal movement get started? Contrary to what some churches are teaching today, the movement did not begin on the day of Pentecost. Some would have you believe that it had its beginning in the first century, when in fact their own literature says differently. Several of the Pentecostal groups give the date of 1901 for the movement's beginning. See the following:

> During the last 21 days of the 19th century, a band of earnest, hungry-hearted ministers and Christian workers in Bethel Bible College, Topeka, Kansas, called a fast, praying earnestly for a great outpouring of the Holy Spirit, which, to their joyful surprise, came upon them in the early hours of the morning on January 1, 1901. The people were heard speaking in other languages as the Holy Spirit gave them utterance, just as it had happened on the day of Pentecost in the year A.D. 30. A great revival immediately broke forth, which soon reached the State of Texas, and thence to Los Angeles, where in the year 1906 it centered in an old building on Azusa Street… (*United Pentecostal Church International*, Manual, 1995, Foreword).

Though some Pentecostal groups give the date of 1901, most historians simply point to 1906 and the Azusa Street Revival. That series was led by an African American preacher, William Seymour. In the Student's Handbook of Facts In Church History, by S.C. McClain, published in 1948, we learn some very interesting details. McClain was an Instructor of Church History at the Pentecostal Bible Institute.

Here, at 1901, the beginning to the twentieth century, history seems in a general way to become silent…why so great a movement as *the Pentecostal movement* with its many branches and millions of members are not mentioned in history. Then we noticed that a new epoch had come; another church period had begun. *It is Pentecost again with all the fruits and gifts being restored in the church* (page 8).

In the great revival outpouring of the Holy Spirit in Los Angeles in 1906, which continued for many months, morning, afternoon and evening services, there were many mighty signs and wonders and miraculous healings. From this great revival ministers and saints returned to their homes telling the glad news of God's great visitation, and the fire spread, causing whole congregations to seek God and to be filled with the Holy Ghost witnessed by speaking in other tongues; also wonderful healings of all kinds of diseases were experienced. Many of these revivals went out as evangelists *with the same results that were seen in the mighty outpouring of the Holy Ghost in Acts 2:4–17* (page 56).

It was during this "revival" period that many claimed to have received the gift of speaking in tongues and other such miracles that had not been taking place in churches since the first century. This new movement grew from there to the far reaches of the United States and then to other countries.

Today, in our society, it is common to meet people from many different denominations who are Pentecostal in their beliefs. It is also common to get invited to visit some of their church services. Over the years we (Max and Curtis) have visited many, many revivals and healing services in Texas. And very often, those visits resulted in further studies with some of the members and leaders of those churches. Those studies sometimes included the Pastor, the Minister or even a man or woman who claimed to be a Prophet or Prophetess. It was often the case that one of the churches would sponsor a nationally known speaker to come to the area and hold a meeting for their group. Many times, it would be billed as a "Holy Ghost Miracle Healing Service" and the general public would be invited to bring the sick to be healed. We would often bring one of our friends who had some injury or illness to those services and let the faith healer attempt a healing on them.

In some of those services we actually videotaped and documented what was happening. What we saw was a failure on their part 100 % of the time. Not even once was something done that could even be said was a "partial" healing.

Today, one of the things that many people want to know is whether any real miracles are actually happening in those services or not. By "real miracles," we mean cases like we read about in the New Testament. We have all seen video clips of such healing services on TV and on-line. In most of those healing revivals, they will begin with the healer talking about all of the past revivals that he has conducted and the many miracles he has done. In many of these services, the preacher will claim to have received information about people in the audience through the gift of discernment. (The gift of discerning of spirits is mentioned in 1 Corinthians 12:10 and is seen in actual practice in Acts 5:1–11.) He will next bring those people to the stage and give details about their lives and ailments that he seemingly could not know. He may also bring audience members to the stage to testify that they have been healed of some malady. Yet, in most of those testimonies there will not be anything visible to see for verification and so we, the observers, must take their word for it that a miracle has taken place. But is it real? That is what most want to know. What follows in this book will be descriptions of some of what we saw in those many services. We will explain what we have learned in those follow-up discussions and studies. And we will tell you about the conclusions we have drawn as a result of those years of extensive and intensive experiences in Pentecostal churches. In this book we will present the Bible passages that Pentecostals use to defend their doctrinal positions and support their claims to miraculous powers. It is worthy to note something ironic about how Pentecostals attempt to use the Bible to support their claims: In the first century, the apostles used miracles to support and confirm their gospel message; yet today, Pentecostals do the opposite and try to use the gospel message to support and confirm that they have miracles. If they actually have miraculous powers, they would not need to try to prove it by the Bible or find evidence for it in the scriptures. Rather, the miracles themselves would stand as self-evidence.

Throughout this book we will present various facts of history and points of doctrine of the Pentecostal movement. We will also share with you many of the personal encounters we have had with faith healers. Our only request is that you, the reader, keep an open mind as you go through the various sections of this book. We ask that you refrain from forming any opinions, pro or con, until you have read and evaluated the material in its entirety. Each chapter will build on the chapter before it. In this book you will be able to do comparisons of what is being claimed by modern-day Pentecostals and the Bible itself. You will then have not just an opinion, but an informed understanding of this very important and critical topic.

John 8:32

And you shall know **the truth,** and **the truth** shall make you free.

2

Miracles in the Bible

In order to understand what miracles are, we need to go to the Bible for our information. Let's begin with a statement from the Apostle Peter in Acts 2:22:

> "Men of Israel, hear these words: Jesus of Nazareth, a Man attested by God to you by **miracles**, **wonders**, and **signs** which God did through Him in your midst, as you yourselves also know..."

In this text, Peter makes the bold claim that Jesus worked miracles. What did Peter mean by this? Did he just mean Jesus did unusual things that were difficult to explain? Was it just surprising things? Peter has something more significant in mind.

He calls upon the miracles of Jesus as testimony that Jesus has been sent by God. That makes it doubly important that we understand miracles. What is a miracle? The topic of miracles is one that people are not only curious about, but one that is central to religion. Yet, most people are confused about miracles—even religious people are perplexed. Did Jesus really work miracles? How do we even define miracles? What are their characteristics? Why did God even work miracles at all? Do miracles continue today? We will understand nothing of miracles if we do not first understand what they are. Let's begin our study of miracles in the Bible by seeing what they are not!

WHAT A MIRACLE IS NOT

A miracle is not just a remarkable thing. The way the word "miracle" is used in the New Testament is not the same as how many use it today. People today use this word in a way that is much looser and in an outright different manner than in the Bible. Anything that is unusual or "beats the odds" is quickly labeled as a miracle. A baseball player who hits a spectacular home run that wins the World Series is called a "miracle." The case of a person who has a terrible car wreck but survives with no injuries is labeled as a "miraculous" event. A person who receives cancer treatment and recovers is said to have had a "miracle." There are many remarkable and unusual things that take place in our world that are not miracles. Yet, most people fail to understand that. A child being born is amazing and remarkable, but childbirth is not a miracle. The birth of a child is accomplished by the natural laws of God. According to Genesis chapter one, all new life—plant and animal—comes through God's laws of reproduction. To call remarkable things "miracles," does a disservice to the real miracles.

A miracle is not just a chance occurrence. Ecclesiastes 9:11 teaches that "time and chance" happen to all men. It is the nature of our world that chance occurrences take place. Sometimes chance occurrence works for our good; sometimes it does not. Sometimes it has no significant impact at all. If a man hits the lottery (a game of chance), he calls it a "miracle." But where is the miracle? Someone had to win it. To call chance "a miracle" tends to cheapen real miracles and creates confusion.

A miracle is not merely something that surprises us. Sometimes it is funny the way we use "miracle." Someone says, "I got a call from the IRS. They called to apologize for collecting too much tax from me. Is that a miracle, or what?" We hope we all understand that things that merely surprise aren't "miracles."

A miracle is not the intervention of God through providence. The Bible teaches that God governs nations; He directs events on earth (Daniel 2:20-21). The Old Testament is a record of how God controlled kings and nations. But it was rare when God used miracles to accomplish his purposes. One such miracle, however, is where 185,000 Assyrian soldiers died at the hand of an angel (2 Kings 19:35). But God also defeated the Egyptian-Assyrian alliance by the hand of Nebuchadnezzar (2 Kings 23:29; Jeremiah 46:2; Daniel 5:26). God did it, but there was no miracle in this case.

God provides our sustenance—that is, the things we need to live—our food, water, and the air we breathe. God even provides through natural means—the sun and rain (Matthew 5:45; 6:11). God accomplishes this through His natural laws. But Jesus also fed 5,000 by miraculously multiplying five loaves and two fish (John 6:1-14). The food and water we consume daily is from God, but no miracle is involved.

God often delivers His people out of trouble. In one case, with the Apostle Paul, God delivered him from a shipwreck without a miracle (Acts 27:22-25). When you read the entire chapter, you see a terrible storm, a violent shipwreck—and all the men escaped safely. God caused it without a miracle. But, in the case found in Matthew 8:25-26, Jesus saved His disciples from being shipwrecked by the use of a miracle. The problem many of us have is a failure to understand how God works. Many of us mistakenly believe that if God acts at all, that makes the event a miracle. To call God's providence "miraculous" leads to uncertainty about what miracles are.

WHAT MIRACLES ARE

In the Bible, a miracle was when God set aside natural laws to cause an event to occur; therefore, it went contrary to the laws of nature. When the laws of nature are suspended, we refer to it as "supernatural," meaning that it was above or outside of natural law. When such an event occurs, we are forced to conclude that God was responsible for the event taking place. Why? Because it was impossible for such an event to have happened naturally or by ordinary means.

When we hear an atheist say that "the Bible is not true because it contains stories of miracles, and miracles are impossible, we answer, "Yes, they are." They are impossible by natural means. There can be no other explanation for them. That's why they are called supernatural events. What is impossible for man is possible for God. The miracle then points to God as the source.

Notice the following examples in the Bible:

Exodus 7:9

"When Pharaoh speaks to you, saying, '**Show** a miracle for yourselves,' then you shall say to Aaron, 'Take your rod and cast it before Pharaoh, and let it become a serpent' " (Exodus 7:9).

John 6:11–14 (KJV)

And Jesus took the loaves; and when he had given thanks, he distributed to the disciples, and the disciples to them that were set down; and likewise of the fishes as much as they would. When they were filled, he said unto his disciples, Gather up the fragments that remain, that nothing be lost. Therefore they gathered them together, and filled twelve baskets with the fragments of the five barley loaves, which remained over and above unto them that had eaten. Then those men, **when they had seen** the miracle **that Jesus did**, said, This is of a truth that prophet that should come into the world.

In these Old and New Testament passages, the word "miracle" is used to convey that a special event had God behind it. Notice some of these additional Bible examples of miracles:

Old Testament:

- Destruction of Jericho (Joshua 5:10–6:26)

- The sun standing still (Joshua 10:13)

- Parting of the Red Sea (Exodus 14:15)

New Testament:

- Water turned to wine (John 2)

- Feeding the multitude with five loaves and two fishes (John 6:9–10)

- Jesus walking on water (John 6:19)

- Raising the dead (Acts 9:36–41)

In all the events listed above, the laws of nature were not only suspended but the events themselves were contrary to the natural order of things. What was otherwise impossible, did in fact actually happen. We would look at any of those and say they could not happen. We would conclude that these things were impossible. But God is able to do what man cannot do.

Mark 10:27

But Jesus looked at them and said, "With men it is impossible, but not with God; for **with God all things are possible**."

So, by definition, that which is impossible by nature cannot happen unless God intervenes. It is then no longer natural but *super*natural. Biblically, a miracle is always a supernatural event. It can be nothing else. That's why we must be very careful in our use of the word "miracle." In addition, when a miracle took place in the Bible, it was described in several important ways. First, it was always complete and not partial like modern-day Pentecostals claim. Second, its effect was immediate and not weeks, months or years later as modern-day Pentecostals claim. If you were to take the time to go through the New Testament and list every miracle recorded, you can put them into several groups.

As we went through the New Testament, we counted thirty-six times that miracles of Jesus were mentioned. There were sixteen accounts of the miracles of the disciples mentioned. And there were seven accounts of large numbers of people being healed at the same time. Some of those miracles of Jesus were duplicate accounts of the same events in the four Gospels.

Group 1 — The miracles of Jesus (36 accounts)
Example: Matthew 8:2–3

And behold, a leper came and worshiped Him, saying, "Lord, if You are willing, You can make me clean." Then Jesus put out His hand and touched him, saying, "I am willing; be cleansed." **Immediately** his leprosy was **cleansed.**

Group 2 — The miracles of the disciples (16 accounts)
Example: Acts 9:32–34

Now it came to pass, as Peter went through all parts of the country, that he also came down to the saints who dwelt in Lydda. There he found a certain man named Aeneas, who had been bedridden eight years and was paralyzed. And Peter said to him, "Aeneas, Jesus the Christ heals you. Arise and make your bed." Then **he arose immediately.**

Group 3 — Cases where large numbers of people were healed (7 accounts)
Example: Acts 5:16

Also a multitude gathered from the surrounding cities to Jerusalem, bringing sick people and those who were tormented by unclean spirits, and they were **all healed.**

Many other miracles could be added to these brief examples. Think about the case where Jesus walked on water (John 6:19). That was a supernatural act; it was above natural law; it was even contrary to natural law. The laws of nature say that a man will sink if he tries to walk on water. Even little children know that. Think of the case where Jesus miraculously turned water to wine (John 2:7-9). No amount of pouring will ever turn water to wine by natural means. This was supernatural. It was contrary to natural law. These few examples should suffice to show us that Jesus caused supernatural acts to take place. A miracle is a supernatural act; the intervention of God in a way that is above natural law; a miracle transcends and is contrary to natural law.

Results of Bible Miracles
When we look at the details of those miracles, how were the results described? Was it a complete miracle or was it a partial one? With

regards to those miracles, in all those cases, the results of the healings were described using words such as "completely," "made whole" or "healed all." So, when Jesus or the disciples healed someone, it was not a partial healing like some claim today where they are told to keep going to the doctor and to keep taking their medicine. Instead, it was a complete healing, every time.

Time Factor of Bible Miracles

When looking at the details of those miracles, how was the time factor described for how long it took for those healings to take place? With regards to those miracles, the time factor was described using words such as "immediately," "the same hour," "that hour," "that very hour" and "straight way." So, when Jesus or the disciples healed someone, there was no delay before the healing took place like some claim today. Instead, their healing took place immediately.

And so, the way the word "miracle" is generally used today is vastly different from how it is used in the Bible. As a result, before anyone can do an evaluation of the claimed miracles in modern-day Pentecostalism, one needs to closely examine those miracles discussed in the Old and New Testaments and then do a comparison with today. Let's do a summary of what we have just seen in this chapter (**Figure 1**).

Comparison of Bible Miracles and "Modern-Day" Miracles

Bible Miracles	Modern-day Pentecostalism
1. Events contrary to the laws of nature	1. Nothing like that documented
2. Healings were complete	2. Claimed healings not complete
3. Healings done immediately	3. Claimed healings delayed
4. Large groups healed together	4. Large groups never healed
5. Miracles admitted by enemies	5. Claimed miracles denied by enemies
6. Miracles confirmed the word	6. Claimed miracles questioned

Figure 1.

After having visited numerous modern-day Pentecostal services and many that were advertised as a "healing service," we can confidently and accurately report that we never, even a single time, saw anything remotely similar to what we read about in the Bible. We challenge every reader to visit some of those services in your area and do your own evaluation. You will see nothing any different than what we have seen and you will have the same conclusions.

A Variety of Terms Used to Describe Miracles

There is one more thing that we want to include in this chapter. The New Testament uses a variety of words to describe supernatural events. These words are sometimes used interchangeably. Sometimes they are used in the same context to denote different elements or effects of supernatural events. Here are three words that are used numerous times to describe the mighty powers of God. We have listed the English words along with the anglicized Greek words used in the texts. The following words are all three found in Acts 2:

> **22** Men of Israel, hear these words: Jesus of Nazareth, a Man attested by God to you by **miracles, wonders**, and **signs** which God did through Him in your midst, as you yourselves also know...

- **Miracle** (δύναμις, *dunamis*). The word means power or mighty works. It refers to the power required to produce the work. God is the source of the power. See John 14:11 for more on this.

- **Wonder** (τέρας, *teras*). The word indicates a sensational event. It refers to the effect produced upon those who saw the miracles, causing them to marvel, be astonished or amazed. See Matthew 8:26–27.

- **Sign** (σημεῖον, *sēmeion*). The word means an indication or token. It refers to the significance of the miracle. A sign means God has acted! See John 3:2.

These terms, each having distinct meaning, cannot be separated from one another. They go together. Though emphasis may be on one element over the other two, one single act can serve as a miracle, wonder and sign. An example is found in Mark 2:1–12. It was a miracle, in that supernatural power had come from God; it was a wonder, in that it caused men to be amazed; it was a sign, in that men came to understand who Jesus was.

In the New Testament, miracles, wonders and signs are supernatural events, by which God authenticated those men who were sent by Him, and by which men proved that what they were speaking was from God. See Hebrews 2:

> ³ how shall we escape if we neglect so great a salvation, which at the first began to be spoken by the Lord, and **was confirmed** to us by those who heard Him, ⁴ God also bearing witness both **with signs and wonders, with various miracles, and gifts** of the Holy Spirit, according to His own will?

What modern-day Pentecostals claim as miracles are nothing like those supernatural events that are recorded in the word of God. While Pentecostals may make claims to have supernatural power, they cannot produce any miracles, signs, or wonders.

We challenge the reader to objectively investigate these things for himself. We believe you will come to the same conclusions that your authors have. Carefully study the scriptures, and then compare what you see in Pentecostal-Charismatic churches with what you find in the Bible. When you see that they cannot produce any miracles, then your mission is to study with them. Help them to see their error. Help them to learn the truth of the gospel. Our mission is not to merely point out where they are wrong; it is to point them to the gospel truth in order that they might be saved.

3

The Providence of God

If you were to visit one of the modern-day Pentecostal churches today, you will very likely hear a sermon on why they believe that there are miracles today. But what you will not hear is a sermon on the Providence of God, or how God sometimes works in a non-miraculous way and within the laws of nature. Why not? It may be because they don't really believe or understand the providence of God. They tend to think that if God acts at all, then it must be a miracle. Let's explore the idea of the Providence of God further.

> **Question:** Do you really believe it is going to help when you pray? When you pray, do you really believe that God is going to answer your prayer? But, do you believe that God can only answer through a miracle? And if God does not answer through a miracle, does this mean that He is doing nothing at all?

James 1:6

Ask in faith, nothing wavering.

This presents a dilemma for those who believe that the Bible teaches that God is not working through miracles today and that those miracles ended at the end of the first century. If that be the case, if the age of miracles has passed, then how is God working and how is He going to answer our prayer if not through a miracle?

DEFINITIONS

Let's do a short review. As we saw in a previous chapter, people today seem to use the word "miracle" in a much looser and different manner than in the Bible. Anything that "beats the odds" is quickly labeled as a miracle. If a baseball player hits a home run that wins the World Series, it will be called "the miracle hit." If there is a car wreck where everyone is killed but one person, the news media will say that it was a miracle that the person lived. If a person diagnosed with cancer is given under a year to live, but then after having chemotherapy they recover, it is called a miracle. This kind of thinking is found throughout popular culture. When the U.S. Olympic team beat the Russians in 1980, the announcer, Al Michaels, exclaimed, "Do you believe in miracles?" It was called, "The Miracle on Ice." When Captain "Sully" Sullenberger successfully ditched U.S. Airways Flight 1549 on the Hudson River in 2009, it was called the "Miracle on the Hudson." While we can be grateful that all passengers survived with no serious injuries, Sullenberger exactly followed ditching protocols (as he had been trained). A miracle involves a supernatural act, a suspending of the laws of nature. There were no supernatural interventions in that case. Sometimes, our culture speaks of the "miracle of childbirth." Childbirth is anything but a supernatural event. It is the most natural thing that ever happens on our planet. Childbirth takes place according to God's natural laws of reproduction. So, let's be careful about how we use the word "miracle." Now, let's find out what the Bible calls a miracle and stick to that definition.

In the Bible, a miracle is when God sets aside natural laws to cause an event to occur, therefore it goes contrary to the laws of nature. When the laws of nature are suspended, we refer to it as "supernatural." We would then be forced to conclude that God was responsible for the event taking place since it was impossible for it to have happened naturally or in nature. Here are some examples of miracles in the Bible.

Old Testament:

- The sun standing still (Joshua 10)

- Destruction of Jericho (Joshua 5:10–6:26)

- Parting of the Red Sea (Exodus 14:15)

New Testament:

- Water turned to wine (John 2)

- Jesus walks on water (John 6:19)

- Feeding the multitude with five loaves and two fishes (John 6:9–10)

- Raising the dead (Acts 9:36–41)

In all of the events listed above, the laws of nature were suspended and the actions that took place were outside of natural law. What was otherwise impossible actually happened. We would look at any of those and say they could not happen. That it was impossible. But, when looking at such cases, we need to remember the power of God. He is able to do what otherwise could not be done. He is not limited by the laws of nature that He put into force.

Matthew 19:26

But Jesus looked at them and said to them, "With men this is impossible, but with God all things are possible."

Mark 10:27

But Jesus looked at them and said, "With men it is impossible, but not with God; for with God all things are possible."

Luke 1:37

For with God nothing will be impossible.

The text above in Luke 1:37 is about the angel Gabriel speaking to Mary about how she will have a child without the aid of a man. Mary is a virgin, so she asked Gabriel, "How can this be, since I do not know a man?" That was the question that provoked Gabriel's answer. It was impossible for this to happen without the intervention of God through a miracle. God would suspend the laws of nature and supernaturally cause Mary to become pregnant. In this case, we can confidently speak of "the miracle of childbirth." There has never been another case like this where God acted contrary to natural law. The conception of Jesus within the body of Mary was a supernatural event.

So, by definition, that which is impossible by nature cannot happen unless God intervenes. It is then no longer natural but supernatural. From this you can see that the word "miracle" is directly related to the word "supernatural." All miracles are supernatural events.

Now let's talk about how God many times works not in the supernatural but within the laws of nature to accomplish His ends. The English word "providence" comes from the Latin word "pro-video." "Pro" means before, "video" means to see, thus "to see before." In those cases, God, knowing the future, sees a need and "provides" for the desired outcome that He has in His mind. But this will take place within the laws of nature and not through a miracle.

BIBLE EXAMPLES OF PROVIDENCE

The following are examples of events in which God caused certain things to happen. In some of them He used miracles. In others He caused the very same outcome to take place through natural means rather than a miracle (**Figure 2**).

Examples of Miracles and Providence

Miracle	Event	Providence
1. Tower of Babel confused languages (Genesis 11:7-9)	← scattered people →	through persecution (Acts 1:8; 8:1-4)
2. Three Hebrew boys (Daniel 3:16-18)	← delivered →	Paul from mob (2 Cor 1:8-10; Acts 19:31-41)
3. Jesus calmed the sea (Mark 4:37-41)	← delivered from death in storm →	Paul in shipwreck (Acts 27:21-44)
4. Sodom and Gomorrah (Genesis 19:23-25)	← cities destroyed →	Jerusalem (Matthew 24)
5. Lame man at gate (Acts 3:2; 4:22)	← sickness healed →	Hezekiah's boil (2 Kings 20:1-7) Put on lump of figs

Figure 2.

Example 1

These are cases of God scattering people. The people were scattered at the tower of Babel by God miraculously confusing their language, whereas God caused the gospel to go to all the world by allowing the disciples to be scattered as a result of persecution. A clear miracle was worked in scattering the people at the tower of Babel, yet no miracle was worked by God in scattering the people in Acts.

Example 2

These are cases of God delivering someone from death. The three Hebrew boys were miraculously delivered from death in the fiery furnace whereas God allowed Paul to be delivered from death at the hands of the mob with the help of the town clerk. In Paul's case God worked in a non-miraculous way. No laws of nature were suspended. No miracle was worked. Yet, God "provided" for Paul to escape!

Example 3

These are cases of people being delivered from death in a stormy sea. In the first case, Jesus calmed the storm by speaking to it, which was obviously a miracle. But in the case of Paul, they were not only caught in a fierce storm, but were actually shipwrecked. The people on the ship thought they were going to drown, yet in the face of certain death, they were all spared. They "just happened" to be in just the right place when the ship wrecked so that none drowned. Paul was the only one who knew that they would be saved because an angel had appeared to him and told him so. God then delivered them in a non-miraculous way! But consider this: If it were not for the angel telling Paul (and ultimately us) that it was God behind them being spared, there would be no way to know for sure. But in this case we are told that it was God at work!

Example 4

These are cases of God destroying cities and the people in them. God miraculously destroyed Sodom and Gomorrah by raining fire from heaven. But in the case of the destruction of Jerusalem in A.D. 70, no miracle was worked. No laws of nature were suspended or broken at all. Yet it was God who brought it all about! Here, God decided to destroy the city of Jerusalem and the people of the city, but He accomplished it through natural means. He brought this judgment upon the Jews because they had rejected Christ and crucified Him. And God carried out this judgment by allowing the Roman army, led by General Titus, to completely destroy the city and the people in it. And if it were not for the fact that the scriptures tell us this, we could not even know God had caused this event to happen! God destroyed Sodom and Gomorrah miraculously and yet destroyed the city of Jerusalem non-miraculously.

Example 5

These are cases of people being healed. Peter heals the lame man in Acts chapter three. It is called a miracle in Acts 4:22. And yet in 2 Kings 20:1–7 a very interesting case of healing is found. Hezekiah is said to have been "sick unto death." He was told by God through the prophet Isaiah that he was going to die. After praying to God and asking Him to spare his life, God told him that he would grant his petition. He then instructed Hezekiah, again through Isaiah, to put a "lump of figs" on the boil and after doing so he recovered. We are specifically told in the account that it was God who healed him. Without that information, we might just attribute it to wise medical advice from Isaiah. But we know that it was God who healed him and through natural means. A clear miracle was worked in the healing of the lame man, yet no miracle was worked in God healing Hezekiah.

THREE ADDITIONAL EXAMPLES OF PROVIDENCE:

Example 6

Genesis 45:5–8 — In reading these verses we see that Joseph's being sold into slavery by his brothers was actually God looking to the future and "providing" for them.

5 "But now, do not therefore be grieved or angry with yourselves because you sold me here; for **God sent me before you to preserve life.** 6 For these two years the famine has been in the land, and there are still five years in which there will be neither plowing nor harvesting. 7 And God sent me before you to preserve a posterity for you in the earth, and **to save your lives by a great deliverance.** 8 So now it was not you who sent me

here, but God; and He has made me a father to Pharaoh, and lord of all his house, and a ruler throughout all the land of Egypt."

The passage says that God's purpose was for Joseph to help provide food for them during the famine that was about to come that they were unaware of. The Israelites were unaware of the coming famine, but God was aware. Keep in mind that if the scriptures did not tell us that it was God who was working behind the scenes in this event, we would not know about what He was doing! This is another case of God working in a non-miraculous manner to accomplish His ends.

Example 7

Genesis 22:1–13 — In this text, Abraham was about to offer his son Isaac as a sacrifice to God. At the last moment, Abraham was stopped by God. Notice some of that text:

> [8] And Abraham said, "My son, **God will provide** for Himself the lamb for a burnt offering." So the two of them went together. … [13] Then Abraham lifted his eyes and looked, and there behind him was a ram caught in a thicket by its horns. So Abraham went and took the ram, and offered it up for a burnt offering instead of his son.

There was no miracle performed here! There were no natural laws suspended. Yet God caused the event to happen the way it did. God "provided" the ram that was offered as sacrifice.

Example 8

Esther 4:11–17 — In this text, Esther, the King's wife, is having to make a difficult decision. The king had been persuaded by his advisers to issue a decree with respect to the Jews in his kingdom: all the Jews must be killed on a certain day. Esther, a Jew herself, is the only one who can help the people of Israel by petitioning her husband, the king. But there is a problem. The law did not permit a person to enter the king's house without having been personally beckoned by the king himself; to do so brought about the death penalty. The queen could not even go in without being beckoned! Esther being fully aware of this law had this conversation with her cousin, Mordecai:

> [13] And Mordecai told them to answer Esther: "Do not think in your heart that you will escape in the king's palace any more than all the other Jews. [14] For if you remain completely silent at this time, relief and **deliverance will arise** for the Jews **from another place**, but you and your father's house will perish. Yet **who knows whether you have come to the kingdom for such a time as this**?"

The point that Mordecai was making was that God was going to accomplish His goal; He would preserve the Jewish people. God would do this even if Esther decided not to act on behalf of her people. The key phrase is found in verse 14 when he says "who knows" whether Esther was put in this position just for this purpose. Mordecai does not know. Esther does not know. Was it simply "luck" that a Jewish woman was married to the king of Assyria at the time when he decreed that all Jews be put to death? The point is that they did not "know." However, both Mordecai and Esther could be assured that somehow, in some way, God would deliver His people. And they could have confidence that God would accomplish His ends even if they did not understand how He might do it. And we can have the same confidence today, even if we do not know how or when God is providentially working to accomplish His purposes!

IS GOD WORKING TODAY AND HOW IS HE WORKING?

Can we understand how God works in the world today? In Daniel 2:21, the prophet said, "He removes kings and raises up kings." Daniel had confidence that God was working in the world of his time. Did Daniel have to know how God "removed kings and raised up kings?" He did not. God's purposes would be accomplished even if he had no knowledge of how God controls the world empires that were on the horizon (Daniel 2:39-44). God was in control of history in Daniel's day. He is in control today—even though we may have no idea of how or when God is working. Did Joseph have to know how God was working in his time in order for God to accomplish His purposes? He did not. So, for us today, we can no more understand how or when God is working than Joseph would have known what God was doing in the life of the Israelites. And Joseph may have never known about God's providence if it had not been supernaturally revealed to him that those specific events had been directed by God! And no more than Paul would have known about those lives spared in the shipwreck if it had not been supernaturally revealed to him by the angel! That is the whole point of this chapter. Since the Bible teaches that the time of revelation has ceased (1 Corinthians 13:8–10), God then is working now through the natural means to accomplish His ends. And without a direct revelation from Him to us explaining how He is working we cannot put our finger on an event and say that we know for sure that God brought about that event. And a direct revelation will not take place today because all the revelation of God to man has now been completed and is within the pages of our Bibles. Yet, we can have confidence that God is still ruling in the kingdom of men (Daniel 4:17). In His word, God has given all that we need in order to serve Him. He has completely furnished us with all that is necessary for our faith and service to Him.

2 Timothy 3:16–17

All scripture is given by inspiration of God…that the man of God may be perfect, thoroughly furnished unto all good works.

Though we cannot know specifically how God is working today, we can have confidence that He is working. Notice these passages.

1 Peter 3:12

For the eyes of the Lord are over the righteous, and his ears are open unto their prayers.

James 5:16

The effective, fervent prayer of a righteous man avails much.

1 Corinthians 10:13

No temptation has overtaken you except such as is common to man; but God is faithful, who will not allow you to be tempted beyond what you are able, but with the temptation will also make the way of escape, that you may be able to bear it.

Matthew 6:33

"But seek first the kingdom of God and His righteousness, and all these things shall be added to you."

These scriptures show very clearly that God is actively working in world events today, but we still cannot single out a specific event and say this is God working at this time and at this place.

"The secret things belong to the LORD our God, but those things which are revealed belong to us and to our children forever, that we may do all the words of this law" (Deuteronomy 29:29).

O the depth of the riches both of the wisdom and knowledge of God! How unsearchable are his judgments, and his ways past finding out! (Romans 11:33).

We should also note an interesting passage describing life in general:

Ecclesiastes 9:11

I returned and saw under the sun that—

The race is not to the swift,
Nor the battle to the strong,
Nor bread to the wise,
Nor riches to men of understanding,
Nor favor to men of skill;
But time and chance happen to them all.

Solomon tells us, through the inspiration of the Holy Spirit, that there is an element of chance in everything. Some things may have happened anyway, but we have no way of knowing for sure. So, we give God the praise!

4

Who Received Holy Spirit Baptism in the Book of Acts?

The question about who received Holy Spirit baptism is critical in understanding God's plan of salvation in the book of Acts. It is also critical in understanding the subject of modern-day Pentecostalism. It is generally believed by most religious teachers that all of the 120 disciples in Acts chapter one were baptized in/with the Holy Spirit when that great event took place in Acts chapter two. Beyond that, most religious teachers hold the view that all believers in some way receive Holy Spirit baptism, even though it may not be manifested in a miraculous way.

Why is this so important? Because it seems as though this one point is the foundation on which modern-day Pentecostalism stands or falls. We have been told by Pentecostals that we are not true Christians, nor are any members of the church to which we belong, because we have not been "baptized in the Holy Spirit." They believe that all saved people will have this type of experience. And they will attempt to prove that point by directing you to Acts chapter one and claim that all the 120 mentioned in verse fifteen received the baptism of the Holy Spirit, not just the Apostles. They will further claim that all the 3,000 new converts in Acts 2:41 also received this miraculous outpouring as well as the 5,000 men mentioned in Acts 4:4. And since they claim that all of those converted in the New Testament received this baptism, then likewise they teach that all today must receive it. But, on the other hand, if the giving of the baptism of the Holy Spirit by Jesus was limited in its scope and if all the 120 did not receive it, then the foundational "rug" has just been pulled from underneath the modern-day Pentecostal movement! So, what does the Bible actually say on this very important subject?

A careful study of the text in the Acts will show that the baptism of the Holy Spirit was received by only a handful of people. Not only was it received by a very few, its purpose was also very specific and limited in nature. Our study will not only show who received it, but will also show its purpose.

THE CASE OF THE APOSTLES

Let us begin by looking at the text from Acts 1:1 to Acts 2:4. Please carefully note that we have highlighted "the apostles" in Acts 1:2. As we move through the text, we have also highlighted the pronouns that follow in verse three and beyond. We have also highlighted other specific words ("numbered with us...this ministry...witness with us...apostleship") that make it clear that the apostles were the ones under consideration. Carefully following the text, you can only conclude that it was the apostles who received Holy Spirit baptism in this instance. It was not the 120 disciples in the upper room.

Acts 1

[1] The former account I made, O Theophilus, of all that Jesus began both to do and teach

[2] until the day in which He was taken up, after He through the Holy Spirit had given commandments to **the apostles** whom He had chosen

[3] to **whom** He also presented Himself alive after His suffering by many infallible proofs, being seen by **them** during forty days and speaking of the things pertaining to the kingdom of God.

⁴ And being assembled together with **them**, He commanded **them** not to depart from Jerusalem, but to wait for the Promise of the Father, "which," He said, "**you** have heard from Me;

⁵ for John truly baptized with water, but **you** shall be baptized with the Holy Spirit not many days from now."

⁶ Therefore, when **they** had come together, **they** asked Him, saying, "Lord, will You at this time restore the kingdom to Israel?"

⁷ And He said to **them**, "It is not for **you** to know times or seasons which the Father has put in His own authority.

⁸ But **you** shall receive power when the Holy Spirit has come upon **you**; and **you** shall be witnesses to Me in Jerusalem, and in all Judea and Samaria, and to the end of the earth."

⁹ Now when He had spoken these things, while **they** watched, He was taken up, and a cloud received Him out of **their** sight.

¹⁰ And while **they** looked steadfastly toward heaven as He went up, behold, two men stood by **them** in white apparel,

¹¹ who also said, "Men of Galilee, why do **you** stand gazing up into heaven? This same Jesus, who was taken up from **you** into heaven, will so come in like manner as **you** saw Him go into heaven."

¹² Then **they** returned to Jerusalem from the mount called Olivet, which is near Jerusalem, a Sabbath day's journey.

¹³ And when **they** had entered, **they** went up into the upper room where **they** were staying: Peter, James, John, and Andrew; Philip and Thomas; Bartholomew and Matthew; James the son of Alphaeus and Simon the Zealot; and Judas the son of James.

¹⁴ **These** all continued with one accord in prayer and supplication, with the women and Mary the mother of Jesus, and with His brothers.

¹⁵ And in those days Peter stood up in the midst of the disciples (altogether the number of names was about a hundred and twenty), and said,

¹⁶ "Men and brethren, this Scripture had to be fulfilled, which the Holy Spirit spoke before by the mouth of David concerning Judas, who became a guide to those who arrested Jesus;

¹⁷ for **he was numbered with us** and obtained a part in **this ministry**."

¹⁸ (Now this man purchased a field with the wages of iniquity; and falling headlong, he burst open in the middle and all his entrails gushed out.

¹⁹ And it became known to all those dwelling in Jerusalem; so that field is called in their own language, Akel Dama, that is, Field of Blood.)

²⁰ "For it is written in the book of Psalms: 'Let his dwelling place be desolate, And let no one live in it'; and, 'Let another take his office.'

²¹ Therefore, of these men who have accompanied **us** all the time that the Lord Jesus went in and out among **us**,

²² beginning from the baptism of John to that day when He was taken up from **us**, one of these must become **a witness with us** of His resurrection."

²³ And they proposed two: Joseph called Barsabas, who was surnamed Justus, and Matthias.

²⁴ And they prayed and said, "You, O Lord, who know the hearts of all, show which of these two You have chosen

²⁵ to take part in **this ministry and apostleship** from which Judas by transgression fell, that he might go to his own place."

²⁶ And they cast their lots, and the lot fell on **Matthias**. And he was **numbered with the eleven apostles**.

Acts 2

¹ When the Day of Pentecost had fully come, **they** were all with one accord in one place.

² And suddenly there came a sound from heaven, as of a rushing mighty wind, and it filled the whole house where **they** were sitting.

³ Then there appeared to **them** divided tongues, as of fire, and one sat upon each of **them**.

⁴ And **they** were all filled with the Holy Spirit and began to speak with other tongues, as the Spirit gave **them** utterance.

Please note, that in Acts 1:2 that it speaks of the "apostles whom He had chosen." If you carefully follow the pronouns ("you, them, they") that follow, you will see that the promise of Holy Spirit baptism was made to the apostles. It was not made to the 120 disciples in the upper room. Note also in verse eight that the baptism of the Spirit would empower the apostles to serve as "witnesses" to Jesus. Please keep that thought in mind because it will come up again later. It is further interesting that, in the larger context of chapter one, only one man would be chosen to be a witness to Jesus, only one man would be chosen as a new apostle taking the place of Judas. It is clear throughout Acts chapter one that the focus is upon the twelve apostles.

While the 120 disciples are introduced in Acts 1:15, they are not the focus of Luke's account. In fact, it does not even say that there were exactly 120 present, but that there were "about" 120 assembled there. Luke, the writer of Acts, is just giving details to help readers form an accurate mental picture of the events that took place. So again, the focus of Luke's account is not on the group of about 120, but on the apostles. See particularly verse 17. It was Judas, an apostle, who was "numbered with us" and obtained a part in "this ministry." Peter is clearly speaking of Judas being numbered with the apostles; it was the ministry of the apostles that he speaks of, not the 120 disciples.

Note in Acts 1:22 that someone must be chosen to become a "witness with us" of Jesus' resurrection. This is not about the 120, but about the apostles being witnesses of the Lord's resurrection. Please understand, that if all those disciples (the 120) who were present were to be witnesses, there would be no need to single out one man to take the place of Judas as a witness!

In verses 24 and 25, the final decision as to who would be the next apostle was left to God. And that was as it should be. Out of the group that was present, there were two men who met the qualifications to be an apostle, a witness of the resurrection. Both "Joseph called Barsabas" and "Matthias" had accompanied the Lord throughout His ministry, beginning from the baptism of John until the day of the Lord's ascension back to heaven. These two men met those qualifications. This could not be said of the 120. These two men were singled out, but the final decision was left to the Lord. The Lord made His will known by means of casting lots. The lot fell upon Matthias, and he was "numbered with the eleven apostles."

Note that chapter one ends with Matthias being "numbered with the eleven apostles." Chapter two begins with those twelve men assembled together on the Day of Pentecost. Many people make the mistake of assuming the pronoun "they" in Acts 2:1 goes all the way back to Acts 1:15, and that it refers to the 120. In getting a proper understanding of this text it is important to remember that the chapter and verse breaks in our modern Bibles were not part of the original text. Those breaks were added hundreds of years later. When you read Acts 1:26 and Acts 2:1 without a break, the most natural conclusion is that "they" who were all with one accord in one place were those mentioned in Acts 1:26. It was "Matthias" and "the eleven apostles." Matthias was numbered with the eleven apostles, thus bringing the number up to twelve once again. When you read these two verses without a break, combining these two verses, as they are in the original text, it is easy to see that both verses are talking about the apostles.

That it was the apostles who received Holy Spirit baptism is further evidenced by the fact that the crowd perceived them all as Galileans. It is apparent from Acts chapters one and two that the apostles were all from Galilee.

Acts 2

6 And when this sound occurred, the multitude came together, and were confused, because everyone heard **them** speak in his own language.

7 Then they were all amazed and marveled, saying to one another, "Look, **are not all these who speak Galileans?**"

Who were the Galileans? Notice Acts chapter 1:

Acts 1

9 Now when He had spoken these things, while they watched, He was taken up, and a cloud received Him out of their sight.

10 And while they looked steadfastly toward heaven as He went up, behold, two men stood by them in white apparel,

11 who also said, "**Men of Galilee**, why do you stand gazing up into heaven? This same Jesus, who was taken up from you into heaven, will so come in like manner as you saw Him go into heaven."

Notice that the angels said, "men of Galilee." Who were these Galileans? If you will go back and read Matthew 4:25, it tells of the areas from which the disciples came. The very first ones were from Galilee, then from Decapolis, then from Jerusalem, from Judea, and then beyond Jordan. The reason the first ones were from Galilee was because that was where Jesus was from. It was from that area that the very first followers came, those who would later become the apostles. Since the context up to Acts 1:9 was dealing with the apostles, it is no coincidence that the angels addressed these men as "Galileans"!

If there is any question about who received the outpouring of the Holy Spirit on the day of Pentecost, it can be answered by just asking who the Galileans were. We have already shown that the apostles were the ones being referred to as Galileans! And this fits perfectly well with the context. It is interesting that those Jews present recognized that those men speaking were from the area of Galilee. There is a verse in Matthew 26 that may shed some light on this:

Matthew 26:69, 73

69 Now Peter sat outside in the courtyard. And a servant girl came to him, saying, "You also were with Jesus **of Galilee.**"... 73 "Surely you also are one of them, for **your speech betrays you.**"

Apparently, there was a recognizable dialect for those who were from the area of Galilee, much like we can recognize someone from New York City today, as distinguished from someone from Birmingham, Alabama. Those Jews who gathered in Jerusalem in Acts chapter two were from all parts of the world as is seen in verses 8-11. Yet they readily perceived that those men speaking were from Galilee.

As an interesting and important point, it should also be noted that in John 11:1 it mentions Mary, Martha, and Lazarus as being from Bethany. Therefore, they were not Galileans. This is an important point simply because after Jesus raised Lazarus from the dead, those three are mentioned over and over again as being with the group following Jesus throughout the rest of His ministry. It is difficult to believe that after following Him throughout the country right up to the time of the crucifixion, they would then be strangely absent from that same group of followers after the ascension. It seems as though if anyone would have been there in Acts chapter one, in addition to the apostles, it would have been Mary, Martha, and Lazarus. Yet they were not Galileans, and all those who received the baptism of the Holy Spirit and spoke in tongues were Galileans!

Another interesting and important point, is that Judas Iscariot was not from Galilee, as the other apostles were. Instead, he was from the town of Kerioth located south of Jerusalem in Judea. Had Judas still been alive and in the group of apostles, those angels would not have likely referred to the group of apostles as "Galileans." But Judas, having died, was not present, and so the reference was accurate in referring to the rest of the apostles as Galileans.

Lastly, notice that Peter did not stand up with the "120" as he spoke.

Acts 2:14

But Peter, **standing up with the eleven**, raised his voice and said to them…

Instead of standing up with the 120, he stood up with the other apostles—all Galileans—and defended them since it was those apostles who were accused of being drunk. Why do you think they were the ones being accused? Simply because they were the ones who had spoken in tongues! The men of Galilee!

That Acts 2:1-4 applies to the apostles (and not the 120) is further evidenced by Acts 2:14. "But Peter standing up with the eleven…" began to address the crowd. "Peter" and the "eleven" makes twelve apostles. Peter did not stand up with the 120, but with the other apostles. Those who make the mistake that "the 120 received Holy Spirit baptism" complicate their mistake by thinking that the 120 received the same power as the apostles and were able to do the same miracles as the apostles. That view will not stand a careful examination of the text. But this is done by modern-day Pentecostals in an attempt to justify their claim that they have the same baptism of the Holy Spirit today as was given on the day of Pentecost. But that is just not the case when we carefully examine these passages.

Remember also, that in Acts 1:2-5, that it was the apostles who were told to wait in Jerusalem until the Holy Spirit had come upon them. This was a command given to the apostles, not to the 120.

As you work your way through Acts chapter two, it becomes increasingly obvious that only the apostles received Holy Spirit baptism on the Day of Pentecost. We have already noted Acts 2:14 where "Peter stood up with the eleven" (not the 120). But notice also Acts 2:32 where Peter speaks of the resurrection of Jesus. He says, "This Jesus God has raised up, of which we are all witnesses." Remember, this is Peter, standing up with the eleven, who says this. Peter's statement harkens back to Acts 1:22, where "one of these must become a witness with us of His resurrection." That was when the lot fell upon Matthias, and he became a witness with the other apostles of the resurrection of Jesus. The text simply will not allow us to conclude that it was the 120 who were witnesses.

In Acts 2:36, Peter begins to draw his lesson to a close. In that verse, he accused the crowd of having crucified the Lord and Christ. When the audience responded to this in Acts 2:37, they spoke to "Peter and the rest of the apostles." The large audience gathered on that day did not speak to the 120, but to the apostles. Luke, in writing the book of Acts, left the 120 back in chapter one, verse fifteen. There is simply no reference whatever to that larger group in Acts chapter two.

Following the baptism of 3,000 souls in Acts 2:38-42, you will find that these new converts "continued steadfastly in the apostles' doctrine." Why would Luke mention "the apostles' doctrine" if the 120 received the same power and ability to witness as the apostles? It was the twelve apostles who were set apart for the special purpose of being witnesses and teachers at this time. When Acts 2:42 speaks of "the apostles' doctrine," it shows the authoritative position of the apostles that had been given them by the Lord. The next verse (Acts 2:43) is also significant. It says, "Then fear came upon every soul, and many wonders and signs were done by the apostles." If the 120 were all working miracles, then Luke could not have said this. It was the apostles who were working the miracles at this time, not the 120. In fact, if you carefully read from this point onward through chapter six, you will find no case where anyone else works any miracles. It was only the apostles at this time.

THE APOSTLES WORKED MIRACLES FOLLOWING PENTECOST

As we move into chapter three, it was the Apostle Peter who worked a miracle by the power given to him by Christ (Acts 3:1-10). Peter made it clear that he and John had not worked the miracle by their own power, but by the power given them by Christ (Acts 3:11-16). That truth was further confirmed in Acts chapter four when Peter and John were arrested. Peter, filled with the Holy Spirit, testified that it was by the name of Jesus that the lame man was healed (Acts 4:1-13). The

Jewish council could not deny that a miracle had been done by the hands of the apostles. In Acts 4:16, they said,

> "What shall we do to these men? For, indeed, that **a notable miracle has been done through them** is evident to all who dwell in Jerusalem, and we cannot deny it."

They could not deny that these apostles had worked a miracle. There is no indication that anyone but apostles were working miracles, not the 120 of Acts 1:15, and not the 3,000 who were baptized on Pentecost in Acts 2:41. It is generally believed by most Pentecostals that all the Christians had access to miraculous powers. But there is simply no record whatever of that being the case.

The council threatened the two apostles and told them "not to speak at all or teach in the name of Jesus" (Acts 4:18). But the apostles continued to speak. Upon being released, Peter and John returned to "their own company" (Acts 4:23 NASB). We understand "their own company" to be the other apostles. The word used in that text that is translated "own" means "pertaining to one's self, one's own, belonging to one's self" (*Strong's*, ἴδιος, *idios*). Being that it is not a broad term, but limited, we would understand it to apply to the apostles. It would then appear that it was the apostles who prayed (Acts 4:24-30), and that God who responded to their prayer by causing the place where they were assembled to shake (Acts 4:31). While this incident is not critical toward understanding who received Holy Spirit baptism, it is supportive of the premise that it was only the apostles who received that miraculous outpouring in Acts chapter two. It is also interesting, that in this case, there is no mention of anyone—apostle or otherwise—working a miracle. Rather, it was God who caused the shaking of the place of assembly without any direct action on the part of any apostle.

As we move into chapter five, we have the matter of Ananias and Sapphira lying to God (Acts 5:1-10). Once again, there appears to be no direct action on the part of Peter or the other apostles, but both Ananias and Sapphira died that day. Their deaths were directly brought about by God, but no miracle was done by the apostles to cause them to die. The most that could be said from this text is that Peter declared to Sapphira that she would die,

> "How is it that you have agreed together to test the Spirit of the Lord? Look, the feet of those who have buried your husband are at the door, and they will carry you out" (Acts 5:9).

The next verse shows that her death came immediately, and she was buried alongside her husband. The response of the people in the next three verses is critical in understanding the unique position of the apostles.

Acts 5

> [11] So great fear came upon all the church and upon all who heard these things.
>
> [12] And **through the hands of the apostles** many signs and wonders were done among the people.
>
> [13] And they were all with one accord in Solomon's Porch. Yet none of the rest dared join them, but the people esteemed them highly.

Note the reaction of the church, and even those beyond the church. Great fear came upon all those who heard what happened to Ananias and Sapphira (Acts 5:11). Their lies had been told in the presence of the apostles. Peter, by the power of the Holy Spirit, knew what was in the hearts of these two. This episode seems to be a case of Peter exercising the gift of "discerning of spirits" mentioned in 1 Corinthians 14:10 or what we commonly refer to as "the gift of discernment." It was revealed to him that they were lying. They lied in the presence of the apostles, and they died in the presence of the apostles. That is the reason why fear came upon all those who heard about it.

As the text continues, it is plainly stated that, "through the hands of the apostles many signs and wonders were done among the people" (Acts 5:12). There is no indication in this text or in any other that miraculous powers were possessed by others in the church at this time. The claim made by Pentecostals that it was the 120 (Acts 1:15) who received Holy Spirit baptism on the Day of Pentecost is a claim made without any scriptural support. Again and again, we see that it was the apostles who were given miraculous power.

That it was the apostles only is further supported by Acts 5:13. That verse tells us that "none of the rest dared join them." We understand "them" to be the church that was assembled in Solomon's porch (Acts 5:12). We might wonder who "the rest" were. Were they the non-believers? Very likely. Because of what happened to Ananias and Sapphira in the presence of the apostles there might have been a healthy fear of joining with the Christians. Hypocrites would especially have reason to fear. The judgment of God in the case of Ananias and Sapphira separated the fakers from the followers, and the make-believers from the true believers. Everyone knew that something dramatic had happened in the presence of the apostles.

But ask yourself this question; if all the 120 had received the same power as the apostles, then why would they be afraid? Even though it was only Peter who had pronounced that Ananias and Sapphira would die, the other eleven apostles did not have this fear.

In Acts 5:14–16 the text tells us that sick people were brought out into the streets of Jerusalem in hope that at least the shadow of Peter passing by might fall on some of them. There was no magical power in Peter's shadow, just like there was no magical power in Jesus' garment in Luke 8:44. The power lay in the name of Jesus. They were healed by Jesus. And, it is vitally important to note, that there were no failures in the cases recorded here. Verse 16 tells us that "they were all healed." Once again, this testifies that God was at work—the God who does not fail. What we see in the Bible text are genuine miracles. This is not what you see on TV today. These Bible miracles were openly and publicly done and apparent to all—apparent even to the enemies of Jesus and the apostles. What we are seeing in these passages are what we should expect to see. Why is that? It is because the Lord gave to the apostles the ability to perform supernatural acts as a way of confirming the message of truth. Mark 16:20 says,

> And they went out and preached everywhere, the Lord work-
> ing with them and confirming the word through the accom-
> panying signs.

In Acts 5:17-32 we have another significant incident. This time it wasn't
just Peter and John who were arrested, but rather the larger body of
the apostles. Verse eighteen tells us that they "laid their hands on
the apostles and put them in the common prison." But, that night, an
angel of the Lord released them from the prison. The apostles went
to the temple and continued their preaching. Once again, they were
arrested and brought before the council. In verse twenty, Peter and
the other apostles answered the council's complaint against them
and said, "We ought to obey God rather than men." The council had
previously told them not to preach any more in the name of Jesus.
And now, in Acts 5:30-32, before the very Jewish leaders who told
them not to preach, the apostles preached the resurrection of Jesus!
Verse thirty-two is a key text.

> "And we are His witnesses to these things, and so also is the
> Holy Spirit whom God has given to those who obey Him."

The apostles were witness to the ministry of Jesus and to His resurrection. They had seen Him alive after His death. But note that they also
claimed that the Holy Spirit was a witness to the truth about Christ.
How was the Holy Spirit a witness to Jesus? By performing miracles,
wonders, and signs by the hands of the apostles. Acts 5:32 closes with
"the Holy Spirit whom God has given to those who obey Him." The
claim that the apostles are making is that God has given them the
Holy Spirit, thus proving that they are obeying God! The apostles are
obeying God. The men on the Jewish council are not obeying God!
The apostles proved they were obeying God by the many miracles
they were working. Once again, there is no evidence of anyone else
working miracles.

THE LAYING ON OF THE APOSTLES' HANDS

"But what about Stephen in Acts 6:8? Didn't he work miracles? He was
not an apostle, was he?" Indeed, the case of Stephen is important to the
study of miracles. He was not an apostle, and he did work miracles.
But if you look carefully at the text, you will see what happened and

how he got this power. The church in Jerusalem was in need of workers who could take care of needy widows among them. The apostles could not devote all their time to this undertaking. Other men could be appointed who would manage this. Acts 6:3–8 shows us how the twelve apostles addressed this matter.

Acts 6

³ "Therefore, brethren, seek out from among you seven men of good reputation, full of the Holy Spirit and wisdom, whom we may appoint over this business;

⁴ but we will give ourselves continually to prayer and to the ministry of the word."

⁵ And the saying pleased the whole multitude. And they chose **Stephen**, a man full of faith and the Holy Spirit, and Philip, Prochorus, Nicanor, Timon, Parmenas, and Nicolas, a proselyte from Antioch,

⁶ **whom they set before the apostles**; and when they had prayed, **they laid hands on them.**

⁷ Then the word of God spread, and the number of the disciples multiplied greatly in Jerusalem, and a great many of the priests were obedient to the faith.

⁸ And Stephen, full of faith and power, did great wonders and signs among the people.

Indeed, Stephen did great wonders and signs among the people. This is the first time any person in the book of Acts worked a miracle who was not an apostle! But note what had just happened to this man (as well as the six other men chosen by the church). The text says these men were "set before the apostles; and when they prayed, they laid hands on them." It was only after the apostles laid hands on these men that they had the miraculous powers of the Holy Spirit. Acts 8:18 teaches that it was through the laying on of the apostles' hands that the Holy Spirit was given.

The case of Stephen does not disprove the premise of this chapter. Remember, our premise and point is that it was only the apostles on the Day of Pentecost who received Holy Spirit baptism. The case of Stephen reinforces our premise and point. It is important that we make a distinction between baptism of the Holy Spirit and the laying on of apostles' hands. While both empowered men to work miracles, signs and wonders, they are not the same. According to John 1:33, Jesus is the one who baptizes with the Holy Spirit. Here are the words of John the Baptist from that text.

John 1:33

"I did not know Him, but He who sent me to baptize with water said to me, 'Upon whom you see the Spirit descending, and remaining on Him, this is He who baptizes with the Holy Spirit.'"

It is Jesus who baptizes with the Holy Spirit. No one else has that power. While the apostles could lay hands on disciples and transmit some of the miraculous spiritual gifts, they could not baptize anyone with the Holy Spirit. That power was reserved for Jesus alone. We hope the reader can see the distinction between Holy Spirit baptism and the laying on of apostles' hands. A failure to make that biblical distinction only leads to confusion and misunderstanding. Holy Spirit baptism is administered by Jesus directly from heaven. The transmission of the miraculous gifts of the Holy Spirit to certain disciples was administered by the apostles.

We have already seen the case of Stephen—that it was after the apostles laid hands on him that he was able to do "great wonders and signs among the people" (Acts 6:5-8). But Stephen was not the only one upon whom the apostles laid their hands. In that list of seven men in verse five you will also find Philip. It is obvious from the text that this is not the Apostle Philip. It is proper to call the man chosen in Acts 6, "Philip, the evangelist" for that is what Acts 21:8 calls him.

Acts 21:8

On the next day we who were Paul's companions departed and came to Caesarea, and entered the house of Philip the evangelist, who was one of the seven, and stayed with him.

Note that he is identified as both an "evangelist" and "one of the seven." This man became an important figure in Acts 8. When a great persecution came against the church in Jerusalem, the disciples were scattered throughout the regions of Judea and Samaria. The apostles were the exception to this; they remained in Jerusalem (Acts 8:1). Philip was among those who were forced to leave Jerusalem. He, along with many others went out from Jerusalem preaching the word of God (Acts 8:4–7). Here is that text.

Acts 8

⁴ Therefore those who were scattered went everywhere preaching the word.

⁵ Then **Philip** went down to the city of Samaria and preached Christ to them.

⁶ And the multitudes with one accord heeded the things spoken by Philip, hearing and seeing the miracles which he did.

⁷ For unclean spirits, crying with a loud voice, came out of many who were possessed; and many who were paralyzed and lame were healed.

Philip went into a city of Samaria as he preached the gospel. Multitudes of people heard his word, and they also saw the miracles which he did! He cast out demons and healed those who were paralyzed and lame. Where did Philip get such power to perform these miracles? He got it from the same place as Stephen. It was by the laying on of the apostles' hands back in Acts 6:6. Philip did not receive Holy Spirit baptism, but he did receive miraculous power through the hands of the apostles—just like Stephen.

Through the work of the gospel that Philip did in Samaria, a new congregation of God's people was begun. A number of people believed the preaching and were baptized (Acts 8:9–13). Philip would soon move on to another place, but who would teach this infant congregation after he was gone? They needed teachers and preachers! Someone needed to lay hands on some of the Samaritans so they would be empowered to teach and edify the church, since the scriptures had not yet been written. Someone needed to give them some of the same spiritual gifts that Philip had.

When the apostles at Jerusalem heard that the Samaritans had been converted, they sent Peter and John (two apostles) to Samaria in order for them to have spiritual gifts (Acts 8:14–18). Why didn't Philip lay hands on them to give them power from the Holy Spirit? He was already in Samaria; why did the apostles have to come to that city? It was because Philip was not an apostle. He could not transmit the gifts of the Holy Spirit to others. Note particularly verse 18:

Acts 8:18

Simon saw that through the laying on of the apostles' hands the Holy Spirit was given.

Notice that this was something Simon saw.

Acts 8

[18] And when **Simon saw that through the laying on of the apostles' hands the Holy Spirit was given,** he offered them money,

[19] saying, "Give me **this power** also, **that anyone on whom I lay hands may receive the Holy Spirit.**"

[20] But Peter said to him, "Your money perish with you, because you thought that the gift of God could be purchased with money!

[21] "You have neither **part** nor portion in **this matter**, for your heart is not right in the sight of God."

What Simon referred to as "*this* power" was what Peter answered as "*this* matter." Simon wanted the "power" to transmit those supernatural spiritual gifts just like Peter and John. But the "matter" of the transmission of those gifts was a "part" of the role and office of being an Apostle. And it was present during the early stages and establishment of the church and was not something that was within God's plan for Simon to have.

The miracles, signs and wonders could be seen! This is just like back in verse 6. In that verse, the Samaritans were "seeing the miracles" which Philip did.

A similar case is seen in Acts 19:1–6. The Apostle Paul came to the city of Ephesus. He found some disciples there who needed further teaching on baptism. After he taught them, he baptized them in the name of the Lord Jesus. Note carefully what Paul did in verse 6.

> And when Paul had laid hands on them, the Holy Spirit came upon them, and they spoke with tongues and prophesied (Acts 19:6).

This is like the previous cases we have seen in Acts chapters six and eight. It was the laying on of the hands of an apostle that transmitted the miraculous spiritual gifts. It was the power of the Holy Spirit in operation as these disciples were able to speak with tongues and prophesied. Two additional examples can also be found.

2 Timothy 1:6

> Therefore I remind you to stir up **the gift of God** which is in you **through the laying on of my hands** (i.e., the Apostle Paul's hands, 2 Timothy 1:6).

Romans 1:11

> For I long to see you, that I may **impart to you some spiritual gift**, so that you may be established.

Paul reminds Timothy of "the gift of God" that he had received. Paul does not specify which gift he had imparted to Timothy, but only that he had received it in the same way as the others, through "the laying on of my hands," the hands of an apostle. And Paul opens the letter to the church at Rome by saying that he had a longing to see them so that he could "impart some spiritual gift" so that they could "be established." Again, the spiritual gifts were needed in each of those congregations in the absence of the written word that we have today. The new revelation given through those gifts would serve to "establish" them.

Who administered this power of the Holy Spirit? What means or medium did God use to empower these men with these miraculous gifts? It was not done as a direct outpouring from heaven. It was administered by the apostles' hands. These cases we have seen in Acts chapters six, eight, and nineteen are not Holy Spirit baptism. These cases are never called Holy Spirit baptism, and we make a mistake that confuses people if we call these cases Holy Spirit baptism!

Jesus is the one who administers Holy Spirit baptism (John 1:33). He administers that directly from heaven. There is no human intermediary in such cases. The case that we saw in Acts chapter two was indeed a case of Holy Spirit baptism. There was no human intermediary. No one laid hands on the twelve apostles who received Holy Spirit baptism in Acts two.

THE CASE OF CORNELIUS

How are we to understand Acts chapter ten? What happened at the house of Cornelius? This account of conversion is critical to the Bible story because this case records the first Gentile conversion. And it is also important because there is another miraculous outpouring of the Holy Spirit in this chapter. As we look at the chapter, we will have to determine whether it was directly from heaven, or whether an apostle laid hands on Cornelius and upon those in his household.

That Cornelius was a Gentile is obvious from the very opening of the chapter. He is a Roman soldier and, even though he is a religious man, he is not a Jew (Acts 10:1-4). He is told by an angel to send for Peter who would tell him what he must do (Acts 10:5-8). As the servants of Cornelius were on the way to get the Apostle Peter, God caused a vision to come upon the apostle (Acts 10:9-16). In the vision, all sorts of animals were presented to Peter as food, but Peter resisted saying, "I have never eaten anything common or unclean." While Peter wondered what the vision could mean, the men sent from Cornelius arrived at the house. Peter, still wondering what the vision meant, was told by the Holy Spirit to go with them. And he went with them to Caesarea (Acts 10:17-23).

When Peter arrived at the house of Cornelius, he made it clear that he would not have come there except that God had directed him to do so (Acts 10:24-33). Peter concluded that the purpose of the vision was to teach him that he "should not call any man common or unclean" (v. 28). Peter went on further to say, "In truth I perceive that God shows no partiality. But in every nation whoever fears Him and works righteousness is accepted by Him" (Acts 10:34-35). Peter is learning that the Gentiles are to be accepted by God!

With this new understanding, Peter preached Christ to the household of Cornelius (Acts 10:36-48). It is recorded within this short text that the Holy Spirit fell on those who heard Peter's sermon.

Acts 10

[44] While Peter was still speaking these words, the Holy Spirit fell upon all those who heard the word.

[45] And those of the circumcision who believed were astonished, as many as came with Peter, because the gift of the Holy Spirit had been poured out on the Gentiles also.

[46] For they heard them speak with tongues and magnify God. Then Peter answered,

[47] "Can anyone forbid water, that these should not be baptized who have received the Holy Spirit just as we have?"

[48] And he commanded them to be baptized in the name of the Lord. Then they asked him to stay a few days.

There is no question that there was a miraculous outpouring of the Holy Spirit in this case. But, was this a case of Holy Spirit baptism, a case where there was a direct outpouring from heaven? Or, did God use a human intermediary, an apostle to lay hands on them? The answer is rather obvious. There was no laying on of apostles' hands in this case. This was something administered directly from heaven by Jesus (John 1:33). This is only the second time in the book of Acts where such an event is recorded, Acts chapter two being the first when the apostles were baptized with the Holy Spirit. All the other cases we have seen involved the laying on of the apostles' hands.

It is important to note that Holy Spirit baptism at the house of Cornelius did not turn these Gentiles into apostles. It is necessary to point that out, because sometimes men make the mistake of thinking that Holy Spirit baptism is what made someone an apostle. That wasn't true in Acts chapter two, and it is not true in Acts chapter ten. The word *apostle* means "one sent." The twelve men in chapter two were personally chosen by Jesus to be His apostles. They were "sent" to be witnesses to the whole world as to what they had seen and heard (Acts 1:8). While Holy Spirit baptism empowered the apostles to do their work, it did not make them to be apostles. They were already apostles even before Jesus sent the Spirit upon them. Holy Spirit baptism at the house of Cornelius certainly did not make these Gentiles to be apostles.

What, then, was the purpose of Holy Spirit baptism at the house of Cornelius? Let us first ask what was its purpose with the apostles? As we have already noted, it was to empower them as witnesses, to reveal and confirm the truth of the gospel as they preached (Acts 1:8). It was given to them to reveal all truth. That's the promise Jesus made to the apostles in John 16:

> "However, when He, the Spirit of truth, has come, He will guide you into all truth; for He will not speak on His own authority, but whatever He hears He will speak; and He will tell you things to come" (John 16:13).

A similar promise was made to the apostles in John 14:

> "But the Helper, the Holy Spirit, whom the Father will send in My name, He will teach you all things, and bring to your remembrance all things that I said to you" (John 14:26).

The Holy Spirit upon the apostles would guide them into all truth, would teach them all things, and would even bring to their remembrance all the things that Jesus had said to them! That's what Jesus promised to them. And, indeed, the New Testament record shows us that was what happened!

But, still, what was the purpose of Holy Spirit baptism at the house of Cornelius? We need only to go to the next chapter (i.e., Acts 11) to see what the early Christians thought about the purpose. Acts 10 is where the events surrounding the conversion of Cornelius were recorded. Chapter eleven is where the aftermath of that conversion is recorded. In that chapter, when Peter came to Jerusalem, he was immediately called upon to give an account of what happened. It was particularly those who were defenders of circumcision who called him on the carpet (Acts 11:1-3).

Peter's defense is recorded in Acts 11:4-17. Peter showed the brethren that what had happened at Caesarea was God's doing—from beginning to end. It was not Peter who initiated the trip to the house of Cornelius (verses 5-14). In fact, it was God working at both ends: God gave a vision to Peter who was in Joppa; and God sent an angel to Cornelius at Caesarea to tell him to send for Peter. God was directing the events—not the Apostle Peter! Verse fifteen is important in Peter's defense. He declares that it was "…as I began to speak, the Holy Spirit fell upon them…" This gives us a different look at the events of Acts chapter ten. Why the difference? Acts chapter ten tells us the facts of what happened, but chapter eleven is more precise. Notice that in Acts 11:4, Luke says, "Peter explained it to them *in order* from the beginning." The phrase "in order" is from the Greek adverb καθεξῆς, *kathexēs*. The word indicates "succession," a successive order. Peter shows what happened first, second, third, etc. Rather than just retell the events that had happened as recorded by Luke in chapter ten, Luke further tells us in chapter eleven that Peter recounted those events in a precise chronological order to those brethren at Jerusalem.

"As I began to speak" would show the outpouring of the Holy Spirit to be toward the front end of Peter's discourse, not at the conclusion of his preaching. This would show to the brethren at Jerusalem that Peter was authorized by God to speak to the Gentiles and to baptize them in water. Once again, Peter shows us that what happened at the house of Cornelius was God's doing—from beginning to end. When Peter says in verse sixteen that he remembered the word of the Lord, how He said, "John indeed baptized with water, but you shall be baptized with the Holy Spirit," he is recalling what Jesus said in Acts 1:8. Peter relates it to what Jesus said to the apostles. He is telling us that what happened to the apostles—a direct outpouring from heaven—has happened again! And notice the last words of verse sixteen. He says the Holy Spirit fell on them "as upon us at the beginning." Peter had to go all the way back to Acts chapter two, on the Day of Pentecost, to find another case like this! Holy Spirit baptism is recorded only twice in the book of Acts!

Peter concludes his point in verse seventeen.

Acts 11:17

"If therefore God gave them **the same gift** as He gave us when we believed on the Lord Jesus Christ, who was I that I could withstand God?"

It was the same gift—the direct outpouring from heaven administered by Jesus—that was given to Cornelius as was given to the apostles. If Peter had resisted, if he had refused to baptize these Gentiles in water, he would have been guilty of fighting against God. Once more, Peter shows that he was not the one responsible for what happened at this house in Caesarea. It was God—from beginning to end.

Now let us see the conclusion that the church in Jerusalem draws from this. It is found in verse eighteen.

Acts 11:18

When they heard these things they became silent; and they glorified God, saying, "Then God has also granted to the Gentiles repentance to life."

That's how the church understood the purpose of Holy Spirit baptism at the house of Cornelius. It was given to prove that the Gentiles could be saved. Let us be careful that we do not assign a different purpose to this grand act of God! If you are a Gentile, then you can thank God for what happened at the house of Cornelius, for it proved once and for all that Gentiles could be saved by the gospel. Later, when an issue was raised about whether or not Gentiles had to be circumcised in order to be saved, Peter pointed back to the house of Cornelius as an answer (Acts 15:1–11).

So, in concluding this section on Holy Spirit baptism in the book of Acts, we can safely say that there are but two instances of that action by Jesus taking place in this book. The first was the outpouring upon the twelve apostles in Acts chapter two. The second, and final account, was the outpouring at the house of Cornelius. The first instance was to *reveal all truth* to the apostles. The second was to *reveal one truth*—Gentile salvation.

5

Laying On of Hands

One of the most common misunderstandings among the modern-day Pentecostals involves what is described in the New Testament as "the laying on of hands." This was briefly discussed in the previous chapter, but we would like to expand on it further here. After a careful study of the various texts, it becomes clear that, as a general rule, the miraculous spiritual gifts mentioned in Mark 16:17–20 and in 1 Corinthians 12:1–10 were transmitted to those Christians through the laying on of the apostles' hands. That is a clear-cut distinction that is beyond dispute. Let's look at some related passages.

Acts 6

⁵ And the saying pleased the whole multitude. And they chose **Stephen**, a man full of faith and the Holy Spirit, and **Philip**, Prochorus, Nicanor, Timon, Parmenas, and Nicolas, a proselyte from Antioch,

⁶ whom they **set before the apostles; and when they had prayed**, they laid hands on them.

⁷ Then the word of God spread, and the number of the disciples multiplied greatly in Jerusalem, and a great many of the priests were obedient to the faith.

> **8** And **Stephen, full of faith and power, did great wonders and signs among the people**.

After having the apostles lay their hands on those men, we read that Stephen then "did great wonders and signs among the people." The gift to work miracles had been transmitted to Stephen through the laying on of the apostles' hands. Another of those seven men was Philip. Notice that he also received the same power by the apostle's hands.

Acts 8

> **5** Then **Philip** went down to the city of Samaria and preached Christ to them.

> **6** And the multitudes with one accord heeded the things spoken by Philip, hearing and seeing **the miracles which he did**.

> **7** For unclean spirits, crying with a loud voice, came out of many who were possessed; and many who were paralyzed and lame were healed.

Both Stephen and Philip had received the miraculous gifts after having the apostles lay their hands on them for that purpose. They both were able to work miracles after the apostles had laid their hands on them. Notice that further in Luke's narrative, Philip had traveled to the city of Samaria to preach. While there, he converted a man named Simon. Remember that back in Acts 1:8 Jesus told them that they were to first begin the preaching in Jerusalem, then go to Judea, then from there go to Samaria, and from there to the rest of the world. The gospel has now reached Samaria as a result of the efforts of the preacher, Philip. Notice how Philip used those miracles to "confirm" the word that he was preaching. Luke says that as a result of "hearing and seeing" those miracles done by Philip, that the people "gave heed" to those things which he spoke. This is exactly what Jesus said was going to happen back in Mark 16:15–20, that the miracles would be used to confirm the word. Now notice further what happened in Samaria as a result of Philip's preaching:

Acts 8

¹³ Then **Simon** himself also believed; and when he was baptized he continued with **Philip**, and was amazed, seeing the miracles and signs which were done.

¹⁴ Now when **the apostles** who were at Jerusalem heard that Samaria had received the word of God, **they sent Peter and John** to them,

¹⁵ who, when they had come down, prayed for them that they might receive the Holy Spirit.

¹⁶ For as yet He had fallen upon none of them. They had only been baptized in the name of the Lord Jesus.

¹⁷ **Then they laid hands on them, and they received the Holy Spirit.**

18 And when Simon saw that **through the laying on of the apostles' hands the Holy Spirit was given**, he offered them money,

¹⁹ saying, "**Give me** this power **also, that anyone on whom I lay hands may receive the Holy Spirit.**"

²⁰ But Peter said to him, "Your money perish with you, because you thought that **the gift** of God could be purchased with money!

²¹ **"You have neither part nor portion in** this matter…"

The passage clearly tells us that Simon "saw" that it was the apostles Peter and John who were able to transmit to others the ability to work miracles through the laying on of their hands. The fact that Simon "saw" this indicates that there was something to be observed when the apostles laid hands on these new Christians. Simon could have seen the gift of tongues, or the gift of prophecy in action. He could have seen the gift of healing if that gift had been transmitted by the apostles. The point is, when the apostles laid hands on the Samaritans, the resulting spiritual gifts could be observed. When Simon foolishly asked if he could purchase from Peter that "power" to be able to also transmit the gifts, Peter responded in the negative and said that Simon did not have a "part in that matter." What matter? The laying on of hands. That was unique to the office that the apostles held. There are three additional passages that mention this "matter."

Acts 19:6

And when **Paul had laid hands on them**, the Holy Spirit came upon them, and they spoke with tongues and prophesied.

2 Timothy 1:6

Therefore I (the Apostle Paul) remind you to stir up the gift of God which is in you **through the laying on of my hands**.

Romans 1:11

For I (the Apostle Paul) long to see you, that I may **impart to you some spiritual gift**, so that you may be established.

In Acts 19 we have another example of Christians receiving miraculous gifts through the laying on of an apostle's hands. This time it was Paul's hands. As a result of that, those Christians began to speak in tongues and to prophesy. The same thing again is mentioned in 2 Timothy chapter one, though it is not revealed which of the spiritual gifts Timothy had received. However, it is quite clear how he received that gift, by the laying on of the Apostle Paul's hands! And then lastly, Paul expressed a desire to go to Rome in order to "impart" spiritual gifts to those Christians. They were still living in the time when new revelation was being given and it would have to be confirmed. That was the purpose of the spiritual gifts, to reveal truth, and to confirm truth. Paul knew that those Christians would need more of their members to possess spiritual gifts and that the only way to receive those gifts was through an apostle's hands. That would then explain why he felt the urgent need to go there!

One of the most important details to note here has a direct application to modern-day Pentecostalism.

When Samaria began to have conversions to Christ as a result of the preaching of Philip, these new disciples did not automatically receive the miraculous gifts that Philip had when they became Christians.

Notice also that Philip could not transmit those gifts to the new converts himself. As a result, the apostles back at Jerusalem sent Peter and John to Samaria. Verses 17–18 tell us that it was through the laying on of apostles' hands, in this case Peter and John, that those new converts received the spiritual gifts. When Simon asked for "this power," he was not referring to the spiritual gifts themselves, but rather, was referring to the power Peter and John had to transmit those gifts to others. That was why Peter and John came all the way from Jerusalem to Samaria. Had those disciples been able to receive the spiritual gifts another way, it would have been unnecessary for the apostles to make that journey. But, again, Peter's reply that Simon did not have part nor lot in this matter, was a reference to the fact that the ability to transmit spiritual gifts was a part of the office and work of an apostle.

In an attempt to find some scriptural example that would prove that there are miracles today, modern-day Pentecostals will many times point to a passage in Acts chapter nine.

Acts 9

¹² And in a vision he has seen a man named **Ananias** coming in and **putting his hand on him, so that he might receive his sight**.

¹⁷ And Ananias went his way and entered the house; and laying his hands on him he said, "Brother Saul, the Lord Jesus, who appeared to you on the road as you came, has sent me **that you may receive your sight** and be filled with the Holy Spirit."

¹⁸ Immediately there fell from his eyes something like scales, and **he received his sight at once**; and he arose and was baptized.

Modern-day Pentecostals will point to this passage and say that verse twelve is an example of a non-apostle, Ananias, laying hands on someone to transmit miraculous gifts. But read the passage very carefully and notice *why* Ananias laid hands on Paul. Luke says that the reason was "so that he might receive his sight." Keep in mind that Paul had not yet been converted and had not been baptized. But he had been blinded by the bright light when Jesus had appeared to him back on the road to Damascus. This passage in Acts chapter nine is very clear concerning the instructions Jesus gave to Paul and to the preacher Ananias. The reason for Ananias laying his hands on Paul was to give Paul back his sight. And as soon as Ananias did so, Paul's sight was returned. After that he arose and was baptized. But be very clear, the laying on of Ananias' hands was not the same as in the other passages we have seen where the miraculous gifts were being transmitted. This case cannot be used by modern-day Pentecostals to try and produce a scriptural example of how they can get one of those gifts in a different manner.

Another text that is often misunderstood by modern-day Pentecostals is 1 Timothy 4:14.

1 Timothy 4:14

Do not neglect the gift that is in you, which was given to you by prophecy with **the laying on of the hands of the eldership**.

There is no indication that the gift given to Timothy was miraculous in nature. It is much more likely that it referred to his work as a teacher of the gospel. It was given to him by prophecy; that is, it was prophesied that he was to receive the gift as a teacher. This would be consistent with Romans 12:6–18 where teaching is one of several non-miraculous gifts listed. In reading that text, it is clear that only one of the eight gifts listed there is miraculous in nature, that being the gift of prophecy. All the other gifts mentioned (teaching, exhortation, etc.) are natural gifts from God, or those acquired through training or appointment.

The point is, whatever one may say about 1 Timothy 4:14, this text does not teach that men who served in the eldership had the ability to transmit miraculous spiritual gifts. Remember, the transmission of miraculous spiritual gifts was done through the laying on of the apostles' hands (Acts 8:18).

It might also be valuable for us to look at 1 Corinthians 14:

1 Corinthians 14:13

Therefore let him who speaks in a tongue **pray that he may interpret** (1 Corinthians 14:13).

The gift of interpretation of tongues is one of the gifts mentioned in 1 Corinthians 12:8–10. Without doubt, it is one of the miraculous spiritual gifts that could be transmitted by the laying on of the apostles' hands. But, does this text teach that all one had to do was just pray—and that no apostle had to be involved in the giving of the gifts? Indeed, that is what some people assume. But there is no record or even an implication of that ever happening.

The better understanding of this text is that prayer would accompany the laying on of the apostles' hands. Please note that in Acts 8:14–18 that prayer is mentioned in conjunction with the laying on of the apostles' hands at Samaria.

Acts 8

14 Now when the apostles who were at Jerusalem heard that Samaria had received the word of God, they sent **Peter and John** to them,

15 who, when they had come down, **prayed for them** that they might receive the Holy Spirit.

16 For as yet He had fallen upon none of them. They had only been baptized in the name of the Lord Jesus.

17 **Then they laid hands on them**, and they received the Holy Spirit.

18 And when Simon saw that **through the laying on of the apostles' hands the Holy Spirit was given**, he offered them money.

We are not surprised that prayer accompanied such events in the book of Acts. Prayer was virtually a part of everything that the apostles and other Christians did in the first century. But prayer alone did not cause Christians to receive miraculous spiritual gifts. God's means of transmitting those gifts to those who were not apostles was through the laying on of the hands of those special servants of Christ—the apostles.

In conclusion, we stated in the beginning that one of the most common misunderstandings among the modern-day Pentecostals involves what is described in the New Testament as "the laying on of hands." We now know that in the New Testament this was a reference to the laying on of the apostle's hands. Through that act those miraculous spiritual gifts were transmitted to the other Christians. Other than the direct outpouring (baptism) of the Holy Spirit on the Apostles (Acts 2) and on Cornelius, the first Gentile convert (Acts 10) those gifts of the Holy Spirit were always transmitted through the laying on of the apostle's hands. And so that leaves modern-day Pentecostals with a real dilemma since there are no longer any apostles who are alive. And more importantly, those gifts are no longer needed as a means of giving new revelation since the New Testament has been completed.

6

Speaking in Tongues

When you think of modern-day Pentecostalism, most will usually think of "speaking in tongues." And you will have a mental picture of someone in an excited state who is speaking or shouting words that nobody can understand. There are churches that not only teach that "tongues" exist today but also claim to have members who are using that gift. On the other hand, many churches today teach that "tongues," and the other miraculous spiritual gifts were limited to the first century when new revelation was being given and do not exist today. And as a result, they say that any church claiming to have those gifts is in reality doing something different than in the Bible. Who is right? Somebody is mistaken. In this chapter we will be looking at what exactly "speaking in tongues" was during the first century as described in the New Testament. We will also be looking at modern-day claims and doing a comparison.

There are several questions that need to be answered in order to understand this dilemma. First of all, what do we mean when we refer to "speaking in tongues" or in an "unknown tongue?" Second, was it unknown to the speaker or to the hearer? Third, is what we see in modern churches that claim to have the gift of tongues today, the same as in the first century? Let's explore these questions.

> **Question 1** — What was "speaking in tongues"
> in the first century?

The first reference to speaking in tongues was given by Jesus in Mark 16 in what is generally referred to as "The Great Commission."

Mark 16

¹⁵ And He said to them, "Go into all the world and preach the gospel to every creature.

¹⁶ "He who believes and is baptized will be saved; but he who does not believe will be condemned.

¹⁷ "And **these signs** will follow those who believe: In My name they will cast out demons; **they will speak with new tongues;**

¹⁸ "they will take up serpents; and if they drink anything deadly, it will by no means hurt them; they will lay hands on the sick, and they will recover."

¹⁹ So then, after the Lord had spoken to them, He was received up into heaven, and sat down at the right hand of God.

²⁰ And they went out and preached everywhere, the Lord working with them and confirming the word through **the accompanying signs.**

Jesus said that "speaking with new tongues" was one of the signs that his followers would use to "confirm" the word that they were preaching. We then have the apostles doing just that in Acts 2.

Acts 2

¹ When the Day of Pentecost had fully come, they were all with one accord in one place.

² And suddenly there came a sound from heaven, as of a rushing mighty wind, and it filled the whole house where they were sitting.

³ Then there appeared to them divided tongues, as of fire, and one sat upon each of them.

⁴ And they were all filled with the Holy Spirit and began to **speak with other tongues,** as the Spirit gave them utterance.

⁵ And there were dwelling in Jerusalem Jews, devout men, from every nation under heaven.

⁶ And when this sound occurred, the multitude came together, and were confused, because **everyone heard them speak in his own language.**

⁷ Then they were all amazed and marveled, saying to one another, "Look, are not all these who speak Galileans?

⁸ "And **how is it that we hear, each in our own language** in which we were born?

⁹ "Parthians and Medes and Elamites, those dwelling in Mesopotamia, Judea and Cappadocia, Pontus and Asia,

¹⁰ "Phrygia and Pamphylia, Egypt and the parts of Libya adjoining Cyrene, visitors from Rome, both Jews and proselytes,

¹¹ "Cretans and Arabs—**we hear them speaking in our own tongues** the wonderful works of God."

¹² So they were all amazed and perplexed, saying to one another, "Whatever could this mean?"

Just as Jesus had said, the apostles went out preaching the new message to unbelievers. A central piece of that message was that they had each seen Jesus alive after he had been crucified. When that claim was met with skepticism, those men would work a miracle by speaking to those hearers in the hearer's local and unique language. And it was a language that was clearly evident to be "unknown" to the speaker. That was what gave it such a tremendous impact. The Christians were able to speak languages that they had never learned. How could they do that? This could only be done if God was behind those men and was confirming their message to be from Him. And this procedure worked to perfection just as Jesus had said. In the Acts 2 account, it says that they spoke with other tongues "as the Spirit gave them utterance" (v. 4). It was the Holy Spirit who was giving the words to those men in a language that they did not know. It was a miracle. And that was the conclusion that the hearers made that day. It says that they were at first "confounded" (v. 6) and they were "amazed and marveled" (v. 7). They realized that those men speaking were "Galileans" and yet were able, as a group, to each speak in the various languages of those foreigners who had assembled in Jerusalem for the Day of Pentecost. The text then lists several of the areas that those listeners were from and that each was hearing a speaker give a message in their native "tongue" or language.

Notice how "tongues" is described in some of these passages:

- Called "gift of the Holy Ghost" (Acts 10:45, KJV)

- Called "the like gift" (Acts 11:17, Cornelius had the same gift as the apostles.)

- Called "spiritual gift" (Romans 1:11)

- Called "gifts" (Ephesians 4:8)

- Called "gift" (2 Timothy 1:6)

- Called "the heavenly gift" (Hebrews 6:4)

Tongues was called a "gift" because something was *given* by the Holy Spirit to these men. They were given a special power. And that power enabled them to speak any language when in foreign lands so that they could preach to those people. There was no language barrier for the apostles! And they could also use the "gift" to preach when in a church service if there was an interpreter present. When this was done in an assembly, those Christians knew that the sermon was directly from God since the speaker did not know the particular language that he was speaking.

When the apostles spoke in tongues to unbelievers back in Acts 2, Peter and the apostles actually spoke in the various languages of those foreign lands:

Acts 2

> [8] And how is it that **we hear, each** in our own language **in which we were born?**
>
> [9] Parthians, and Medes, and Elamites, and the dwellers in Mesopotamia, and in Judaea, and Cappadocia, in Pontus, and Asia,
>
> [10] Phrygia, and Pamphylia, in Egypt, and in the parts of Libya about Cyrene, and strangers of Rome, Jews and proselytes,
>
> [11] Cretes and Arabians—we do hear them speak in our tongues the wonderful works of God.

There was no need for an interpreter because they spoke directly to those groups, each in their own different language. Those unbelievers heard them speak "the wonderful works of God" (Acts 2:11) and they heard them "magnify God" (Acts 10:46). That is what caused the multitude to be "amazed." They rightly concluded that God must be the source of the message. It "confirmed" the word to them just as Jesus had said back in Mark 16:20.

One of the problems that many Bible students have when studying this topic is the use of the word "tongue" in the King James Translation. There are many references to "tongue" or "tongues" in the New Testament. Here are a few:

- "new tongues" (Mark 16:17)
- "other tongues" (Acts 2:4)
- "kinds of tongues" (1 Corinthians 12:10)
- "diversities of tongues" (1 Corinthians 12:28)
- "unknown tongue" (1 Corinthians 14:2)
- "other tongues" (1 Corinthians 14:21)
- Simply "tongues" in many passages

You will notice in the King James Version (KJV) that the word "unknown" is inserted in italics in many of those passages. This is letting the reader know that the italicized word was added in the English version but was not in the original Greek. The word "unknown" was added for clarity in order to give the reader the proper understanding in English of the Greek sentence. In the year 1611, when the KJV was translated, they used the word "tongue" in the same way that we use the word "language" today. In that time, they would ask, "What *tongue* do you speak?" Today, we would ask, "What *language* do you speak?" Most of the newer translations do not use the word "tongue" but rather translate using the English word "language." In fact, let's do a comparison of two different translations of a passage in Acts 22:

Acts 22:2 (KJV)

And when they heard that he spake in the Hebrew **tongue** to them, they kept the more silence.

Acts 22:2 (NKJV)

And when they heard that he spoke to them in the Hebrew **language**, they kept all the more silent.

Luke, in writing the book of Acts, said in Acts 22:2 that Paul spoke to them in the Hebrew language or tongue. Now, go back and read all the passages that contain the word "tongue" and instead read them with the word "language." As simple and basic as this point is, it is apparently what has caused confusion for many today on this important topic. Many do not understand that to "speak in tongues" in the Bible was simply speaking in a language that the speaker had not learned, thus it was a miracle witnessed by those hearers. And this is especially important when we realize that this basic misunderstanding is prevalent in modern-day Pentecostal churches.

What some people today call "speaking in tongues" are merely unintelligible sounds and gibberish. When the apostles on Pentecost spoke in tongues, they did not jabber with disconnected syllables coming from the mouth. They spoke actual languages that could be understood, languages that men from the various provinces had learned.

Question 2 — When the word "unknown" is used in describing the gift of "tongues," to whom is it unknown?

Is it unknown to the one hearing? Is it unknown to the one speaking? Or is it unknown to both the speaker and hearer? When the apostles were using tongues as a sign to unbelievers, then the tongue or languages were not unknown to the ones hearing. It certainly was known by the hearers in Acts 2 since the text says so. This was a public use of the gift of tongues to unbelievers. But notice this passage in 1 Corinthians 14:23–28 concerning the use of "tongues" in the church assembly of believers:

1 Corinthians 14

²³ Therefore **if the whole church comes together in one place**, and all speak with tongues, and there come in those who are uninformed or unbelievers, will they not say that you are out of your mind?

²⁴ But if all prophesy, and an unbeliever or an uninformed person comes in, he is convinced by all, he is convicted by all.

²⁵ And thus the secrets of his heart are revealed; and so, falling down on his face, he will worship God and report that God is truly among you.

²⁶ How is it then, brethren? Whenever you come together, each of you has a psalm, has a teaching, has **a tongue**, has a revelation, has **an interpretation**. Let all things be done for edification.

²⁷ If anyone speaks in a tongue, let there be two or at the most three, each in turn, and let one interpret.

²⁸ But **if there is no interpreter, let him keep silent** in church, and let him speak to himself and to God.

In this passage we have teaching on how the gift of tongues was to be used differently when it was for believers in the church assembly. Paul, through the inspiration of the Holy Spirit, commands that they are "to keep silent" if there is "no interpreter" present in the assembly.

Further, he also says that even when there is an interpreter present, there can only be "two or at the most three" who can speak in tongues in that assembly. It should be obvious that the one with the "gift of tongues" had the discretion of when to speak and use the gift versus when to keep silent. If there was no interpreter present, then he was told not to use the gift at that time. If others had already spoken, he was not to use the gift at that time. And if he chose to use the gift and to speak in tongues to the congregation, he was to do it "in turn" which means he was to wait until the other speaker had finished. And the point of these guidelines when speaking in tongues in the assembly, was so that it was "for edification" (v. 26) and that things would be done "decently and in order" (v. 40). But, if they went ahead and spoke in tongues without an interpreter, then they would be speaking in a language that nobody in the church assembly understood. And there would be no benefit because they would not understand the message. Even if they knew the speaker was miraculously speaking a language that he did not know and that God was the source of that message, the message would still not be comprehended by the audience and would not serve to edify the church. And so, they were told to not speak in tongues in those assemblies unless an interpreter was present.

So, when used in an assembly, an interpreter would always be needed and thus required. It appears that when used publicly and outside of the assembly for the benefit of unbelievers, an interpreter would never be needed because they were speaking to people in their language, though in a language that the speaker did not know. Thus, it was "unknown" to him. And it would be an obvious miracle to the hearer and confirm to them that the message given in that language must actually be coming from God and thus be heeded. So, we can summarize by saying that the primary purpose for speaking in "unknown tongues" was for a sign for unbelievers (1 Corinthians 14:22) and a secondary purpose can be found when used in the church assembly for the giving of revelation.

As a note, there is an interesting and seldom discussed passage in this chapter:

1 Corinthians 14 (KJV)

14 For **if I pray in an unknown tongue**, my spirit prayeth, but my understanding is unfruitful.

15 What is it then? I will pray with the spirit, and I will pray with the understanding also: I will **sing** with the spirit, and I will sing with the understanding also.

This passage discusses *praying* and *singing* in an unknown tongue. Apparently, those disciples who had received the "gift of tongues" through the laying on of an apostle's hands were not only using that gift in the church assemblies to give a message or sermon, but were also using it when offering prayers and at times when singing. The same thing that was said about the guidelines for "speaking in tongues" in the assembly was also said regarding praying and singing "in tongues," in the assembly. Paul said that if he prayed in an unknown tongue, that even though his "spirit prays," his "understanding is unfruitful." He said that he also wanted to pray and sing "with my understanding." It is apparent that this means that those speaking, praying, or singing in an unknown tongue did not even themselves understand what they were saying unless someone else gave an interpretation. With an interpretation, they would then have "an understanding" along with everyone else in the assembly.

1 Corinthians 14 (NKJV)

16 Otherwise, if you bless with the spirit, **how will he who occupies the place of the uninformed say "Amen" at your giving of thanks, since he does not understand what you say?**

17 For you indeed give thanks well, but the other is not edified.

Paul concludes by saying that when the guidelines are followed that were given by the Holy Spirit and the gift of tongues is only used in the assembly when an interpretation is given, then the others present would understand the message and be able to say "Amen."

So, in answering whether speaking in an "unknown tongue" meant that it was unknown to the speaker, the hearer or both, let us give a simple answer to that question. When speaking away from an assembly, to unbelievers, it was "unknown" to the speaker but was known to the hearers. But when speaking to a church assembly of believers, it was "unknown" both to the speaker and to the hearers (the audience), thus the need for an interpreter.

Question 3 — What is happening in current churches who claim to have the gift of tongues?

After having visited many modern-day Pentecostal churches, we can confidently say that what is happening in those churches is not the same as what we read about in the New Testament, but is different.

DIFFERENCES THAT MUST BE ANSWERED

- Modern-day Pentecostal church "tongues" are *not* real languages like they were in the New Testament. Why not?

- How are the gifts transmitted since there are no apostles today who can "lay on hands" like in the New Testament?

- Do modern-day Pentecostals have control over when the gift of "tongues" is used as they did in the New Testament?

- If modern-day Pentecostal church "tongues" are real, then how do they confirm or convince unbelievers?

- Why are modern-day Pentecostal churches not following the guidelines for "tongues" set forth by the Holy Spirit in 1 Corinthians 14?

- If modern-day Pentecostal churches have real "tongues," then which of the different groups is God really confirming that their message is the truth, since they disagree with each other?

- If modern-day Pentecostal churches have real "tongues," then why are not the other miraculous spiritual gifts also present?

Modern-day Pentecostals must change what "speaking in tongues" was in the New Testament in order for them to make the claim of having that gift today. They must change it to something other than a real language. And they do. We have attended many of those churches today and after watching and listening to them, we questioned why it was not understood by the audience. The answer sometimes would be that "They are speaking a heavenly language that nobody can understand." Well, they are correct in the "nobody can understand" part, but incorrect in it being a heavenly language. Sometimes they will quote 1 Corinthians 13:1 and claim that they are speaking with the "tongues of angels."

> **Though** I speak with the tongues of men and **of angels**, but have not love, I have become sounding brass or a clanging cymbal (1 Corinthians 13:1).

But, notice that Paul never said that he had spoken with the "tongues of angels." He was using a figure of speech called *hyperbole* which is defined in the dictionary as:

"An obvious and intentional exaggeration. An extravagant statement or figure of speech not intended to be taken literally."

Paul used that figure to make his point of the importance of love. In fact, he did not even say that he had spoken with the tongues of angels, but only *"though* I speak with..." His point was simply that "if" he had spoken with the tongues of angels and did not have love, then he would be like sounding brass or a clanging cymbal. But, he did not say that he had actually spoken with the tongues of angels. In all of the cases in the Old and New Testaments where angels actually did speak to men, those men always understood what the angel was speaking.

Paul in fact used a series of hyperboles in this text.

1 Corinthians 13:2

> **Though** I have the gift of prophecy, and understand all mysteries and all knowledge, and **though** I have all faith, so that I could remove mountains, but have not love, I am nothing.

Even with Paul being an apostle, that office did not give him the ability to "know everything" like God does, but only what was revealed to him. Paul never said that he had that degree of understanding, but only "if" he had it and did not have love, he would be nothing. Neither did Paul say that his faith had ever moved a mountain. Once more, this is hyperbole. He is telling his readers that even if he had miraculous faith to such a high degree, without love, he would be nothing.

And lastly, he said in verse three, "*though* I bestow all my goods to feed the poor, and *though* I give my body to be burned, but have not love, it profits me nothing." We have no information that Paul gave his body to be burned. In each of these verses, the hyperbole is used to say that even *if* Paul had done those things, without love it would not have been of any benefit. So, he never said that he had spoken with the tongues of angels, but only that "if" he had done so and did not have love, then it was of no benefit. This passage does not help present day Pentecostals in their attempt to define what it is that is happening when they claim to be "speaking in tongues."

Today, those claiming to have tongues, do not even claim to have had apostles lay hands on them to transmit that gift like in the New Testament. For the most part, and what we have seen after visiting those many services, is that modern-day "tongue speakers" just have it come on them. And in many cases, they are actually taught how to do it. Or they may simply watch others and imitate what they see them doing. And in many of those cases you can hear several people speaking the same unintelligible words.

As an interesting side note, after having visited many Pentecostal services over the years and having heard many of their members speak in what they said was "unknown tongues," we began to notice something odd. We started listening very carefully to exactly what was being said and we wrote it down. And what became apparent was that many of those "tongue speakers" were saying the same thing. They almost always start with these words, "andelae shastama..." We know a little Spanish and "andale" means to "go" or to "hurry." But we don't think that these so-called tongue speakers are speaking Spanish. And "shastama" does not seem to be a real word at all.

So, what they are doing is simply repeating what they have heard others in their church say which is to repeat meaningless gibberish that cannot be translated because it is not a real language, unlike in the New Testament examples. In fact, if you tried to make up a fake language by simply speaking some "nonsense," then it would sound exactly the same as what they are doing in those churches.

One of the interesting things that we have done is to simply ask one of the members to speak in tongues. Most of the time they will say that they cannot do it at will but only as the Spirit comes over them. In other words, they do not have control of the "gift of tongues," if they actually have it. This is a convenient way for them to get out of having to give a demonstration and be tested. Also, this is unlike in the New Testament where they did have control over their use of the gift. In fact, if you think about the guidelines given in 1 Corinthians chapter fourteen of how the gift of "tongues" was to be used in the church assemblies, they were told not to speak when there was no interpreter present—but that they could indeed speak if one was present. In other words, it was up to the Christian who had the gift of tongues, to decide whether to use the gift or not. That is totally different than what you will see today if you visit a Pentecostal church. Not only do they say they have no control over its use, which we do not believe, but you will see several men speaking at the same time, and you will see men and women speaking when no interpretation is given. This simply causes confusion which goes against the point being made in 1 Corinthians 14. In the first century, when "speaking in tongues" to other believers at a church assembly, they apparently were giving new revelation in the absence of the written word. By giving it in tongues would guarantee to all who were present that it was from God and not just made up. Is this what is happening today? No, it is not. And today, what do these "modern-day tongues" do for an unbeliever who is present in one of their assemblies. In fact, one of Paul's points to the church in Corinth is very similar to what we see in churches today:

1 Corinthians 14:23

> Therefore if the whole church comes together in one place,
> and all speak with tongues, and there come in those who are
> uninformed or unbelievers, **will they not say that you are
> out of your mind?**

Paul's point was that if an unbeliever came into a church assembly
where members with the "gift of tongues" spoke to the congregation
all at the same time and with no interpreter, that unbeliever would
conclude that they were "mad" or as we might say today, "crazy."

Remember what we saw earlier from Mark 16:15-20. "Tongues" was
one of the gifts given by Jesus to His apostles. Verse 20 of that text
shows that tongues was one of the gifts that the Lord used to confirm
the message of the apostles. The apostles went out and preached everywhere, the Lord working with them, confirming their message
through the signs that accompanied their preaching.

Modern-day "tongues" does not confirm anything at all. Which of the
different Pentecostal groups are we to believe has the real tongues, if
any? One group is teaching that God is confirming that there are three
persons in the Godhead while another group is teaching that God is
confirming that there is only one. And what about the charismatic
Catholics? What are they confirming? And what are the Mormons
confirming with their tongues? Can you see the confusion here? When
we compare the alleged "tongues" in all the modern-day Pentecostal
groups, they all appear and sound the same. They are not real languages and cannot be interpreted. But when we compare them to what
happened in the New Testament, we can see an obvious and distinct
difference. There they miraculously spoke real languages that they
had not learned. That is different than what we see today.

And if a modern Pentecostal church claims to have the gift of tongues
today, why do they not also have all of the other miraculous spiritual
gifts as well? We have not seen anybody raising the dead, have you?
And we have not seen any of those faith healers make a televised trip
up to the hospital emergency room and heal all those injured people

who are being brought in by ambulance. Have any of you seen that happen? Of course not.

Some of the Pentecostal groups teach that all the saved will speak in tongues as a sign of salvation. But, when we look at 1 Corinthians chapter twelve we can clearly see that was certainly not the case in the New Testament.

1 Corinthians 12

²⁹ Are all apostles? Are all prophets? Are all teachers? Are all workers of miracles?

³⁰ Do all have gifts of healings? **Do all speak with tongues?** Do all interpret?

³¹ But earnestly desire the best gifts. And yet I show you a more excellent way.

Paul, through the inspiration of the Holy Spirit, asks rhetorical questions directly related to this topic. One of those questions was, "Do all speak with tongues?" The answer to all those questions is "No." All were not apostles. All were not prophets. All were not teachers. All were not workers of miracles. All did not have the gift of healings. And, all the saved in the first century did *not* speak in tongues. Therefore, tongues could *not* have been a sign of salvation as is being claimed by many churches today. Tongues, when it was given in the first century church, was limited in how it was received (through the laying on of apostles' hands), limited in its operation (confirming the word) and limited in its duration (used until the written word was completed).

The unknown "tongues" that we see today in modern-day Pentecostal churches is not the same as in the New Testament. Today, they are not real languages and cannot be interpreted. They do not confirm anything to unbelievers, and they do not give any new revelation to believers. Therefore, they serve no purpose. But what they actually do is to show us how some have misunderstood the scriptures and are involved in ridiculous practices—like being taught to speak in tongues—and their actions are simply make-believe as people have to get worked up into an emotional frenzy in order to speak in tongues. They are pretending to have a special power from God, that in reality they do not have.

SOME FINAL THOUGHTS AND QUESTIONS ABOUT SPEAKING IN TONGUES

Sometimes people ask us, "How do you explain the claims to tongues that men make today?"

We think we have already answered that question. But just to be clear, let us say that most of the time what you see is nothing more than an emotional experience. It is often necessary for those who claim to speak in tongues to be whipped into an emotional frenzy in order to produce their phenomena. Many people think they need a sign that God has accepted them. They have been taught that the gift of tongues is such a sign. If they have tongues, it means they are close to God and are spiritual people. They do not, however, speak actual languages by the Spirit of God.

For other tongue-speakers, it is less an emotional experience, and more a learned experience. Most of the readers of this book may not know "how tongues are supposed to sound." But, if we have been exposed to those who profess to speak in tongues and have learned the sounds from them, it would be easy—consciously or unconsciously—to reproduce those sounds. Some people are actually taught "how to speak in tongues" by repeating tongue-twisting phrases.

It is worthy of note that this same non-miraculous phenomenon is found among many religions, including both the Hindus and Muslims.

The following questions may be asked of those who claim to speak in tongues by the Holy Spirit.

1. Do you speak a language known to others in the world?
   See Acts 2:6, 8, 11.

2. Are your tongues used as a sign to unbelievers?
   See 1 Corinthians 14:22.

3. Do several speak in tongues at once in your assemblies?
   See 1 Corinthians 14:27.

4. Do your people speak in tongues only with an interpreter?
   See 1 Corinthians 14:28.

5. Are your assemblies conducted in an orderly fashion?
   See 1 Corinthians 14:40.

These are questions that we have asked numerous times to a variety of professing tongue-speakers. The Bible answers to these five questions are found in the texts above. Are we surprised when those professing to speak in tongues answer differently than what these verses teach? We ought not to be surprised because what they have is not what Christians in the early church had.

The gift of tongues in the New Testament is to be understood as the miraculous ability to speak a foreign language that could be understood by those who had learned that language.

The gift of tongues was received in one of two ways: 1) It was received by some through Holy Spirit baptism; 2) It was received by others through the laying on of apostles' hands. In either case, its purpose was to reveal and/or confirm a message from God.

Modern tongue-speaking is not Biblical tongue-speaking at all and is a phenomenon common to some religions that do not profess Jesus as the Christ. The present practice of tongue-speaking has no biblical basis. In fact, most who claim to practice it violate plain passages of scripture when they do it.

7

The Witnesses

In the New Testament, there were Christians who were said to be "witnesses." What exactly did this mean, and can we be witnesses today?

Acts 1:8

> But you shall receive power when the Holy Spirit has come upon you; and you shall be **witnesses** to Me in Jerusalem, and in all Judea and Samaria, and to the end of the earth.

Jesus, in speaking to the Apostles, told them just prior to his ascension to heaven, that they would "be witnesses" to Him. Later in the chapter when a replacement for Judas was being made, we read:

Acts 1

> [21] Wherefore of these men which have companied with us (apostles) all the time that the Lord Jesus went in and out among us,
>
> [22] beginning from the baptism of John, unto that same day that he was taken up from us, must one be ordained **to be a witness with us of his resurrection.**

The "us" is a reference to Peter and the other ten apostles who were present. Therefore, Peter claims that all the apostles were "witnesses of the resurrection." He said that they had been accompanying Jesus from the beginning of his ministry, "beginning from the baptism of John." Peter also said they had followed Jesus "unto that same day that he was taken up from us" which is a reference to the ascension after His death. Peter then stated that the replacement for Judas had to have been a witness of the resurrection like all the other apostles.

> **Question** — How could anyone be a witness of that if no one was there inside the tomb to see the event—that is, the actual moment when Jesus arose from the dead? No one was in the tomb at the moment of resurrection.

> **Answer** — After Jesus was raised from the dead He appeared to many people. Anyone who saw Him alive after He had been crucified would have been an "eyewitness" to the fact that He was indeed raised from the dead! That is what is meant by "a witness with us of His resurrection."

Why would this be a qualification that the replacement for Judas would have to meet? Because the claim that Jesus had been raised from the dead would be the central theme of the message that these apostles would preach to the world. It was God's plan for the apostles to be eyewitnesses to the resurrection of Jesus. (See Acts 10:39-41.) Eyewitness testimony is testimony of the highest order. In the pages of the New Testament (and particularly in the book of Acts) we have a permanent record of the testimony of those men who had personally seen Jesus alive after He had been crucified.

There are numerous references throughout the New Testament to the apostles being witnesses of the resurrection. Take time to look up the following passages and see how they preached, claiming that they were "witnesses" of the resurrection.

Acts 2:32 (Peter)

"This Jesus God has raised up, of which we are all **witnesses**."

Acts 3:15 (Peter)

"...whom God raised from the dead, of which we are **witnesses**."

Acts 4:33 (Luke)

And with great power the apostles gave **witness** to the resurrection of the Lord Jesus.

Acts 5:29–32 (the apostles)

"And we are his **witnesses**."

Acts 10:39–41 (Peter)

"And we are **witnesses**. ...Him God raised up the third day, and showed him openly...who did eat and drink with him after he rose from the dead."

Acts 22:15 (Jesus to Paul)

"For you will be His **witness** to all men of what you have seen and heard."

Acts 23:11 (Jesus to Paul)

"So you must also **bear witness** at Rome."

Acts 26:16 (Jesus to Paul)

"For I have appeared to you for this purpose, to make you a minister and a **witness** both of the things which you have seen and of the things which I will yet reveal to you."

1 Peter 5:1 (Peter)

I who am a fellow elder and a **witness** of the sufferings of Christ.

Hebrews 2:3–4 (author of Hebrews)

[S]alvation...was confirmed unto us by them that heard Him [a reference to the original twelve], God also **bearing witness**, both with signs and wonders...

2 Peter 1:16–19 (Peter)

For we did not follow cunningly devised fables…but were **eyewitnesses** of His majesty.

1 John 1:1–2 (John)

That which was from the beginning, which we have heard which we have seen with our eyes, which we have looked upon, and our hands have handled… and we have seen it, and **bear witness**.

Please take note of the last scripture given in the list above. The text of First John points to something that we should not miss. John says, "…we have seen with our eyes, which we have looked upon…" To have "seen with the eyes" and to have "looked upon" sounds like the same thing, but it is not. To have "looked upon" is stronger. The first reference is "to see, to look at, or to behold" with the eyes (*Strong's*). The second reference, to have "looked upon," is to "look closely or to view attentively" (*Strong's*). This second reference carries the idea of examination. It can easily be understood in the case of Thomas in John 20:26-29. Thomas was one of those witnesses chosen by Jesus.

John 20

²⁶ And after eight days His disciples were again inside, and Thomas with them. Jesus came, the doors being shut, and stood in the midst, and said, "Peace to you!"

²⁷ Then He said to Thomas, "**Reach your finger here, and look at My hands; and reach your hand here, and put it into My side. Do not be unbelieving, but believing.**"

²⁸ And Thomas answered and said to Him, "My Lord and my God!"

²⁹ Jesus said to him, "Thomas, because you have seen Me, you have believed. Blessed are those who have not seen and yet have believed."

You can see from this text that Jesus allowed Thomas to examine Him—to see and touch the wounds in Jesus' body. The Apostle John was present when Jesus allowed this examination. There was no doubt to Thomas or to any of the apostles that Jesus was alive. They had seen and examined Him. And, as First John 1:2 says, "our hands have handled." These men were to be Jesus' witnesses to the world!

Peter, John, Paul, and all of the other apostles truly were witnesses of the resurrection of Jesus. The original twelve accompanied Jesus during His ministry on the earth. They then saw Him put to death. Afterwards, He appeared to them empowering them to testify that He had indeed been raised from the dead. Jesus also appeared to Paul giving him the ability to make the same testimony.

But what about today? We have seen many Pentecostal churches today with a quotation of Acts 1:8 posted behind the pulpit admonishing their people to "be witnesses" today. So, there is obviously a misunderstanding among many as to what being "a witness" means. Most simply equate it with telling someone how their life has changed since following Jesus. They call it "witnessing." And although that is admirable, that is not what being "a witness" means in the New Testament.

Let us give an illustration to clarify. Think for just a minute about a car accident that your friend saw. He was an eyewitness. What if he told you every single detail of that accident? You would then know as much about it as he knew, even though you did not see it. Now suppose that both of you were called on to testify at a hearing about the accident. You may be asked to get up and tell what you know to have happened. However, as soon as it becomes apparent that you were not personally an eyewitness, your testimony will be ruled second hand, or hearsay. But your friend who was there would then be called on to testify as to what he had personally seen, as an eyewitness. Though you could have given a correct account, you still were not an eyewitness, and your testimony would not be as convincing as his. Our courts today recognize the importance of that kind of evidence. It can constitute *proof*, considering the reliability of the witness. Since the apostles were told in Acts 1:8 that they would be the ones to first begin the preaching of the gospel, it would be important that they be able to answer the skeptics by saying, "We are eyewitnesses!" That, in essence, is what they claimed in Acts 2:32. They could then further produce proof by *confirming* their words with miracles!

The testimony of the apostles was indeed powerful! They could testify that they had seen Jesus alive following his resurrection, and they could further verify it by performing signs and wonders (Mark 16:20).

Nobody today then is a *witness* in the sense that "witness" was used in the New Testament.

8

A More Excellent Way

If you were to visit a modern-day Pentecostal church, you will likely hear a sermon on how there are those today with the miraculous spiritual gifts. On the other hand, there are many who will say that those gifts were only present during the giving of new revelation in the first century. Which is correct? Let's explore this further by examining some very clear passages in the New Testament.

We understand that Paul, through the inspiration of the Holy Spirit, had much to say in the book of 1 Corinthians on the subject of miracles. The apostle devoted three chapters of that book to supernatural spiritual gifts—chapters twelve, thirteen, and fourteen. Those three chapters can be viewed in the following way (**Figure 3**).

The Topics of 1 Corinthians 12–14

Passage	Topics Addressed
1 Corinthians 12	Explains how the supernatural spiritual gifts all work together
1 Corinthians 13	Explains how these gifts were temporary in nature from the beginning
1 Corinthians 14	Explains how these gifts were to be regulated in the church assemblies

Figure 3.

1 Corinthians 12. Chapter twelve discusses the various "spiritual gifts" and how they all work together in the church assembly. The gifts have value to the group when they are used to edify the church. The spiritual gifts were giving new revelation to the church and giving confirmation of that revelation.

1 Corinthians 13. Chapter thirteen discusses the temporary nature of the gifts. The church was told that those gifts were given for a particular purpose and when that purpose was fulfilled, then those gifts would end.

1 Corinthians 14. Chapter fourteen gives guidelines of how those gifts were to be used (and sometimes not used) when in a church assembly. This chapter regulates the use of the gifts during that time when the miraculous gifts of the Spirit were active among the early Christians. When those gifts were used correctly, they fit perfectly into God's plan for the building up of the early church. But when used incorrectly, they only caused problems. And yet, in the middle of all those verses and at the end of chapter twelve, Paul makes a statement that many have been perplexed as to its meaning.

> But earnestly desire the best gifts. And yet I show you **a more excellent way** (1 Corinthians 12:31).

What is the "more excellent way" to which Paul referred? This phrase is consistent with the context of the next section, chapter thirteen, about the temporary nature of the spiritual gifts. The phrase "a more excellent *way*" is pointing to something that would continue when the gifts had ceased in the early church. The Corinthian church was one that was in disarray. They had confusion, conflict, and division in their assemblies. (See 1 Corinthians 1:10–11; 11:18–19.) Part of the conflict was over the use of these miraculous spiritual gifts. Some in that church believed that the gift of tongues was a greater gift than the others. Some of the members may have believed they were un-important if they did not have the same spiritual gifts as others (see 1 Corinthians 12:15–30). Verse 25 points to the fact that there were schisms (division) over the spiritual gifts. Brethren were arguing and contentious with one another over the gifts. It was in this context that

Paul said "I show you a more excellent way" (v. 31). The excellent way is found in chapter thirteen. The spiritual gifts were only temporary, but there was something that was permanent. The spiritual gifts were giving partial revelation, but there was coming a complete and final revelation of God's will to man. When the gifts ceased, there was something that would not cease, something that would abide. It is our duty to study the context and to learn what would continue after the gifts ceased. When we have learned that, then we will know what "the more excellent way" is. What follows now is a simple exercise in proper Bible study. So, let's review the context.

Chapter twelve is addressing the nature of spiritual gifts and how they operate. Notice how this chapter begins:

1 Corinthians 12:1

Now concerning spiritual gifts, brethren, I do not want you to be ignorant.

Paul begins the discussion of spiritual gifts by telling them that he wants them to understand these gifts. Unfortunately, there are those even today who do not understand spiritual gifts. Paul's teachings were inspired by the Holy Spirit. The Holy Spirit wanted men to know how spiritual gifts would fit into God's plan for mankind's salvation. He writes in verse four that there are "diversities of gifts" which means that there are different gifts. But he says in verse seven that in spite of this fact, all of the gifts come from God and are given "for the profit of all." In verses eight through ten he gives a list of nine gifts:

1. The word of wisdom
2. The word of knowledge
3. Faith (a miraculous measure of faith)
4. Gifts of healings
5. The working of miracles
6. Prophecy
7. Discerning of spirits
8. Different kinds of tongues
9. The interpretation of tongues

He then goes on in verses eleven through thirty to explain how the supernatural spiritual gifts, the giving of divine revelation to man, are given by God to individual members so that they can all work together. As part of that, he uses the analogy of a man's body and how all the various body parts work together. No one part of the body should be in conflict with the other parts. All of the parts of the body should work together for the benefit of the whole. The final thoughts of this section of chapter twelve looks at how God has placed the various gifts and persons in the church as it has pleased Him. Since this order and arrangement was God's plan, the Corinthians should not be jealous of one another, and should not have conflicts over spiritual gifts.

As a side note, please observe that the Apostle Paul makes an interesting and important statement in verse thirty. He asks a rhetorical question, "Do all speak with tongues?" With such questions the answer is always obvious. All of the early Christians did not have the gift of tongues. Compare that truth to the modern Pentecostal claim that "all born again Christians will speak in tongues." That claim was not true among the early Christians, and is not at all true today! Let's look at chapter thirteen.

1 Corinthians 13

¹ Though I speak with the tongues of men and of angels, but have not love, I have become sounding brass or a clanging cymbal.

² And though I have the gift of prophecy, and understand all mysteries and all knowledge, and though I have all faith, so that I could remove mountains, but have not love, I am nothing.

³ And though I bestow all my goods to feed the poor, and though I give my body to be burned, but have not love, it profits me nothing.

⁴ Love suffers long and is kind; love does not envy; love does not parade itself, is not puffed up;

⁵ does not behave rudely, does not seek its own, is not provoked, thinks no evil;

⁶ does not rejoice in iniquity, but rejoices in the truth;

⁷ bears all things, believes all things, hopes all things, endures all things.

⁸ Love never fails. But whether there are prophecies, they will **fail**; whether there are tongues, they will **cease**; whether there is knowledge, it will **vanish away**.

⁹ For we know **in part** and we prophesy **in part**.

¹⁰ But when that which is perfect has come, then that which is **in part** will be **done away**.

¹¹ When I was a child, I spoke as a child, I understood as a child, I thought as a child; but when I became a man, I put away childish things.

¹² For now we see in a mirror, dimly, but then face to face. Now I know **in part**, but then I shall know just as I also am known.

¹³ And now abide faith, hope, love, these three; but the greatest of these is love.

Paul clearly tells us that those spiritual gifts were only temporary. In verse eight he mentions prophecies, tongues, and knowledge. These three represent the longer list of spiritual gifts just mentioned in the previous chapter. In chapter twelve, verse eight Paul had mentioned the gift of "the word of knowledge." Verse ten had mentioned "prophesy" and "tongues." This is the same thing that was done by Jesus in Mark 16:17-20. There, Jesus only mentioned five gifts that are representative of all the gifts that would be used to confirm the word. This use of a representative list to stand for the whole list is called "synecdoche" (pronounced "sin-EK-do-key," emphasis on the second syllable). Paul uses synecdoche here in 1 Corinthians thirteen. Even though he mentions only prophecy, tongues, and knowledge, this partial list stands for the whole found in chapter twelve, verses eight through ten. In chapter thirteen, he said that those gifts would "fail" (v. 8), "cease" (v. 8), "vanish away" (v. 8), be "done away" (v. 10), and "put away" (v. 11). When would that happen? He said that would happen when "the perfect" has come. The "perfect" or completed revelation is a reference to the time when the written scriptures would be finalized. Keep in mind that during the beginning of the New Testament period there was no written New Testament.

Verse ten says, "*when* that which is perfect is come." That process was finalized by about the end of the first century (the last book of the New Testament, Revelation, was written in about A.D. 96) and therefore those spiritual gifts would end as God's final word to mankind was complete; thus, the gifts would no longer be needed. The church would no longer have to rely on "partial" revelation because the revelation had been completed or "perfected" ("*that* which is perfect") when it was put in written form. The word rendered "perfect" is the Greek word τέλειος, *teleios*, which is defined by *Vine's Greek Dictionary* as "having reached its end (τέλος, *telos*), finished, complete." Paul uses this word in contrast to that which is "in part," imperfect, or incomplete. It is the "part" contrasted with the "whole," complete or finished.

It is important to understand that the Greek word translated "perfect" does not have the same meaning as our English word. The way we use our English word, "perfect," carries the idea of something having no faults; we even use it to mean "sinless." But the Greeks would use that word to describe a project that was being built; when that project was finished, they would say that it was *teleios* or completed. They would use the same word in describing a child growing up to an adult, he would be *teleios* or complete, grown. In 1611, when the King James Translation was made, they used the English word "perfect" in the same way that the Greeks used the word *teleios*. On the other hand, many of the newer translations render it "complete" which more accurately fits our current use of those words. Unfortunately, the use of "perfect" in the KJV has caused many to falsely conclude that it is referring to something other than the giving of revelation and instead incorrectly believe it refers to the second coming of Jesus. This conclusion is totally at odds with the clear context in that section of the book. The context is about God giving revelation to mankind through the various spiritual gifts. The gifts gave partial revelation. The early church was looking toward the time when they would have a complete revelation.

Again, Paul clearly tells us that the "part" is the spiritual gifts. Since we know that those gifts were used to give revelation to man, then "the complete" must also be in reference to the giving of revelation to man. The substance of the "part" must be the same as the substance of the whole, complete or "perfect." Nobody who cuts a part (piece) of an apple pie would expect it to be anything other than apple pie (the whole). The part is always of the same substance as the whole. And the same thing is true in the context of our discussion. So, again, what does "that which is perfect" stand for? It is the completed revelation of God's will—the written word. James referred to the word as "the perfect law of liberty" in James 1:25. When the revelation is completed in written form, then there would be no more need for partial, oral revelation. Paul said when that happens then "that which is in part shall be done away." In verse eleven, he compares this process to a child coming to maturity. A child grows year by year into an adult. When he becomes an adult, he puts away the things of his childhood. When Paul wrote these things the church was in its childhood and needed these special gifts to reveal God's will because, at that time, they did not have the completed revelation. But when God's revelation was complete, those temporary gifts would cease. When the scriptures grow book by book into a completed form, the things of the church's childhood would no longer be needed. Paul used this same illustration in Ephesians of which we will discuss later.

He then follows in chapter fourteen by giving new revelation detailing the guidelines of how those gifts were to be used while they were still in effect. He even contrasts their use in the church assemblies as opposed to their use outside the assembly. Notice the phrases "yet in the church" (v. 19), "if the whole church comes together in one place (v. 23), "or an uninformed person *comes in*" (v. 24), "Whenever you come together" (v. 26), "in the church" (v. 28), "to another who *sits by*" (v. 30) and "in the churches" (v. 34). These are all references to church assemblies and how those spiritual gifts were to be used there.

Now what about the passages in chapter thirteen that discuss "love"? Doesn't this seem a bit out of place to put these eight verses in the middle of three long chapters that are going into great detail teaching the church about the purpose and use of the spiritual gifts? No, these verses are not out of place if you understand why they are there. The subject of love is inserted, not just by Paul, but by the Holy Spirit, in order to have a transition or segue in the context. It is used to place an emphasis on a critically important point that will be made. Keep in mind that, up to the writing of this letter to the church at Corinth, the congregations had apostles' hands laid on some members in order to transmit those spiritual gifts to them in the absence of the completed written word. Those who received those gifts then had the power to work miracles, speak prophetically, and use the gift of tongues in giving revelation. How great it must have been to have one of these gifts and to be able to use it in the teaching of the gospel! Imagine what a shock it might have been to find out that the "gift" or power was going to end! And so, that brings us back to the original passage in question:

1 Corinthians 12:31

But earnestly desire the best gifts. And yet I show you **a more excellent way**.

Remember that Paul began chapter twelve by saying that he had something important to teach them about spiritual gifts so that they would not be "ignorant" on the subject. After detailing to the church how all of the gifts work together for the good of all, he begins a transition to informing them that the gifts were going to end. He begins that transition with 1 Corinthians 12:31 and describes what he is about to reveal as a "more excellent *way*" than the way that revelation was being given at that time through the gifts. The more excellent "way" is the same as what he is about to call "that" which is perfect, the words "excellent" and "perfect" being synonyms. Chapter thirteen then begins by discussing love. Paul uses a figure of speech called hyperbole, which is where something is exaggerated for effect in order to make a point. He uses several examples of hyperbole in verses one through three.

1 Corinthians 13

¹ **Though I speak with the tongues** of men and **of angels**, but have not love, I have become sounding brass or a clang-ing cymbal."

> ² And **though** I have the gift of prophecy, **and understand all mysteries and all knowledge,** and though I have all faith, so that I could remove mountains, but have not love, I am nothing.
>
> ³ And **though I bestow all my goods to feed the poor,** and **though I give my body to be burned,** but have not love, it profits me nothing.

Paul, even with the gift of "tongues" did not speak with the tongues or languages of angels (v. 1). And though Paul was an Apostle, that office did not give him the ability to "know everything" (v. 2) like God does, but only what was revealed to him. And we have no information that Paul gave his body to be burned (v. 3). In all of these verses, the hyperbole is used to say that even *if* Paul had done those things, without love it would not have been of any benefit. He next goes on to elaborate about love (vv. 4–7). The transition fully takes place in verse eight where he says "love never fails. *But...*" He then begins telling them about something that will fail.

1 Corinthians 13

> ⁸ **Love never fails.** But whether there are prophecies, **they will fail;** whether there are tongues, **they will cease;** whether there is knowledge, **it will vanish away.**
>
> ⁹ For we know in part and we prophesy in part.
>
> ¹⁰ But **when** that which is perfect **has come, then that which is in part will be done away.**

Love has been interjected as something that "never fails" in order to contrast and emphasize this new revelation being given for the first time that those spiritual gifts are about to end ("fail" or "cease").

At this point we want to go back to chapter twelve and make some comparisons with 1 Corinthians 13 as well as with Ephesians 4, noticing how the same words are used (see **Figures 4–7** on pages 104–107).

A Comparison between 1 Corinthians 12:1–11 and 13:8

Now concerning spiritual gifts, brethren, I do not want you to be ignorant…   1 Corinthians 12:1

Supernatural Gifts	Citation
1. for to one is given the **word of wisdom** through the Spirit,	1 Corinthians 12:8a
2. to another **the word of knowledge** through the same Spirit,	1 Corinthians 12:8b
3. to another **faith** by the same Spirit,	1 Corinthians 12:9a
4. to another **gifts of healings** by the same Spirit,	1 Corinthians 12:9b
5. to another the **working of miracles,**	1 Corinthians 12:10a
6. to another **prophecy,**	1 Corinthians 12:10b
7. to another **discerning of spirits,**	1 Corinthians 12:10c
8. to another **different kinds of tongues,**	1 Corinthians 12:10d
9. to another the **interpretation of tongues.**	1 Corinthians 12:10e
But one and the same Spirit works all these things, distributing to each one individually as He wills.	1 Corinthians 12:11
Love never fails. But whether there are **prophecies**, they **will fail**; whether there are **tongues**, they **will cease**; whether there is **knowledge**, it **will vanish away.**	1 Corinthians 13:8

Figure 4.

Notice that three of the supernatural spiritual gifts of chapter twelve, (knowledge, prophecy and tongues) are repeated in chapter thirteen in the list of things that will end (**Figure 5**).

Supernatural Spiritual Gifts Will End
(1 Corinthians 13:8–10)

Love never fails.	1 Corinthians 13:8a

Supernatural Gifts	Citation
1. But whether there are **prophecies**, they will **fail**;	1 Corinthians 13:8b
2. whether there are **tongues**, they will **cease**;	1 Corinthians 13:8c
3. whether there is **knowledge**, it will vanish away.	1 Corinthians 13:8d
For we know **in part** and we prophesy **in part**.	1 Corinthians 13:9
But when that which is perfect has come, then that which is **in part** will be done away.	1 Corinthians 13:10

Figure 5.

Notice that the passage says that the gift of "prophecy" is given as a "part" of the revelation from God as well as the gift of "knowledge" (**Figure 6**).

Prophecy and Knowledge are "Part" of Revelation
(1 Corinthians 13:9–12)

Text of 1 Corinthians 13:9–12	Citation
For we know in **part** and we prophesy in part.	1 Corinthians 13:9
But when that which is **perfect** has come, then that which is in part will be done away.	1 Corinthians 13:10
When I was **a child**, I spoke as a **child**, I understood as a **child**, I thought as a **child**; but when I became a **man**, I put away **childish things**.	1 Corinthians 13:11
For now we see in a mirror, dimly, but then face to face. Now I know in part, but then I shall know just as I also am known.	1 Corinthians 13:129

Figure 6.

Notice that Paul compares the incomplete revelation as to being "a child." And he compares the complete revelation as to being "a man." He calls the use of spiritual gifts "childish things."

An interesting comparison can be made to the language used in 1 Corinthians 13 and how similar it is to what is used in Ephesians 4 concerning the nature of the spiritual gifts (**Figure 7**).

Spiritual Gifts in Ephesians 4:8, 12–16

Text of Ephesians 4	Citation
Therefore He says: "When He ascended on high, He led captivity captive, And gave **gifts** to men."	Ephesians 4:8
...for the equipping of the saints for the work of ministry, for the edifying of the body of Christ,	Ephesians 4:12
till we all come to the unity of the faith and of the knowledge of the Son of God, to **a perfect man**, to the measure of the stature of the fullness of Christ;	Ephesians 4:13
that we should no longer be **children**, tossed to and fro and carried about with every wind of doctrine, by the trickery of men, in the cunning craftiness of deceitful plotting,	Ephesians 4:14
but, speaking the truth in love, may **grow up** in all things into Him who is the head—Christ—	Ephesians 4:15
from whom the whole body, joined and knit together by what every joint supplies, according to the effective working by which every **part** does its share, causes growth of the body for the edifying of itself in love.	Ephesians 4:16

Figure 7.

Notice how similar Ephesians 4 is to 1 Corinthians 13. In Ephesians 4, Paul again alludes to the temporary nature of the miraculous spiritual gifts. They were never intended by God to be a permanent fixture in the church. They were given to serve a purpose and when that purpose was fulfilled, they would end. The gifts being called a "part" referred to partial revelation and were given "till" (Ephesians 4:13) the church matures through this knowledge. The church is then compared to a "child" maturing into a "man." This would happen book by book as the partial revelation was being given and recorded for us in a permanent form. Notice this interesting comparison between 1 Corinthians 13 and Ephesians 4 (**Figure 8**).

Comparison of 1 Corinthians 13 and Ephesians 4

Text of 1 Corinthians 13:9–12	Citation
Love never fails. But whether there are prophecies, they will fail; whether there are tongues, they will cease; whether there is knowledge, it will vanish away.	1 Corinthians 13:8
For we know in **part** and we prophesy in **part**.	1 Corinthians 13:9
But when that which is **perfect** has come, then that which is in part will be done away.	1 Corinthians 13:10
When I was a child, I spoke as a **child**, I understood as a child, I thought as a child; but when I became a man, I put away childish things.	1 Corinthians 13:11

Text of Ephesians 4:13–16	Citation
till we all come to the unity of the faith and of the knowledge of the Son of God, to a **perfect man**, to the measure of the stature of the fullness of Christ;	Ephesians 4:13
that we should no longer be **children**, tossed to and fro and carried about with every wind of doctrine, by the trickery of men, in the cunning craftiness of deceitful plotting,	Ephesians 4:14
but, speaking the truth in love, may grow up in all things into Him who is the head—Christ—	Ephesians 4:15
from whom the whole body, joined and knit together by what every joint supplies, according to the effective working by which every **part** does its share, causes growth of the body for the edifying of itself in love.	Ephesians 4:16

Figure 8.

In 1 Corinthians 13 and Ephesians 4, Paul uses the same symbolism when describing not only spiritual gifts, but the fact that those gifts were going to end when God's revelation was completed. Notice the duplicate words "part," "child," "children" and "man." In both texts, Paul uses the example of how a child grows into adulthood to describe the establishment of the church. Just as the child grows up to be a perfect (or complete) man, so also does the revelation of God's will come to maturity, and the things of childhood are "put away." As each of the members of the body of Christ do their "part," with those spiritual gifts each providing partial revelation, the church is slowly coming into maturity. This happens year by year with a child. And it was happening book by book with the New Testament as new revelation was being given and it was being written down for future generations to come.

Paul said in Ephesians 4:16 that this process would "cause the growth of the body," and we know that the "body" is a reference to the church (Ephesians 1:22–23). And it did. The church came to the "unity of the faith and the knowledge of the Son of God to a perfect man" (verse thirteen). This all happened when the new revelation was completed and the New Testament was written at the end of the first century.

Notice again this passage in 1 Corinthians 13:

1 Corinthians 13

¹¹ When I was a child, I spoke as a child, I understood as a child, I thought as a child; **but when I became a man**, I put away childish things.

¹² For **now** we see in a mirror, dimly, **but then** face to face. **Now** I know in part, **but then** I shall know just as I also am known.

¹³ And **now** abide faith, hope, love, these three; but the greatest of these is love.

Paul said, in comparing the process of completing the revelation of the New Testament, that it is like a "child" who "becomes a man." When he (the church) was a child, he spoke as a child and understood as a child. In other words, in the beginning of the church, the members only had limited understanding of God's will, since it had only been partially revealed.

Paul further compared the process of completing the revelation of the New Testament to looking into a mirror. When he (the church) does so he only can see "dimly" which is a reference to the type of mirrors they had in the first century that did not show as clear of an image as we have in our mirrors today. Again, in the beginning of the church, the members only had a "dim" understanding of God's will, since it had not been completely revealed. However, what they had in an incomplete revelation was yet sufficient for their salvation. Paul further said that once he "became a man" that he "put away childish things." After that, when he then looked into that mirror, he no longer saw himself "dimly," but "face to face." There was coming a time, Paul said, when the church would no longer rely on those spiritual gifts to "know in part," but would have the full revelation of God, "but then I shall know even as I am known."

As an important note, and to elaborate on a point that was made earlier, the use of "love" may also have been chosen for the textual transition because of the problems that the Corinthian church was having. These problems are alluded to in 1 Corinthians 12:23 where it discusses how some members may have thought some to be "less honorable" than themselves. Verse twenty-five says that "there should be no schism in the body," a reference to divisions. 1 Corinthians 14:40 seems to indicate that their services were not being conducted in an orderly manner. So, in choosing the subject of love as a transition to give the new revelation on the gifts being done away, God was able to also give them much needed teaching on the need for love in the church. Even though those spiritual gifts were going to end or "fail," Paul said that "love never fails." The gifts would cease; love would endure.

To understand more about why Paul taught that love would not end, consider these facts about the church at Corinth. It was a troubled church. It was plagued with almost every imaginable problem: division, immorality, corrupt worship, exalting men, lawsuits against one another, marriage issues, etc. And, in the context of chapters twelve through fourteen, this church abused the miraculous spiritual gifts!

In thinking about the "more excellent way" (1 Corinthians 12:13), there are two sets of thoughts to consider. First, there were the temporary spiritual gifts which were set in contrast to the permanent and complete final revelation. Good Bible students know that having a complete and final revelation is more excellent than having the temporary gifts.

Second, there was the jealousy, confusion, and disruption over the use of the spiritual gifts. These brethren had lost their way. In their issues over the gifts, they had neglected one of the most fundamental elements of the gospel. They failed to love each other! Love should have been the ruling principle in all their dealings with one another. It is the one thing that would always abide and would never cease. The miraculous spiritual gifts, as valuable as they were, would be in use for only a limited time.

Consider these facts about the thirteen verses of 1 Corinthians 13 (**Figure 9**):

Facts about 1 Corinthians 13

Text of 1 Corinthians 13:9–12	Citation
Love is the vital, life-giving element—without which, the gift of tongues is only noisemaking.	Verse 1
Miraculous insight and miraculous faith—without love, Paul would be nothing; he would be unsaved.	Verse 2
Sacrifice and even martyrdom—without love for God and man, profits him nothing.	Verse 3
Love demonstrates itself in actions—both positive and negative. The Corinthians erred on this, violating these principles.	Verse 4
This text presents four negatives. Love is not disgraceful; is not about self; it is not roused to anger; it is not grudging.	Verse 5
A contrast: love knows how to rejoice; it does not take joy in unrighteous deeds, but in God's truth.	Verse 6
Love is forbearing, it believes the best of others, it hopes for the best, and it endures all situations.	Verse 7

Text of 1 Corinthians 13:9–12	Citation
The value of love as contrasted with temporary things. Love does not fail. It doesn't mean that if someone loves you, they will always love you. It is about the eternal nature of love as contrasted with temporary spiritual gifts—the gifts of prophecy, tongues, and knowledge are only examples; as mentioned earlier, this is a partial list of miraculous spiritual gifts. The gift of prophecy would be done away; the word used here means to be "abolished," to become "idle." The gift of tongues would cease; the word used here means "to quit, come to an end." The word of knowledge would be done away (it is the same word that is used with the gift of prophecy—to vanish, make void). By contrast, love—would never be voided, vanish, be abolished, quit, or come to an end—this more excellent way is set in distinct contrast to the temporary gifts.	Verse 8
The miraculous gifts provided only partial knowledge and partial prophecy—partial revelation.	Verse 9
The early church looked for the time in the future when the "perfect" (complete, whole) of knowledge and prophecy would be made known. (This verse is not about Jesus but is about God revealing parts of His will through spiritual gifts—contrasted with when His whole will would be revealed in a complete form.)	Verse 10
The church was like a child—in its infancy. But the days of maturity were coming. When that took place, the childhood things (miraculous spiritual gifts) would be done away.	Verse 11
In the time of spiritual gifts complete clarity was not known. But it was coming.	Verse 12
The final verse: The greatest of these is love because it will not only outlast spiritual gifts, it will continue on when faith and hope no longer abide.	Verse 13

Figure 9.

Why is love the greatest? Because it endures into eternity. Though "now" (the present time—after the gifts are gone) there are three that abide—faith, hope, and love. But not in eternity. In eternity *faith* becomes sight. (See 2 Corinthians 5:6–8.) When we see Jesus, it will no longer be a matter of faith (believing and trusting the evidence about who Jesus is). We will see Him and be in His very presence. (See 1 John 3:1–2.) In eternity, our *hope* is realized. (See Romans 8:24–25;

1 John 2:25.) We will no longer hope to see Jesus, or hope for eternal life—we will have it in His presence. While both faith and hope are realized, *love* will continue on. We will be with the ultimate object of our love—the Lord Jesus. (See 1 Peter 1:6–9.) Love for God is never ending; love for brethren will be more perfectly experienced in heaven than ever on earth.

All three—faith, hope and love—abide *now* in this present age, whereas the spiritual gifts do not! The fact that love is the greatest does not demean or denigrate faith and hope. In fact, in the circumstances of life *now*, each has value. When the days are dark, dreary and difficult, we need to trust God; we need faith to sustain us. When we are tired, weak, worn and weary, we must remind ourselves of a better place. We need hope to motivate us. When we have been wronged, hurt or disappointed, we need to love like the Father loves, like Jesus loves (Matthew 5:43–48).

But in eternity, it will only be love. We will look back on faith and hope and be glad as we bask in the blessings of God's love. Forever blessed, forever happy, forever with our Lord Jesus. How sad it was that the Corinthians were disputing and arguing over the spiritual gifts when love was the one thing that would abide.

So, in conclusion, we hope you can see two powerful thoughts about the "more excellent way" (1 Corinthians 12:13). First, there were the temporary spiritual gifts which were set in contrast to the permanent and complete final revelation. We have the blessing of a complete and final revelation. That is more excellent than having the temporary gifts. You might even call the early giving of revelation through the gifts "a less excellent way," since it was imperfect, incomplete revelation. What we have today with our Bibles—a completed revelation—is better than what the Corinthians had. Revelation is no longer being given since it has been completed.

Second, there was the jealousy, confusion, and disruption in the Corinthian church over the use of the spiritual gifts. These brethren were disputing over who had the best gifts, and had failed to live by the one enduring thing that would outlast all the gifts. They failed to love each other! Love is the one thing that would always abide and would never cease. The miraculous spiritual gifts, as valuable as they were, would be in use for only a limited time.

As a footnote, Eusebius, a Christian Greek historian (A.D. 260–339) and a bishop at Caesarea wrote the book, *Ecclesiastical History*. In his book he made a reference to those "miraculous events performed *of old.*"

> [H]ere he confirmed those miraculous events **performed of old** against the wicked, and which have been discredited by so many, as if belonging to fiction and fable, but which **have been** established in the sacred volume, as credible to the believer (Eusebius, *Ecclesiastical History*, p. 392).

It is interesting that Eusebius, writing in the third century and writing about events of the church that had happened in the first century up to his day, spoke of the miraculous in the past tense. If those miracles that had existed at the beginning of the church were still taking place in his day, would not he have spoken in the present tense and even made reference to them? But he did not do so. He spoke in the past tense because those miracles had ceased sometime near the end of the first century when the books of the New Testament were completed. And so, if those miraculous spiritual gifts ended somewhere near the end of the first century as the New Testament said that they would, then what is happening in modern-day Pentecostal churches? It cannot be the same. We will further explore exactly what is happening today in those churches in a later chapter.

9

The Case of Cornelius

In a previous chapter, we briefly discussed the story of Cornelius that is found in Acts chapter ten. Cornelius was the first Gentile convert. The case of his conversion is quite unique. Many Bible students have misunderstood exactly what happened to Cornelius and its significance for us today.

In this chapter we want to further explore some of the misconceptions that many modern-day Pentecostals (and others) have regarding this case of conversion. In the New Testament, two entire chapters of the Book of Acts are devoted to explaining what happened to Cornelius. We are fortunate in that we have been given much information with many specific details. We will then use those details to address common misconceptions about Cornelius. These misconceptions are held not only by modern-day Pentecostals but also by many Bible students in general.

Cornelius is first introduced in Acts chapter 10. The first misconception that we will address involves his receiving of the baptism of the Holy Spirit. How did it happen and what was its purpose? The second misconception involves his actual conversion. It says that he was a "devout man" who feared God and whose prayers had been "heard," yet was not saved. How can that be? Let's look at each of these points in detail.

THE MISCONCEPTION CONCERNING CORNELIUS RECEIVING THE BAPTISM OF THE HOLY SPIRIT

This is a misconception held by many who believe that all Christians in the New Testament received the baptism of the Holy Spirit. And as a result of that mistaken belief, they also believe that Cornelius was just like all the other Christians when he received it. But that is not the case and is not supported by the text.

This misunderstanding grows out of a larger misunderstanding about the Holy Spirit. It is common for Pentecostals (and others) to make an error with "spirit" passages. Years of experience and interaction with a variety of religious people has shown that when they see "spirit" in a given text, they automatically think "Holy Spirit." That is the first leap. (The New Testament word for spirit is "pneuma." It can be used of the Holy Spirit or of the spirit of man. Vine's Expository Dictionary lists more than a dozen different ways that "pneuma" is used. Certainly, all of those uses do not refer to the Holy Spirit.)

But when men make the assumption that all (or most) spirit passages refer to the Holy Spirit, they make a serious error. That is the first leap. The second leap is when they take all Holy Spirit passages and misunderstand them to mean "Holy Spirit baptism." So, they move from "spirit" to "Holy Spirit" to "Holy Spirit baptism." This is done so frequently that it is almost automatic in their minds.

Thus, when a passage speaks of Christians having received "the spirit," they automatically think "Holy Spirit baptism." A case in point is found in Romans 8:14-16. If you read that text carefully, you will see at least three different uses of "spirit."

Romans 8 (NKJV)

¹⁴ For as many as are led by the **Spirit of God**, these are sons of God.

> [15] For you did not receive the **spirit of bondage** again to fear, but you received the **Spirit of adoption** by whom we cry out, "Abba, Father."

> [16] The **Spirit** Himself bears witness with our **spirit** that we are children of God…

In verse 14, it is clear that the use is in respect to the Holy Spirit as the text refers to the "Spirit of God." Note that in verse 15 that the first use of "spirit" is not capitalized. It is important to remember that the choice of capitalizing "spirit" is a choice made by the editors and translators of the text. When Paul wrote these verses, he made no such distinction (as the Greek language of the time was written in uncial form—that is, all upper-case letters. The cursive form, lower-case letters, came along about 400 years after the writing of the New Testament.)

It is apparent that in the New King James translation that the translators believed the second use of "spirit" should be capitalized as a reference to the Holy Spirit. We think a careful examination of the verse will reveal that to be a faulty conclusion on their part. Both uses of "spirit" in that text have to do with the disposition by which a man serves God. Christians do not serve God with a spirit (disposition or attitude) of bondage like a slave would. Instead, Christians serve God with the spirit of adopted sons. It is by this spirit of adoption that we cry out to God with "Abba, Father." He has made us His sons, not slaves. A proper understanding of this verse would conclude that the second reference to "spirit" is not a reference to the Holy Spirit.

Note that in verse 16 that "spirit" is again found twice. The first reference is to the Holy Spirit and the testimony He has given us in His word. He bears witness of the truth. The second reference is to the "spirit" (or soul, the inward invisible part) of man. This second reference is plainly not a reference to the Holy Spirit, but to ourselves. The Holy Spirit's testimony agrees with our testimony that we are God's children. Both bear witness to the same truths. The Holy Spirit has given His testimony as to what we must do to be saved; and our spirit gives testimony that we have done what the Spirit of God says.

Thus, the two are in agreement and we can be certain that we are children of God.

From this brief text, we hope we can all see that there are a variety of uses of "spirit" in the New Testament. It is context that determines the use. Thus, it is faulty Bible study that assumes that every reference to "spirit" is a reference to the Holy Spirit.

Numerous passages teach that Christians do indeed have the Holy Spirit. (See Matthew 28:19, Romans 8:9, Romans 8:11, etc.) But just because the Bible says that the Holy Spirit dwells in Christians does not mean that Christians have Holy Spirit baptism. Making an error in that respect is one of the mistakes that Pentecostals and others make.

As noted in the beginning of this section, Pentecostals (and others) believe that Cornelius was just like all other Christians in that he received Holy Spirit baptism. Evidence would show that all Christians did not receive Holy Spirit baptism. Cornelius did indeed receive Holy Spirit baptism, but his circumstance is very different from other Christians.

Here are some of the passages that describe what happened to Cornelius in Acts 10 and 11:

- Acts 10:44—the Holy Spirit fell upon **all those who heard** the word

- Acts 10:45—The gift of the Holy Spirit had been poured out **on the Gentiles also.**

- Acts 10:47—these...who have received the Holy Spirit **just as we** have.

- Acts 11:15—the Holy Spirit fell upon them **as upon us at the beginning.**

- Acts 11:17—God gave them **the same gift as He gave us** when we believed.

Notice, in Acts chapter eleven, that when Peter was explaining how this event at the house of Cornelius had taken place, he did not say that Cornelius had received the Holy Spirit "just like all other Christians." He did not say that because all the other Christians had not received the baptism of the Holy Spirit. Up to that time only the apostles had received it. Instead, Peter had to go all the way back to "the beginning," to the day of Pentecost in Acts chapter two. That is what he was referencing when he said in Acts 10:47 that they had received the Holy Spirit "just as *we* have." The "we" was a reference to Peter and the rest of the apostles.

Why would Peter have to go all the way back to "the beginning" to find an example of Holy Spirit baptism? The answer is simple. There were no cases of Holy Spirit baptism between Acts 2 and Acts 10! If Holy Spirit baptism was common to all Christians, then it would have happened thousands of times between Acts 2 and Acts 10. One of the things that made the event at the house of Cornelius so unusual was that there was no other example of such a thing happening in those chapters between Acts two and Acts ten.

Furthermore, Peter also had to go all the way back to the day of Pentecost when he said in Acts 11:17 that "God gave them *the same gift as He gave us* when we believed." Again, the phrase "the same gift" is a reference to the baptism of the Holy Spirit that the apostles ("us") received on the day of Pentecost. Peter's statements clearly show that only a select few, received the baptism of the Holy Spirit, not all the saved as many modern-day Pentecostals teach.

When the word "baptism" is used to describe this event (the "baptism" of the Holy Spirit) it describes both the way the Holy Spirit was given to them and the effect. It is a "baptism' that is administered only by Christ; He is the one who baptizes with the Holy Spirit (see John 1:33). It is called "baptism" because those who received it were "overwhelmed" by the Holy Spirit. Just as one who is baptized in water is "immersed" or "overwhelmed" by the water, so also those who received Holy Spirit baptism were "immersed" or "overwhelmed" by the power of the Holy Spirit. The only two recorded cases of such an event are found in Acts chapter two and Acts chapter ten. But a word of caution is necessary here! Cornelius, just like the apostles, received a direct outpouring from heaven that was administered by Christ—but that did not make him an apostle! An apostle had to have personally seen Jesus following His resurrection in order to be a witness for Him (Acts 1:21–22). Thus, Cornelius was not made an apostle by the baptism of the Holy Spirit. Additionally, Cornelius did not have the same special powers that the apostles had. The apostles were given unique powers that others did not have. See 2 Corinthians 12:12. They had special powers that identified them as true apostles of Christ. There is no indication that Cornelius had such powers.

What was the result of Cornelius being baptized with the Holy Spirit?

Acts 10

46 For **they heard them speak with tongues and magnify God**. Then Peter answered,

47 "Can anyone forbid water, that these should not be baptized who have received the Holy Spirit just as we have?"

48 And he commanded them to be baptized in the name of the Lord.

Remember that Paul had said in 1 Corinthians 14:22 that "tongues are for a sign, not to those who believe but to unbelievers." In this case of Cornelius, tongues were a sign to the Jewish Christians who *did not believe* that they were to teach the Gentiles. This "sign" convinced them to change their view.

Acts 11:18

When they heard these things they became silent; and they glorified God, saying, "Then God has also granted to the Gentiles repentance to life."

Following the conversion of Cornelius, Peter returned to Jerusalem and recounted everything that had taken place at the house of Cornelius (Acts 11:1–18). After Peter explained everything that had happened to Cornelius, those Jewish Christians back in Jerusalem held their peace, conceding that God's desire was for the gospel to also be taken to the Gentiles.

It is abundantly clear from the texts of Acts chapters ten and eleven that the purpose of Holy Spirit baptism at the house of Cornelius was to show that the Gentiles could be saved. Peter argued that they could not forbid them to be baptized in water (Acts 10:47) due to the fact that God had sent this miraculous sign upon Cornelius and his household. In response to what God had done in sending the Holy Spirit upon these Gentiles, Peter said, "Who was I that I could withstand God?" (Acts 11:17). To refuse to baptize those Gentiles would have been fighting against God!

THE MISCONCEPTION CONCERNING CORNELIUS' NEED TO BE SAVED AND THE ROLE OF WATER BAPTISM

The dilemma for many who read the story involves how he could be described as a righteous man and yet not be saved. Let's look at the following passages:

Acts 10

¹ There was a certain man in Caesarea called **Cornelius**, a centurion of what was called the Italian Regiment,

² **a devout man** and one **who feared God** with all his household, who gave alms generously to the people, and **prayed to God always**.

²² And they said, "Cornelius the centurion, **a just man**, one who fears God and has a good reputation among all the nation of the Jews, was divinely instructed by a holy angel to summon you to his house, and to hear words from you."

³¹ and said, "Cornelius, **your prayer has been heard**, and your alms are remembered in the sight of God."

So, we see in these passages that Cornelius was described as a man who was "devout," he "feared God," he "prayed to God always;" he was a "just man," and his prayers had "been heard" by God, he was considered "righteous" and that God remembered that he was kind and generous in giving alms to the needy. And yet, in chapter 11 where Peter is recounting the story to those Christians back at Jerusalem, he said that the angel who appeared to Cornelius told him that he needed to "be saved."

1 Corinthians 11

> [13] "And he told us how he had seen an angel standing in his house, who said to him, 'Send men to Joppa, and call for Simon whose surname is Peter,
>
> [14] 'who will tell you words by which you and all your household will **be saved**.'"

So, in spite of Cornelius being described as a righteous man, he was not a saved man. How can that be? Well, the answer is not as complicated as it might seem. First of all, we need to discuss his background.

In Genesis chapter 12:1–7, God made three promises to Abraham. He promised that He would give him a land (verses 2 and 7). God promised that a great nation would come from him (verse 2). And then in verse three was found the "blessing promise" or (as it is often called) the "seed promise." Please note that in Genesis 18:22, as God has more to say about His promises to Abraham, that it says, "In your seed all the nations of the earth shall be blessed, because you have obeyed My voice." This is why we often speak of that third promise as "the seed promise."

The Old Testament, from Genesis chapter twelve onward is a history of God fulfilling His first two promises to Abraham. God did indeed build a great nation from the lineage of Abraham. And He also gave to Abraham's descendants the land of Canaan—the Promised Land. But, in addition to that, the Old Testament is a history of the lineage leading up to Jesus—the promised seed of Abraham!

God had given the Nation of Israel their own laws to keep them separate from the other nations. These laws, as an example, regulated what foods they could eat. Some food was considered "clean" and some "unclean." These different types of food are mentioned in the story of the conversion of Cornelius (Acts 10:10–17, 28 and 11:5–9). These are also referenced in Romans chapter 14 where it discusses how some of the Jewish Christians would not eat certain meats. So, God had given the nation of Israel certain laws that would set them apart from the other nations.

Deuteronomy 14:2

"For you are **a holy people** to the LORD your God, and **the LORD has chosen you** to be a people for Himself, a special treasure above all the peoples who are on the face of the earth."

And yet, in the New Testament, when what is commonly referred to as "The Great Commission" was given by Jesus (Mark 16:15) to those first Christians, who were Jews, they were commanded to take the gospel to "all nations," which would have included the Gentiles. However, in the beginning of their preaching, they only preached to the Jews.

Now those who were scattered after the persecution that arose over Stephen traveled as far as Phoenicia, Cyprus, and Antioch, preaching the word to no one but **the Jews only** (Acts 11:19).

This possibly is a result of what is usually referred to as "the limited commission" in the first part of Jesus' ministry where he had prohibited them from going to the Gentiles.

Matthew 10

⁵ These twelve Jesus sent out and commanded them, saying: "**Do not go into the way of the Gentiles**, and do not enter a city of the Samaritans.

⁶ But go rather to the lost sheep of the house of Israel.

It is obvious that Jesus was operating on a timetable and that God's plan was to first take the gospel to the Jews and then after that to the Gentiles. And yet, it took a miracle to get the church to take the gospel to the Gentiles as we see with the case of Cornelius, the first Gentile convert.

Back in the Old Testament, we sometimes mistakenly conclude that only the Jews served God. That may have generally been so, but there were cases of other nations and people who served Him. You may remember the story of Jonah who was sent to preach to the wicked people of Nineveh. We read in Jonah chapter three that the people repented of their wickedness after Jonah preached to them. So, we then have Gentiles at Nineveh who served God.

And then there is the story of Melchizedek (Genesis 14:18) who was a righteous man outside of Abraham's lineage. There was Jethro, Moses' father-in-law, who was a priest of Midian who apparently was one of God's servants. There were other righteous men outside of the Law of Moses who obeyed those laws God had given them through prophets of their time. Remember that the Old Testament is a history of the offspring of Abraham—the Jewish nation. It is not a history of all the nations of that time. Those nations were under law to God, though their laws were not written down and recorded in Scriptures like the Jewish law was. Cornelius is an example of one who followed what he understood to be right before God! He could be considered as a righteous Gentile. His case is unique in that he lived during what many Bible students call "the transition period;" the period when the Old Testament was coming to an end and the New Testament was just beginning. We are told that the Old Testament Law ended at the death of Jesus (Hebrews 9:16–17). But the first sermon was not preached until the day of Pentecost in Acts chapter two, approximately fifty days after Jesus' death and resurrection. And that was only to a Jewish audience. The gospel was not preached to the Gentiles until approximately ten years later in Acts chapter ten with Cornelius. So, if a faithful Jew had died during the period after the death of Jesus but before that first sermon, surely he went to heaven as a righteous man. And if a righteous Gentile died after the day of Pentecost but before the gospel had been preached to the Gentiles, surely he went to heaven as well. But when Cornelius, as a righteous Gentile living in that transition period, has the new gospel preached to him, he must obey it in order to continue to be a righteous man and thus be "saved." If Cornelius had refused to obey the gospel in Acts chapter ten, he would have been just as lost as any other sinner.

So, who was Cornelius? We are told that he was a centurion who was in the Roman army and was over one hundred soldiers. He was told by the angel that his prayers had been heard by God contrasted to what the man said in John 9:31 that God does not hear the prayers of sinners. And we are told the same thing in 1 Peter 3:12.

John 9:31

Now we know that **God does not hear sinners**; but if anyone is a worshiper of God and does His will, He hears him.

1 Peter 3:12

For the eyes of the Lord are over the righteous, and his ears are open unto their prayers: but **the face of the Lord is against them that do evil**.

Both of these passages are addressing people who oppose the will of God. Cornelius is a man who wants to know the will of God. Thus, these passages would not apply to him.

To get the full story of the conversion of Cornelius, you need to read all of Acts chapters ten and eleven. Here are some key excerpts from those chapters that will help us understand how Cornelius was converted.

Acts 10

34 Then Peter opened his mouth and said: "In truth I perceive that God shows no partiality.

35 "But in every nation whoever fears Him and works righteousness is accepted by Him.

36 "The word which God sent to the children of Israel, preaching peace through Jesus Christ—He is Lord of all.

44 While Peter was still speaking these words, the Holy Spirit fell upon all those who heard the word.

45 And those of the circumcision who believed were astonished, as many as came with Peter, because the gift of the Holy Spirit had been poured out on the Gentiles also.

46 For they heard them speak with tongues and magnify God. Then Peter answered,

47 **"Can anyone forbid water, that these should not be baptized who have received the Holy Spirit just as we have?"**

48 **And he commanded them to be baptized in the name of the Lord.**

Cornelius then was baptized just like all of the Jews were on the day of Pentecost. It is interesting that God chose the Apostle Peter to go to Cornelius rather than the Apostle Paul, whose mission it was to go to the Gentiles. It was Peter whom God had chosen to preach the first sermon to those Jews on the day of Pentecost in Acts chapter two and so God also chose Peter to preach the first sermon to the Gentiles in Acts chapter ten. Paul summarized God's plan to take the gospel to both Jew and Gentile in Romans chapter one:

Romans 1:16 (KJV)

For I am not ashamed of the gospel of Christ: for it is the power of God unto salvation to everyone that believeth; **to the Jew first, and also to the Greek.**

It is significant that God had to help Peter overcome his prejudice against Gentiles in this great story. When Peter arrived at the house of Cornelius, he made it clear to him that he was there because God had directed him to be there. Peter would not have gone to the house of a Gentile except that God had shown him that he must do so. God did several things in this chapter to overcome Peter's reluctance to preach to the Gentiles.

First, in Acts 10:9–16, through a vision he showed Peter that he must not call "common what God had cleansed." While Peter did not initially understand what this meant, he later realized that God was talking about the Gentiles, that he must not call them "common or unclean" (Acts 10:28).

Second, the Holy Spirit told Peter to go to the house of Cornelius, "doubting nothing" (Acts 10:19–20). The implication is that Peter would not have gone to the house of Cornelius except that the Spirit told him to go.

Third, when he arrived at Cornelius' house, he told him that it was "unlawful for a Jewish man to go to one of another nation" (Acts 10:28). It was at this point that Peter explained that God had shown him that he should not call any man common or unclean.

Peter told Cornelius that he had come to his house "without objection" (Acts 10:29). This statement in itself indicates that Peter would have objected to this whole situation if God had not directed him to go to this Gentile house. Peter made it abundantly clear that he was there because God directed him to be there. He did not go of his own accord! Peter would have resisted at every point, but God was working out His plan to take the gospel to the Gentiles.

Even when it came to the matter of baptizing these Gentiles, Peter made it clear that it was God who was in charge of this whole matter! When Peter reported this to the church at Jerusalem, he said, "Who was I that I could withstand God?" (Acts 11:17). Peter wanted the brethren in Jerusalem to know that he had not gone to the house of Cornelius by his own will. He had not preached to the Gentiles of his own will. He had not baptized Cornelius by his own will. The whole matter was God's will from beginning to end. Peter was only the tool that God had used to direct this whole affair.

It is argued by many religious teachers that the outpouring of the Holy Spirit at the house of Cornelius is proof that Cornelius was saved before baptism. The truth is, the outpouring of the Holy Spirit proved that Cornelius *could be saved*, that *he could be baptized!* Remember, the preacher on this occasion is the same as the preacher in Acts chapter two. Peter did not preach anything different on salvation in Acts ten than what he preached in Acts two. In Acts 2:38 he told them to repent and be baptized for the remission of sins. We must not accuse Peter of preaching a different gospel to the Gentiles.

The case of Cornelius forever settles the issue of Gentile salvation. By this outpouring of the Holy Spirit, it was confirmed for all time that Gentiles could be accepted into God's family through faith, repentance, and baptism.

And so, in conclusion we can see that the conversion of Cornelius was unique in a number of ways. First, he was a righteous Gentile who happened to be living in the transition period in between the Old Testament period coming to an end and as the New Testament period was just beginning. And second, he received the baptism of the Holy Spirit before he was saved as a sign that Gentiles could be saved. And third, to convince the Jewish members of the church that they were to now go and convert Gentiles as well as Jews. Yet, the case of the conversion of Cornelius in no way gives modern-day Pentecostals any evidence or proof that they are still receiving that same outpouring of the Holy Spirit today.

10

Demon Possession

If you visit one of the modern-day Pentecostal churches, you might see them claiming to be casting out a demon from someone at the assembly. They believe that there are many today who are demon-possessed just as in the period of the New Testament. And so consequently, those demons need to be cast out. On the other hand, there are many who believe and teach that demon possession was limited to that time in the first century when new revelation was being given that would result in the scriptures that we have today. So, who is right? Let's delve into this topic and see if we can answer that question.

Many religious people today attribute just about anything evil or bad to demon possession. There are those who believe that Hitler was demon-possessed. Some would say the same about Charles Manson. We have been to Pentecostal churches where it was said that if a person had a drinking problem, then they were possessed by a "whiskey demon"! We have heard references to "tobacco demons" making it difficult for a smoker to quit. The list could go on and on. You could list just about any vice, addiction or just a bad habit and someone in a Pentecostal church will attribute it to a demon. Many people who hold to such views do so without ever having gone to the Bible to see what is revealed on the subject. Let's see what the Bible actually says concerning demon possession.

WHAT ARE DEMONS?

The Bible speaks of fallen angels. Those fallen angels may indeed be the demons of the New Testament period. It is not an unreasonable view.

Revelation 12

7 And war broke out in heaven: Michael and **his angels** fought with the dragon; and the dragon and **his angels** fought,

8 but they did not prevail, nor was a place found for them in heaven any longer.

9 So the great dragon was cast out, that serpent of old, called the Devil and Satan, who deceives the whole world; he was cast to the earth, and **his angels** were cast out with him.

2 Peter 2:4

For if God spared not **the angels that sinned**, but cast them down to hell, and delivered them into chains of darkness, to be reserved unto judgment

Jude 1:6

And **the angels which kept not their first estate**, but left their own habitation, he hath reserved in everlasting chains under darkness unto the judgment of the great day.

Matthew 25:4

Then shall he say also unto them on the left hand, Depart from me, ye cursed, into everlasting fire, prepared for the devil and **his angels**.

It cannot be said with certainty exactly when this war took place. Since Revelation chapter twelve says that Satan and his angels were cast out "to the earth," it seems logical that it happened after or during the creation. An important point to note is that the lake of fire mentioned in Matthew 25 was actually prepared for the Devil and his angels and it is this very place, according to that passage, that the wicked men will go as well.

Some may object to the view that is presented here, that the demons are fallen angels. While we cannot prove conclusively that the demons of the New Testament period are fallen angels, that view is as good as any and it certainly fits the context of those passages. We do not know of a better view.

CASES OF DEMON POSSESSION

Case 1

Matthew 9:32

As they went out, behold, they brought to him a dumb man possessed with a devil.

Case 2

Mark 1:23–26 (Luke 4:33–35)

23 Now there was a man in their synagogue with an unclean spirit. And he cried out,

24 saying, "Let us alone! What have we to do with You, Jesus of Nazareth? Did You come to destroy us? I know who You are—the Holy One of God!"

25 But Jesus rebuked him, saying, "Be quiet, and come out of him!"

26 And when the unclean spirit had convulsed him and cried out with a loud voice, he came out of him.

Case 3

Matthew 12:22 (Luke 11:14)

Then one was brought to Him who was demon-possessed, blind and mute; and He healed him, so that the blind and mute man both spoke and saw.

Case 4

Matthew 8:28–33 (Mark 5:1–16, Luke 8:27–33)

28 When He had come to the other side, to the country of the Gergesenes, there met Him two demon-possessed men, coming out of the tombs, exceedingly fierce, so that no one could pass that way.

29 And suddenly they cried out, saying, "What have we to do with You, Jesus, You Son of God? Have You come here to torment us before the time?"

30 Now a good way off from them there was a herd of many swine feeding.

31 So the demons begged Him, saying, "If You cast us out, permit us to go away into the herd of swine."

32 And He said to them, "Go." So when they had come out, they went into the herd of swine. And suddenly the whole herd of swine ran violently down the steep place into the sea, and perished in the water.

33 Then those who kept them fled; and they went away into the city and told everything, including what had happened to the demon-possessed men.

Case 5

Matthew 17:14–21 (Mark 9:17–29, Luke 9:38–42)

14 And when they had come to the multitude, a man came to Him, kneeling down to Him and saying,

15 Lord, have mercy on my son, for he is an epileptic and suffers severely; for he often falls into the fire and often into the water.

16 So I brought him to Your disciples, but they could not cure him."

17 Then Jesus answered and said, "O faithless and perverse generation, how long shall I be with you? How long shall I bear with you? Bring him here to Me."

[18] And Jesus rebuked the demon, and it came out of him; and the child was cured from that very hour.

[19] Then the disciples came to Jesus privately and said, "Why could we not cast it out?"

[20] So Jesus said to them, "Because of your unbelief; for assuredly, I say to you, if you have faith as a mustard seed, you will say to this mountain, 'Move from here to there,' and it will move; and nothing will be impossible for you.

[21] However, this kind does not go out except by prayer and fasting.

Case 6

Acts 16

[16] Now it happened, as we went to prayer, that a certain slave girl possessed with a spirit of divination met us, who brought her masters much profit by fortune-telling.

[17] This girl followed Paul and us, and cried out, saying, "These men are the servants of the Most High God, who proclaim to us the way of salvation."

[18] And this she did for many days. But Paul, greatly annoyed, turned and said to the spirit, "I command you in the name of Jesus Christ to come out of her." And he came out that very hour.

Case 7

Acts 19:13–16

[13] Then some of the itinerant Jewish exorcists took it upon themselves to call the name of the Lord Jesus over those who had evil spirits, saying, "We exorcise you by the Jesus whom Paul preaches."

[14] Also there were seven sons of Sceva, a Jewish chief priest, who did so.

¹⁵ And the evil spirit answered and said, "Jesus I know, and Paul I know; but who are you?"

¹⁶ Then the man in whom the evil spirit was leaped on them, overpowered them, and prevailed against them, so that they fled out of that house naked and wounded.

NATURE OF DEMONS

What can we conclude after looking at all of the cases of demon possession in the New Testament?

1. *They are evil (Luke 7:21; 8:2; Acts 19:12–13).*

Luke 7:21

²¹ And that very hour He cured many of infirmities, afflictions, and **evil spirits**; and to many blind He gave sight.

Luke 8:2

² and certain women who had been healed of **evil spirits** and infirmities—Mary called Magdalene, out of whom had come seven demons,

Acts 19:12–13

¹² so that even handkerchiefs or aprons were brought from his body to the sick, and the diseases left them and the **evil spirits** went out of them.

¹³ Then some of the itinerant Jewish exorcists took it upon themselves to call the name of the Lord Jesus over those who had **evil spirits**, saying, "We exorcise you by the Jesus whom Paul preaches."

2. *Some are more wicked than others.*

Matthew 12:43–45 (Luke 11:24–26)

⁴³ "When an unclean spirit goes out of a man, he goes through dry places, seeking rest, and finds none.

44 Then he says, 'I will return to my house from which I came.' And when he comes, he finds it empty, swept, and put in order.

45 Then he goes and takes with him seven other spirits **more wicked than himself**, and they enter and dwell there; and the last state of that man is **worse than the first**. So shall it also be with this wicked generation."

This is not a case of an encounter with demons, but rather, is simply teaching being done by Jesus about the nature of demons!

3. *Some are stronger than others.*

    Matthew 17:21 (Mark 9:29)

    However, **this kind** does not go out except by prayer and fasting.

4. *They were able to come and go out of a man at will.*

    Matthew 12:43–44 (Luke 11:24)

    43 "When an unclean spirit goes out of a man, he goes through dry places, seeking rest, and finds none.

    44 Then he says, 'I will return to my house from which I came.' And when he comes…"

    Notice also that in this teaching of Jesus about demons, this hypothetical case was not one where the demon was cast out by one of the disciples because in those cases the demon could never return!

5. *They were able to possess animals.*

    Matthew 8:32 (Mark 5:13, Luke 8:33)

    And He said to them, "Go." So when they had come out, they went into the herd of swine. And suddenly the whole herd of swine ran violently down the steep place into the sea, and perished in the water.

6. *They were able to speak through the mouth of the one possessed.*

Mark 1:23–26 (Luke 4:33–35)

²³ Now there was a man in their synagogue with **an unclean spirit**. And he cried out,

²⁴ saying, "Let us alone! What have we to do with You, Jesus of Nazareth? Did You come to destroy us? I know who You are—the Holy One of God!"

²⁵ But Jesus rebuked **him**, saying, "Be quiet, and come out of him!"

²⁶ And when the unclean spirit had convulsed him and cried out with a loud voice, **he** came out of him.

As a note, at first there seems to be a discrepancy between these two accounts. In Mark 1:26 it says the demon had "torn" him before coming out. Yet, in Luke's rendering in Luke 4:35, it says the demon "did not hurt" him when coming out. This is simply a translation problem in the King James Version. If you will notice other translations, such as the NIV, these two passages are clearer. Mark 1:26 says that the evil spirit "shook the man violently and came out of him with a shriek." Luke 4:35 says the demon "threw the man down before them all and came out without injuring him." So apparently, as the demon was being cast out, he gave out a scream, threw the man's body to the ground, yet did him no serious bodily harm.

7. *They knew and feared Jesus and his disciples.*

Mark 1:24 (Luke 4:34)

"**Let us alone!** What have we to do with You, Jesus of Nazareth? Did You come to destroy us? I know who You are—the Holy One of God!"

Matthew 8:29

And suddenly they cried out, saying, "What have we to do with You, Jesus, You Son of God? **Have You come here to torment us before the time**?"

Luke 8:31

And **they begged Him** that He would not command them to go out into the abyss.

They recognized Jesus on sight and immediately asked whether He had come to destroy them "before the time." That seems to indicate that they knew there was a time coming when He would destroy them. They also asked that He not send them "out into the deep," which seems to be a reference back to 2 Peter 2:4 where Peter talks about the angels that fell being cast out of Heaven and into a place called Tartarus, where they would await the Judgment Day. It is interesting to note that in not one of the cases of demon possession did the demon blaspheme God, Jesus, or the disciples.

Acts 19

[15] And the evil spirit answered and said, "**Jesus I know, and Paul I know; but who are you**?"

[16] Then the man in whom the evil spirit was leaped on them, overpowered them, and prevailed against them, so that they fled out of that house naked and wounded.

Not only did the demons recognize Jesus, but they also knew who the disciples were. They had good reason to fear them as well since they had been given the power also to cast those demons out of men and send them back to "the abyss."

8. *They were able to affect the actions of those they possessed.*

- made dumb (Matthew 9:32)
- made dumb and blind (Matthew 12:22)
- made dumb, blind and epileptic (Mark 9:17–27)
- great strength (Acts 19:16)
- great strength, out of mind (Mark 5:1–5)
- power of soothsaying (Acts 16:16)

9. *General sickness was not attributed to demons.*

Matthew 4:24

Then His fame went throughout all Syria; and they brought to Him all sick people who were afflicted with various diseases and torments, and **those who were demon-possessed**, epileptics, and paralytics; and He healed them.

In this passage there is a distinction made between those possessed with demons and those which were lunatic and those with palsy. So, there is actually a difference between demon possession, mental illness and physical illness.

10. *The demons all had a dreaded fear of being sent back to the "pit or the "abyss." Notice these passages concerning the case of the man possessed with "Legion," who went into the swine.*

Luke 8:31 (KJV)

And they besought him that he would not command them to go out into **the deep**.

Luke 8:31 (NKJV)

And they begged Him that He would not command them to go out into the **abyss**.

Matthew 8:29 (KJV)

And, behold, they cried out, saying, What have we to do with thee, Jesus, thou Son of God? art thou come hither to torment us **before the time**?

Matthew 8:29 (NIV)

"What do you want with us, Son of God?" they shouted. "Have you come here to torture us before **the appointed time**?"

It is interesting that these demons understood that they only had a limited amount of time on the earth where they would be given the freedom to possess men. They also understood where they would go when they were cast out. The KJV calls it "the deep." The NKJV says "the abyss." This apparently is a reference to that part of Hades called Tartarus in 2 Peter 2:4 (in the Greek) to which they were sent when they fell from their place in Heaven.

PURPOSE OF DEMON POSSESSION

The question that would naturally arise at this point is, *why* did God allow the demons the freedom to leave Tartarus and come to earth and possess men? Did these demons have the freedom to just roam the earth and do whatever they willed? After looking at the previous passages it is obvious that they did not. They only could do what God allowed them to do. The reason that God allowed them to possess men was simply so that Jesus and His disciples could cast them out, thus demonstrating the Lord's power over Satan and his angels. It is interesting that there are no cases of demon possession to be found in the Old Testament. (The case of King Saul having an evil spirit from the Lord [1 Samuel 18:10] is not a case of demon possession; rather, it had to do with Saul's bouts of depression, and could be soothed by David playing music for Saul.) The reason why demon possession is not found in the Old Testament scriptures is because the demons were loosed only for a definite and limited amount of time. And this was during the period of time that corresponded with the age of miracles, or spiritual gifts. One of the works that Jesus was to perform while on earth was the destruction of the workings of Satan through those demons, and it is obvious that the demons knew this. That is why they had such fear and dread of Jesus and His disciples. In the case found in Mark chapter one, the demon asked Jesus if He was come to destroy them. Mark records that He "rebuked him, saying, 'Be quiet, and come out of him!' " The substance of Jesus' answer was, "Yes, He was come to destroy them." And He "rebuked" the demon for even asking! Notice this interesting passage where one of the purposes is actually discussed:

1 John 3:8

> He who sins is of the devil, for the devil has sinned from the beginning. **For this purpose** the Son of God was manifested, that He might destroy the works of the devil.

This passage tells us about one of the purposes for Jesus' coming to earth, to "destroy the works of the devil." One of those works was the freedom of Satan's angels to possess men's bodies, and that work was destroyed by Jesus and His disciples! The ability to cast out demons was just one of the spiritual gifts that Jesus gave the disciples. Yet, it fits perfectly well with the other spiritual gifts as far as their basic design and purpose was concerned.

Mark 16

> [17] And these signs will follow those who believe: In My name they will **cast out demons**; they will speak with new tongues;

> [18] they will take up serpents; and if they drink anything deadly, it will by no means hurt them; they will lay hands on the sick, and they will recover."

> [19] So then, after the Lord had spoken to them, He was received up into heaven, and sat down at the right hand of God.

> [20] And they went out and preached everywhere, **the Lord working with them and confirming the word through the accompanying signs**. Amen.

The casting out of demons was just one of the signs that would be given to show that the disciples were in fact sent with a message from God. However, after the message had been completely given to man, and confirmed, then those spiritual gifts were no longer needed. Thus, the gift of casting out of demons was no longer needed. The ending of those gifts would coincide with the ending of the demons being permitted to possess men!

THIS HAD BEEN PROPHESIED

Zechariah 13:2

> It shall be in that day," says the LORD of hosts, "that I will cut off the names of the idols from the land, and they shall no longer be remembered. I will also cause the prophets and the **unclean spirit** to depart from the land."

It is interesting to compare where the cases of demon possession are found in the Bible.

- (Old Testament) There were no cases.

- (The four Gospels) There were numerous cases.

- (Book of Acts) There were only a few cases.

- (The Epistles) There were no cases (demons are only mentioned).

Not only are there no cases of demon possession mentioned after the book of Acts, but 2 Peter 2:4 tells us that by the time that epistle was written, all of those "fallen angels" had been cast into Tartarus or "hell." Thus, Peter confirms that the prophecy of Zechariah 13:2 had been completely fulfilled.

CONCLUSION

In the beginning of this chapter, we stated that if you visit one of the modern-day Pentecostal churches, you might see them claiming to be casting out a demon from someone at the assembly. They believe that there are many today who are demon-possessed just as in the period of the New Testament. And so consequently, those demons need to be cast out. However, after reviewing the many passages offered it is obvious that the scriptures teach that demon possession was limited to that time in the first century when new revelation was being given that would result in the scriptures that we have today. Nobody today has the power to cast out demons because that power is not needed since nobody today is demon-possessed.

In several instances, when we have visited a faith healing service as observers, we witnessed preachers claiming to cast out a demon from someone. And those men and women who they said were demon-possessed did not display those super-human attributes seen in those New Testament cases. Instead, the one supposedly with a demon would usually fall to the floor and be motionless. The preacher would then lay hands on them and pronounce the demon to have been cast out. But, purely from an observer's viewpoint, there was nothing to verify that the claimed demon possession was real; and if that could not be verified to be real, then there was no reason to believe that the casting out was real. We only heard and saw claims. So, again, when we compare the true cases of demon possession found in the New Testament with the claimed cases in modern-day Pentecostal churches, they are not the same.

Rather than simply believe and teach what the Bible has to say on this subject, many religious teachers today continue to teach that men are still being possessed by demons. They also teach that this causes these men to smoke, drink, kill and any other terrible sin that they might commit. And in that way, it takes away any responsibility that those men might have had for committing those sins. But think about this for just a minute. In which one of those cases of demon possession in the Bible did Jesus ever rebuke the person possessed with the demon? In none of the cases did He do that! He simply cast the demon out, thus helping the one possessed. The reason the person possessed was not rebuked was because they were not responsible for their action while a demon had control of their body! And it appears that may be what some want today, to be able to say that they are not responsible for their actions. But that will not work.

Romans 14:12

So then every one of us shall give account of himself to God.

Today, since demon possession is no longer taking place, any sin that we commit will be held to our account on the Day of Judgment.

11

Jesus' Name Baptism

If you decided to visit one of the modern-day Pentecostal churches, you first need to understand that they are not all the same. Though they all share the belief that the miraculous gifts are for today, they differ on many other doctrines. And as a result, there are several large denominational groups that are markedly different from each other. One of these is the United Pentecostal Church (UPC), which teaches a peculiar doctrine on baptism. This is the same group that believes that there is only one person in the Godhead. They are known as "Oneness" Pentecostals. You may also find this same belief under the "Apostolic Church" name. We have found that this group believes essentially the same as the United Pentecostals but they reject the UPC organization. These groups teach an unusual doctrine concerning water baptism.

Those churches holding to this view teach that when a person is baptized in water, the one doing the baptizing must say a certain set of words for the baptism to be valid. This set of words is typically called "a baptismal formula." And it is not just any set of Bible words.

Pentecostal preachers will insist that the words found in Matthew 28:19 are the wrong words. Here is what Jesus said as He was giving the Great Commission to His disciples:

Matthew 28:19

"Go therefore and make disciples of all the nations, baptizing them in the name of the Father and of the Son and of the Holy Spirit."

Because of their belief that there is only one person in the godhead, they believe Jesus to be the Father, the Son, and the Holy Spirit—all three. Thus, they conclude that the name of the Father is "Jesus," and that the name of the Son is "Jesus," and the name of the Holy Spirit is "Jesus."

When a baptism is administered and someone says the words of Matthew 28:19 at that baptism, it is insisted that the baptism is invalid. They argue that the "name" (not "names") in that verse means only one name should be uttered—the name of "Jesus."

Thus, in their theology, a baptism in water is only valid if the name of Jesus is uttered. They insist that the person doing the baptizing must say, "I baptize you in Jesus' name" at the point of water baptism. If those exact words are not stated at the baptism, then it is not valid, no sins have been forgiven and the candidate just got wet. Let's briefly examine the validity of this doctrine.

This erroneous doctrine grows out of a misunderstanding of the biblical use of "name." According to *Vine's Expository Dictionary of New Testament Words*, the Greek word ὄνομα, onoma, translated "name," generally refers to that by which a person or thing is called. *Vine's* says that sometimes the name represents the title of that person. *Vine's* states that *name* "implies authority, character, rank, majesty, power, excellence, etc., of everything that the name covers" (Volume 3, pp. 99–100) and gives many references including the following:

Matthew 18:5

"Whoever receives one little child like this **in My name** receives Me."

Matthew 24:4–5

And Jesus answered and said to them: "Take heed that no one deceives you. For many will come **in My name**, saying, 'I am the Christ,' and will deceive many" (Matthew 24:4-5).

Notice this additional passage where "name" is used:

Colossians 3:17

And whatever you do in word or deed, do all **in the name of** the Lord Jesus, giving thanks to God the Father through Him.

In this passage, Paul tells us that "whatever" we do "in word" (what we speak) or "in deed" (what we do), we must have authority from the Lord. This passage is telling us what to *do*, not what to *say*. If "in the name of" means a certain set of words must be uttered when one is baptized "in the name of Jesus," then what does that interpretation do with Colossians 3:17? According to the modern Pentecostal logic, it must likewise mean that a certain set of words must be uttered whenever we do anything ("whatever you do")! However, we all agree that Colossians 3:17 is a reference to doing things "by the authority" of Christ. It is just like in the old cowboy movies where the sheriff would yell, "Stop in the name of the law!" He was not saying "the law" even had a name, or that the robber had to say a name when he stopped, but he was simply making an appeal to the legal "authority" that he had been given by law. Stop and ask yourself this question:

If you are told to do something "in the name of…," are you told:

A. What to do?

B. What to say?

It is obvious that you are told "**A.** what to do." And since Colossians 3:17 tells us that whatever we do in word or deed is to be done "in the name of Jesus," that is telling us that we must have scriptural authority from Jesus for what we are saying or doing. On the other hand, if this passage in Colossians means what the United Pentecostal Church folks tell us, that a formula of words must be said, then think of an example of how this passage could possibly be carried out. You can make no sense of it that way.

Now what about the subject of water baptism? When one is baptized "in the name of Jesus Christ" according to the New Testament, one is baptized *by the authority* of Jesus Christ. Passages that tell us to be baptized in His name do not speak of some type of formula of words that must be uttered! Being baptized "in the name of Jesus" tells us what to *do*, not what to *say*! It is about action we take; not words we say. And if it was telling us what to say, then which variation would you be required to use? It is important to note that there is no standard form of words in the book of Acts when people were baptized. Yet, Pentecostal preachers are insistent upon an exact form of words.

1. In the name of **Jesus Christ**? (Acts 2:38)

2. In the name of **the Lord Jesus**? (Acts 8:16)

3. In the name of **the Lord Jesus Christ**? (Acts 10:48)

And if you must say his name, which will you choose?

1. And his name will be called: **Wonderful** (Isaiah 9:6)

2. And his name will be called: **Counsellor** (Isaiah 9:6)

3. And his name will be called: **Mighty God** (Isaiah 9:6)

4. And his name will be called: **Everlasting Father** (Isaiah 9:6)

5. And his name will be called: **Prince of Peace** (Isaiah 9:6)

6. And His name is called: **The Word of God** (Revelation 19:13)

7. On his thigh a name written: **KING OF KINGS and LORD OF LORDS** (Revelation 19:16)

8. They shall call his name: **Emmanuel** (Matthew 1:23)

9. For the LORD, whose name is: **Jealous** (Exodus 34:14)

10. I am the LORD, that is my name: **LORD, Yahweh, Jehovah** (Isaiah 42:8)

Pentecostal preachers attach a mystical or magical significance to the utterance of the name "Jesus." But we need to remember that the way we pronounce the Lord's name in English is not how it was pronounced in Greek ('Ιησοῦς, Iēsous) or Hebrew (יְשׁוּעָה, Yeshua). If there is a mystical power in getting the name right, why would they think they can pronounce it in English and it be right? Which words are valid, and which are not? These are questions that our Oneness friends cannot answer. Further, it shows a basic inconsistency in the dogmatism of their doctrine!

It was never intended that His name should be uttered to invoke some mystical power. Though there is a Bible example of someone mistakenly thinking that to be the case:

Acts 19:13

> Then some of the itinerant Jewish exorcists took it upon themselves to **call the name of the Lord Jesus** over those who had evil spirits, saying, "We exorcise you **by the Jesus whom Paul preaches**."

We can see through the remainder of the context that just calling the name of "Jesus" had no power or significance in and of itself. This was not a set of magical words that were said to cast out these demons. The New Testament apostles who actually had the power to cast out demons in Jesus' name did so not by uttering the right words, but by acting on the right authority. Jesus gave His apostles power to cast out demons in His name (Mark 16:17). Once again, this was not a matter of saying a special set of words; rather, it was acting on the authority Jesus had given to them. Notice the Great Commission:

Matthew 28:19

"Go therefore and make disciples of all the nations, baptizing them **in the name of** (1) the Father (2) and of the Son (3) and of the Holy Spirit."

This simply means that when you baptize someone, you are doing so by the authority of the Father, Son, and Holy Spirit. It says nothing about what is to be *said*, but just what is to be *done*. In fact, none of the cases of conversion mentioned in Acts give us any information at all concerning what may have been said at those baptisms, if anything at all was said. To speculate would be just that, speculation.

There certainly would not be anything wrong in stating what you were doing at the baptism; that would serve for the benefit of those who might be watching. But there is no passage that tells us, much less commands us, as to what must be said, what should be said, or what was said. We should not do as some and let common sense be the first thing thrown out the window when beginning a religious discussion!

Finally, it is interesting to note that most denominations have a Creed Book or Church Manual. The manual for the United Pentecostal Church has always been virtually impossible for an outsider to get since church officials will not give one out to anyone but a United Pentecostal Church preacher. However, after many years we both finally acquired one. And no, we are not United Pentecostal Church preachers nor have we converted to that faith! This is brought up because we want to quote a statement from the manual. This is from the foreword to the 1995 edition:

> During the last 21 days of the 19th century, a band of earnest, hungry-hearted ministers and Christian workers in Bethel Bible College, Topeka, Kansas, called a fast, praying earnestly for a great outpouring of the Holy Spirit, which, to their joyful *surprise*, came upon them in the early hours of the morning, on January 1, 1901. ...
>
> With the coming of the Holy Spirit, the word of the Lord became *a new book*. Truths which had been *hidden* for many

years were made clear. *In the year 1914 came the revelation* on the name of the Lord Jesus Christ. The pivotal doctrines of the absolute deity of Jesus Christ and the baptism in His name *became* tenets of faith. ... The power which was *hidden* in the name of Jesus began to be revealed. Literally thousands were rebaptized into the name of Jesus Christ...

It is very important to understand that the officials of the United Pentecostal Church themselves readily admit that the doctrine that they teach concerning a formula of words that must be uttered over a candidate for baptism is a new doctrine! The manual tells us that they believe a new revelation concerning this doctrine was given in 1914. Before that we are told that it had been "hidden." This should answer once and for all the controversy over whether this doctrine had been taught by the apostles in the New Testament. If new revelation on this doctrine was received in 1914 that had been hidden before, then clearly it was not a doctrine that had been previously taught in the Bible. Now the question must be asked, "Was this alleged revelation truly from God?" We will continue to believe that it was no more from God than was Joseph Smith's alleged revelation concerning the Book of Mormon. We will stick with the written revelation in God's word, the Bible, and not allow ourselves to be led astray by some man claiming to have received something new!

In dealing with Pentecostal people on this doctrine it is often difficult to get them to see what the real issue is. They think the issue is about getting the right baptismal formula; that is, the right set of words said over a person at their baptism. But the real issue is not over a right set of words that must be said. Rather, it is about whether any words at all are required to be said over a person at baptism.

In misunderstanding this matter, the Pentecostals will assume the thing they must prove. That is, they assume all "Jesus' name" passages are about something to be said. You will have to work hard to get them past this assumption. Typically, they have been indoctrinated over and over to the point where they just can't see anything in those passages except a baptismal formula of words.

The way we have got some of them to see the truth is to continue to ask, "Do these verses tell us what to say? Or do they tell us what to do? Once you get them to see that issue, then the light goes on!

12

The Gift of the Holy Spirit

What Is the gift of the Holy Spirit in Acts 2:38? Some consider it to be a controversial text. It is a text that has traditionally been the subject of much disagreement regarding the Holy Spirit.

Acts 2:38

> Then Peter said to them, "Repent, and let every one of you be baptized in the name of Jesus Christ for the remission of sins; and you shall receive **the gift of the Holy Spirit.**"

It is a favorite verse of the Pentecostals today as they claim that this verse promises the "baptism of the Holy Spirit" to all believers. We noted in a previous chapter that whenever some of these folks see "Holy Spirit," they automatically think, "Holy Spirit Baptism." But it is evident that the baptism of the Spirit was never promised to or given to all Christians. On the other hand, whatever this text promises, it is for all believers.

Others say this passage has to do with miraculous spiritual gifts. Yet, the evidence in the early chapters of the book of Acts is that no one but the apostles had spiritual gifts. It is not until Acts 6:6–8 that the record shows anyone other than the apostles having spiritual gifts.

Stephen did wonders and signs after the apostles laid hands on him. All Christians did not have spiritual gifts. The promise of Acts 2:38 is for all who obey the gospel. Because we understand the Bible's teaching on the limited nature of miraculous spiritual gifts, it is reasonable for us to conclude that the "gift of the Holy Spirit" in Acts 2:38 is *not* a promise of miraculous gifts of the Spirit.

But the question yet remains. What is the gift of the Holy Spirit? Some argue that it is a gift *from* the Holy Spirit. Others argue that it is the Holy Spirit *Himself* as the gift. It is the premise of this chapter that the gift of the Holy Spirit in Acts 2:38 is the promised gift of salvation spoken of by the Spirit through the Old Testament prophets. We will demonstrate that premise in the pages to come.

UNWARRANTED ASSUMPTIONS ABOUT ACTS 2:38

One of the problems that we find as we discuss this text with others is that they often make assumptions about "the gift of the Holy Spirit" that are not justified. Sometimes people just assume or assert the thing that is to be proven. Assumptions and assertions prove nothing. Here are some of the unwarranted things people say about the text.

1. "The Holy Spirit Himself is the gift."

Though that is possible, to merely make the assertion does not prove anything.

2. "The grammar proves the gift is..."

Some say the Greek grammar proves that the Holy Spirit *is* the gift. Others say that the grammar proves it is a gift *from* the Spirit. It appears that the Greek (and English) text would not prove either position. It could be the Spirit as the gift; it could be a gift from the Spirit. We are not persuaded that a solid argument can be made either way based on the grammar.

3. "The gift of the Holy Ghost in Acts 10:45 involved speaking in tongues. It must be the same thing here."

Though that is possible, must a word or phrase always have the same meaning, though used in different contexts? Doesn't the phrase "like gift" in Acts 11:17 indicate that different gifts could be given? A comparison might help us here. Below are several references where "gift of God" is found. Note the differences in the meaning of these texts, though "gift of God" is used in each.

Ecclesiastes 3:13

…that every man should eat and drink and enjoy the good of all his labor—it is the **gift of God.**

John 4:10

Jesus answered and said to her, "If you knew the **gift of God,** and who it is who says to you, 'Give Me a drink,' you would have asked Him, and He would have given you living water.'"

Romans 6:23

For the wages of sin is death, but the **gift of God** is eternal life in Christ Jesus our Lord.

1 Corinthians 7:7 (KJV)

For I would that all men were even as I myself. But every man hath his proper **gift of God,** one after this manner, and another after that.

Ephesians 2:8

For by grace you have been saved through faith, and that not of yourselves; it is the **gift of God…**

In which of these texts is "God" the gift? Look at each one carefully. In Ecclesiastes 3:13, the "gift of God" is to enjoy the good of one's own labor. In John 4:10, the "gift of God" is blessings in Christ. In Romans 6:23, the "gift of God" is eternal life through Jesus. In 1 Corinthians 7:7, the "gift of God" is celibacy (controlling one's lusts while unmarried). In Ephesians 2:8, the "gift of God" is salvation. In which of these texts was God Himself personally the gift? None. If God Himself was not the gift in these cases, why must the Holy Spirit personally be the gift in other places? The best way to study the meaning of any passage or phrase is to study it in context. How does the phrase in Acts 2:38 fit into the larger context of Acts chapter two?

A STUDY OF THE CONTEXT OF ACTS 2:38

Peter's sermon centers on the fulfillment of the prophecy from Joel 2:28–32. He quotes from this Old Testament prophet in Acts 2:16–21. Here are those two texts.

Joel 2

28 And it shall come to pass afterward That I will pour out **My Spirit** on all flesh; Your sons and your daughters shall prophesy, Your old men shall dream dreams, Your young men shall see visions.

29 And also on My menservants and on My maidservants I will pour out My Spirit in those days.

30 And I will show wonders in the heavens and in the earth: Blood and fire and pillars of smoke.

31 The sun shall be turned into darkness, And the moon into blood, Before the coming of the great and awesome day of the LORD.

32 And it shall come to pass **That whoever calls on the name of the LORD Shall be saved.** For in Mount Zion and in Jerusalem there shall be deliverance, As the LORD has said, Among the remnant whom the LORD calls.

Acts 2

16 "But **this is what was spoken by the prophet Joel:**

17 'And it shall come to pass in the last days, says God, That I will pour out of **My Spirit** on all flesh; Your sons and your daughters shall prophesy, Your young men shall see visions, Your old men shall dream dreams.

18 'And on My menservants and on My maidservants I will pour out My Spirit in those days; And they shall prophesy.

19 'I will show wonders in heaven above And signs in the earth beneath: Blood and fire and vapor of smoke.

20 'The sun shall be turned into darkness, And the moon into blood, Before the coming of the great and awesome day of the LORD.

21 'And it shall come to pass **That whoever calls on the name of the LORD shall be saved.'** "

The key verse is Acts 2:21, "whoever calls on the name of the Lord shall be saved." (Note carefully that this is parallel to Joel 2:32.) Peter uses Joel's prophecy not merely to explain the outpouring of the Spirit, but to introduce salvation in the name of Jesus Christ. This is Peter's subject. This is what he sets out to proclaim.

The outpouring of the Spirit that took place on the Day of Pentecost would result in salvation through the Lord (Christ). The first thing Peter must do is establish who the Lord is upon whom they must call. That, in fact, is the primary thrust of his proclamation beginning at verse 22 down through verse 36. Follow the series of questions related to the verses below.

Acts 2

22 "Men of Israel, hear these words: Jesus of Nazareth, a Man attested by God to you by miracles, wonders, and signs which God did through Him in your midst, as you yourselves also know—

23 "Him, being delivered by the determined purpose and fore-knowledge of God, you have taken by lawless hands, have crucified, and put to death;

24 "whom God raised up, having loosed the pains of death, because it was not possible that He should be held by it.

25 "For David says concerning Him: 'I foresaw the Lord always before my face, For He is at my right hand, that I may not be shaken.

26 'Therefore my heart rejoiced, and my tongue was glad; Moreover my flesh also will rest in hope.

27 'For You will not leave my soul in Hades, Nor will You allow Your Holy One to see corruption.

28 'You have made known to me the ways of life; You will make me full of joy in Your presence.'

29 "Men and brethren, let me speak freely to you of the patriarch David, that he is both dead and buried, and his tomb is with us to this day.

30 "Therefore, being a prophet, and knowing that God had sworn with an oath to him that of the fruit of his body, according to the flesh, He would raise up the Christ to sit on his throne,

31 "he, foreseeing this, spoke concerning the resurrection of the Christ, that His soul was not left in Hades, nor did His flesh see corruption.

32 "This Jesus God has raised up, of which we are all witnesses.

33 "Therefore being exalted to the right hand of God, and having received from the Father the promise of the Holy Spirit, He poured out this which you now see and hear.

34 "For David did not ascend into the heavens, but he says himself: 'The Lord said to my Lord, "Sit at My right hand,

35 Till I make Your enemies Your footstool." '

36 "Therefore let all the house of Israel know assuredly that God has made this Jesus, whom you crucified, both Lord and Christ."

Questions

- Who is the Lord upon whom they must call? Read Acts 2:22–24. It is Jesus.

- Of whom did David speak in prophecy? Read Acts 2:25–29. It is Jesus.

- What promise was made to David? Read Acts 2:30. The Messiah (Christ) would be raised up to sit on David's throne.

- For what purpose was Jesus raised from the dead? Read Acts 2:30-33. To be exalted to God's right hand.

- When Jesus ascended into heaven, He received the "promise of the Holy Spirit," Acts 2:33. What did He receive? Did He receive the Holy Spirit, or did He receive something promised by the Holy Spirit? He received what the Holy Spirit promised—to be seated on David's throne. This is what is addressed in the immediate context.

The "promise" of Acts 2:33 is equal to "sworn" and "oath" in verse 30. (Verse 33, correctly understood, is a powerful argument against premillinnialism. King Jesus reigns!)

Who has ascended into heaven and reigns there? Read Acts 2:34-36. It is Jesus. What evidence had been offered as proof of this? See Acts 2:33b. The outpouring of the Spirit was demonstrated by miraculous tongues of fire that sat upon each of the apostles, by their ability to speak foreign languages which they had never learned, and the sound of a rushing mighty wind. Acts 2:33 says, "He poured out this which you now see and hear." The tongues of fire and these other supernatural phenomena were miraculous signs proving that Jesus was at the right hand of God!

From verse 36, what have the Jews just learned about their condition? They are lost; they have killed the Lord and Christ. In these verses (22-36) Peter has established that Jesus is the Lord upon whom men must call for salvation. Peter demonstrates that Jesus is Lord by showing the fulfillment of the prophecy of Psalm 110 (Acts 2:34). He demonstrates that Jesus is the Christ by showing Him to be the rightful heir to David's throne and by affirming that He indeed is seated on David's throne at the right hand of the Father in heaven (Acts 2:30-33). Jesus has fulfilled the Davidic prophecies from Psalm 16 (as well as numerous other scriptures).

In response to Peter's preaching, the Jews ask, "What shall we do?" (Acts 2:37). What do you think they want when they ask the question? They are asking about salvation. We must keep this question in its context. They are not asking "What shall we do for lunch?" The question is incomplete without the context. They are asking, "What shall we do" *to be saved*? They are lost. Remember the language of Acts 2:21.

Peter's answer in Acts 2:38–39 relates to his primary theme in Acts 2:21. The issue is one of salvation. Let's analyze Peter's answer in Acts 2:38–39.

- Peter has already identified *who* the Lord is upon whom they must call (Acts 2:22–36).

- He now tells them *how* to call upon Him, "repent and be baptized."

- He tells *why* they must call upon Him, "for the forgiveness of sins."

- He tells them the *result* of calling upon Him, "...receive the gift of the Holy Spirit."

The *result* of calling upon Him in Acts 2:21 was expressed as "shall be saved." Who made that promise that was found in Acts 2:21? The Holy Spirit made that promise of salvation! (See 2 Peter 1:20–21 for help. It was the Holy Spirit who guided Joel and the other prophets.)

Who was the promise in Acts 2:21 for? It was for "whosoever calls..." Who is the promise in Acts 2:39 for? It was for "you, your children, and those afar off." This explains who the "whoever" is in Acts 2:21. Do not think Acts 2:39 refers to a different promise. It does not!

We are forced by the context to conclude that "the gift of the Holy Spirit" in Acts 2:38 is *the promised gift of salvation* that was foretold by the Holy Spirit through the Old Testament prophets.

Look back to Acts 2:33. When Jesus "received...the promise of the Holy Spirit," He received what the Holy Spirit had promised in Old

Testament prophecy. So it is in Acts 2:38-39. When we "receive the gift of the Holy Spirit" we receive that promised gift of salvation which He (the Holy Spirit) promised through the Old Testament prophets. Someone may ask, "Why do you call it a 'promise'?" Because that is what Peter calls it in Acts 2:39. The scriptures declare salvation to be a promise (see Acts 13:23, 32; Romans 1:2, etc.). The scriptures also declare salvation to be a gift (see Romans 5:15-18; 6:23, etc.).

When we carefully examine Acts 2:38, we will conclude that the *purpose* of obedience to Christ in baptism is "for the remission of sins;" the *result* of having the remission of sins is that we receive salvation, the gift promised by the Holy Spirit. (See Luke 1:77 for a parallel thought. Salvation comes through the remission of sins.)

It is of further interest that, in Acts 1:16, Peter again attributes the writings of the prophets to the Holy Spirit. This is typical of Peter. See the following passages.

Acts 1:16

"Men and brethren, this Scripture had to be fulfilled, which the Holy Spirit spoke before by the mouth of David concerning Judas, who became a guide to those who arrested Jesus

Acts 4:25 (ASV)

"…who by the Holy Spirit, by the mouth of our father David thy servant, didst say, 'Why did the Gentiles rage, And the peoples imagine vain things?' "

1 Peter 1

[11] searching what, or what manner of time, the Spirit of Christ who was in them was indicating when He testified beforehand the sufferings of Christ and the glories that would follow.

[12] To them it was revealed that, not to themselves, but to us they were ministering the things which now have been reported to you through those who have preached the gospel to you by the Holy Spirit sent from heaven—things which angels desire to look into.

2 Peter 1:21

> . . . for prophecy never came by the will of man, but holy men
> of God spoke as they were moved by the Holy Spirit.

CONCLUSION

From studying the context of Acts chapter two, we conclude that the
gift of the Holy Spirit in Acts 2:38 is the promised gift of salvation
that was spoken of by the Old Testament prophets.

Does this mean we do not "have" the Holy Spirit? Not at all. Many
passages affirm our relationship with the Holy Spirit. See Matthew
28:19, Romans 8:9, and 1 Corinthians 6:19–20.

Do not be intimidated by those who claim they have received the bap-
tism of the Holy Spirit. They have not. The only two recorded cases of
Holy Spirit baptism are those of the apostles in Acts chapter two and
Cornelius in Acts chapter ten. All Christians in the first century did
not receive Holy Spirit baptism. And contrary to what modern-day
Pentecostals teach, no Christian receives it today.

13

False Teachers and Prophets

The Bible has a lot to say about false teachers. In some cases, a man or woman may simply be mistaken in what they believe and teach, though they may have honest hearts. In other cases, there are those who may have been deceived by someone into believing and practicing some form of religious error, though again, they may have honest hearts. But then, and unfortunately, there are cases where some intentionally teach error in order to profit materially from their followers. Among the many times we have visited Pentecostal churches and studied with their members, we have seen people who we believed to be in each of the above categories. The vast majority appear to have simply been mistaken in their studies of key passages. But there certainly are those people, some of whom are preachers, who have all of the characteristics of someone who is a deceiver. This should not come as a surprise to anyone since multiple warnings are given in both the Old and New Testaments on this very topic. Let's take a look at some of those passages and then you can make up your own mind on the subject of modern-day Pentecostalism.

In Matthew 7:13–14, Jesus warns us that the way that "leads to life" is "narrow" and "difficult" and the way that leads to "destruction" is "wide" and "broad."

Matthew 7

¹³ Enter by the narrow gate; for **wide** is the gate and **broad** is the way that leads to destruction, and there are **many** who go in by it.

¹⁴ Because **narrow** is the gate and **difficult** is the way which leads to life, and there are **few** who find it.

We conclude from this that it is a lot easier to follow error than to follow truth. It is easier to go down the wide path than it is the narrow one. He actually says that in comparison to the broad way, the narrow way to life is "difficult." He then follows with an explanation that provides one of the reasons for this and it involves "false prophets."

Matthew 7

¹⁵ **Beware of false prophets**, who come to you in sheep's clothing, but inwardly they are ravenous wolves.

¹⁶ **You will know them by their fruits.**

He could not be any clearer than that. Jesus warns us, "Beware." He then gives us more information about those "false prophets" so that we can avoid being adversely affected by them. More information is later given by Jesus in chapter twelve. In that passage Jesus further explains what He means by "their fruits."

Matthew 12

³³ Either make the tree good and its fruit good, or else make the tree bad and its fruit bad; for **a tree is known by its fruit**.

³⁴ "Brood of vipers! How can you, being evil, **speak** good things? For out of the abundance of the heart the mouth **speaks**.

³⁵ "A good man out of the good treasure of his heart brings forth good things, and an evil man out of the evil treasure brings forth evil things.

Jesus Himself gives us a commentary in the discussion recorded in chapter twelve regarding what He had meant back in chapter seven when He referred to "knowing" a false prophet "by their fruits." He first uses the figure of a wolf in sheep's clothing to describe them. When you think of a false prophet or a false teacher, what do you think of? Probably what comes to mind is some man you have seen on TV or on the internet who is clearly a con man and who is bilking his followers. Some men are easily identified as frauds by all but the most gullible. But that is not the illustration that Jesus gives. He is talking about a false prophet who does not have the appearance of being one. His appearance is that of someone who is good, someone who wants to help others and of someone who appears to be simply following the scriptures. In other words, this false prophet is disguising himself and his wicked ways with outward appearances of goodness and righteousness. In fact, he could not make it very far in that venue if his followers could easily see him for who he really is. He has a disguise (a wolf in sheep's clothing). And yet, Jesus' warning tells us how we can see through that disguise. That can be done by simply listening to his words and carefully scrutinizing them. Do his teachings match exactly with the scriptures? Also, keep in mind that in order for a false teacher to get very far, he usually mixes a little error in with a lot of truth. And in order to see this one must carefully examine his teachings for what they contain.

Listen to these similar warnings given by the Apostle Paul:

Ephesians 4:14

That we should no longer be children, tossed to and fro and carried about with every wind of doctrine, **by the trickery of men**, in **the cunning craftiness of deceitful plotting.**

2 Corinthians 11

[13] Such are **false apostles, deceitful workers**, transforming themselves into the apostles of Christ.

[14] And no marvel; for Satan himself is transformed into an angel of light.

¹⁵ Therefore it is no great thing if his ministers also be transformed as the ministers of righteousness; whose end shall be according to their works.

Listen to the similar warning given by the Apostle John:

1 John 4:1

Beloved, **do not believe every spirit**, but **test the spirits**, whether they are of God; because many false prophets have gone out into the world.

We are warned by the Apostle John, through the inspiration of the Holy Spirit that many false prophets are in the world. And we are told that we must not only "not believe" them but that we must also "test" them. In other words, we must be very skeptical at first when someone in a teaching capacity is claiming to speak for God. We have met preachers and healers that we have confidently concluded were con men but saw many around them naively falling for their deception. Some of those naïve folks were very hesitant to even consider that they had been deceived.

Much information is given through the prophet Jeremiah in the Old Testament concerning false teachers and false prophets detailing just exactly how they operate. Notice the following:

Jeremiah 5

³⁰ An astonishing and horrible thing Has been committed in the land:

³¹ **The prophets prophesy falsely**, And the priests rule by their own power; And **My people love to have it so**...

Jeremiah 14

¹³ Then I said, "Ah, Lord GOD! Behold, the prophets say to them, 'You shall not see the sword, nor shall you have famine, but I will give you assured peace in this place.'"

¹⁴ And the LORD said to me, "**The prophets prophesy lies in My name.** I have not sent them, **commanded them, nor spoken to them; they prophesy to you a false vision, divination, a worthless thing, and the deceit of their heart.**"

Jeremiah 23

¹⁶ Thus says the LORD of hosts: "**Do not listen to the words of the prophets who prophesy to you. They make you worthless;** They speak a vision of their own heart, **Not from the mouth of the LORD.**

²¹ **I have not sent these prophets**, yet they ran. **I have not spoken to them**, yet they prophesied.

³² "Behold, I am against those who prophesy **false dreams**," says the LORD, "and tell them, and cause My people to err by **their lies and by their recklessness**. Yet I did not send them or command them; therefore they shall not profit this people at all," says the LORD.

These men had all the appearances of being sent from God, yet God said that He had not sent them. They said that they spoke the commandments of God, yet God said that He had not given those commandments. God said that those claiming to have had a vision had in fact only had a "false vision." That those things had only come from "the deceit of their heart." He warns those following them, "do not listen" to their words. Because their vision is only from "their own heart" and not a vision from "the mouth of the Lord." God said that He had not sent those men, "yet they ran" and He had not spoken to them, "yet they prophesied." And then God concludes with the shocking statement that the way that this had happened is that the people "love to have it so." We have seen many today who clearly fit into this description and it is difficult to get them to see through the deception. It would appear that they "love to have it so" because the false teacher tells them what they want to hear.

Very similar language is given by the Holy Spirit through the prophet Ezekiel:

Ezekiel 13

¹ And the word of the LORD came to me, saying,

² "Son of man, prophesy against the prophets of Israel who prophesy, and say to **those who prophesy out of their own heart**, 'Hear the word of the LORD!' "

³ Thus says the Lord GOD: "**Woe to the foolish prophets, who follow their own spirit and have seen nothing!**

⁶ "They have envisioned futility and **false divination**, saying, 'Thus says the LORD!' But **the LORD has not sent them**; yet they hope that the word may be confirmed.

⁷ "Have you not seen **a futile vision**, and have you not spoken **false divination**? You say, 'The LORD says,' but **I have not spoken**."

⁸ Therefore thus says the Lord GOD: "**Because you have spoken nonsense and envisioned lies, therefore I am indeed against you**," says the Lord GOD.

⁹ "My hand will be against the prophets who envision **futility** and who divine **lies**…"

Notice the similar description and warnings given concerning how those false prophets were working. Those false prophets were not getting their information from God as they claimed but it was actually only coming from "their own hearts." They were called "foolish prophets" because they were not following God but were in fact only following "their own spirit." Rather than telling their audience something that God had shown them, God tells us that those prophets had actually "seen nothing." Their words were simply described as "nonsense." God called what they were doing "lies." Finally, He said that He was "against" those false prophets.

Having been to many faith healing services over the years, we do not know if we could better describe what we saw than the words spoken by the prophet Jeremiah and the prophet Ezekiel.

We must concede the possibility of being deceived ourselves. We did a search in the New Testament to see how many times a warning was given about being deceived and found the list to be quite long. Each of these gives a different way that someone might be deceived. Listen to a few of them:

Matthew 24:4 (Jesus)

Take heed that no man **deceive you**.

Romans 7:11 (Paul)

For sin, taking occasion by the commandment, **deceived me**.

1 Corinthians 6:9

Do you not know that the unrighteous will not inherit the kingdom of God? **Do not be deceived.** [Paul then gives a list of sins that can deceive.]

1 Corinthians 15:33

Do not be deceived: Evil company corrupts good habits.

Galatians 6:7

Do not be deceived. [He then warns against sowing to the flesh.]

Titus 3:3

For we ourselves were also once foolish, disobedient, **deceived**, serving various lusts and pleasures, living in malice and envy, hateful and hating one another.

2 Timothy 3:13

But evil men and impostors will grow worse and worse, **deceiving and being deceived**.

1 Corinthians 3:18

Let no one deceive himself. If anyone among you seems to be wise in this age, let him become a fool that he may become wise.

Ephesians 5:6

Let no man deceive you with vain words...

1 John 1:8

If we say that we have no sin, **we deceive ourselves,** and the truth is not in us.

In these passages, we see warning after warning about being deceived. Most of these verses are referring to being deceived by some sin. And most of these warnings are to Christians. But not all. Have you ever talked with someone that you knew was deceived? Years ago, we had a friend who had fallen in with what we believe to be a cult. They had their own prophet and some very rigid rules for their followers. No matter how much we tried to talk to our friend about it, he would not even consider the possibility that he had been deceived. And that brings up two interesting questions.

> **Question 1** — Does a person who is deceived, believe that he (or she) is deceived?

No, they will say that they "know" that they are not deceived. But think about it. The very nature of being deceived is that you do not know or believe that you are deceived. So, a person who *is* deceived will always say that they are *not* deceived.

Question 2 — Are you deceived?

Let that question sink in for a moment. If you are deceived, you are not going to think so. So, our feeling on the matter is not a good test for whether we really are deceived or not. So, how then will we know? How can we be sure that we are *not* deceived?

John 8:32

And you shall know **the truth,** and **the truth** shall make you free.

In our opinion, one of the most important things to do to make sure that we are not deceived, is to acknowledge that it could happen. It is significant to note that many people believe it is a point of weakness to admit the possibility that it could happen. The reverse is actually true. The person who stands in the truth has no problem with someone questioning or examining his beliefs. Truth never has anything to lose by investigation. If this man is wrong in his beliefs, he wants to know it. That makes his position strong, and he can admit the possibility that he may have been deceived. The person who says it could never happen to them will probably be one of the first to be deceived. And, furthermore, he is likely to be among the last to submit to an open examination of his beliefs. To acknowledge the possibility of being deceived is to reduce the probability of it happening. After acknowledging that we could be deceived, we must diligently study God's word to make sure that we are not being deceived.

2 Timothy 2:15 (KJV)

Study to shew thyself approved unto God, a workman that needeth not to be ashamed, rightly dividing the word of truth.

What is this "workman" doing? He is "rightly dividing the word of truth." So, one of the things that sets apart someone who truly *is* deceived from someone who is *not* deceived is *how* they are studying. We must "rightly divide." And that means that we must study properly without bias, find the context of the passages that we are studying and search for any historical or geographical information which may help. When we do that, as the verse says, we are "showing ourselves approved unto God." And it says that we would not need to ever "be ashamed" of what we believe. When we "rightly divide" the word as we study, we can then have confidence that we have not been deceived.

14

Questions and Objections
(With Answers)

After reading the previous material, there will obviously be numerous questions that will come to mind. Those who are members of Pentecostal churches will have a number of objections as well. In this chapter, we will attempt to cover all such questions and objections that we have heard raised over the years concerning this very interesting and important subject.

QUESTIONS

1. What is the Bible definition of a miracle?

2. What was the purpose of a miracle in the New Testament?

3. Isn't it a miracle anytime God takes action on the earth?

4. Did all of the 120 in Acts chapter one receive the baptism of the Holy Spirit?

5. Does the phrase Holy Spirit always mean the Baptism of the Holy Spirit?

6. Can we be "witnesses" today as in Acts 1:8?

7. What is the significance of the writer telling us in Acts chapter 2 that on the day of Pentecost all who spoke in tongues were "Galileans?"

8. What is speaking in tongues in the New Testament?

9. When "speaking in tongues," was the miracle at the mouth of the speaker or at the ear of the hearer?

10. In the New Testament, didn't all the saved speak in tongues?

11. Is "speaking in tongues" and "the gift of tongues" the same thing?

12. When modern-day Pentecostals claim to "speak in tongues," is it a real language?

13. Are modern-day Pentecostals speaking in "the tongues of angels?"

14. Are modern-day Pentecostals speaking a heavenly language?

15. Did Cornelius, in Acts chapter 10, speak in tongues before he was saved?

16. When someone received the gift of "speaking in tongues" in the New Testament, could they use it at their discretion, and did they have control over when they used it?

17. When modern-day Pentecostals claim to be "speaking in tongues," why are the interpretations given in Old English?

18. How were the spiritual gifts transmitted in the first century?

19. When a person received one of the gifts from an apostle in the New Testament, could he then in turn transmit it to someone else?

20. Could a man with a gift personally and actually work a miracle?

21. How many apostles were there in the New Testament?

22. What were the qualifications to be an apostle in the New Testament?

23. Was Barnabas one of the apostles?

24. Are there apostles today?

25. What were the "signs of an apostle?"

26. How could a person get a spiritual gift after the apostles had died?

27. The New Testament speaks of "trying" or "testing" men claiming to be apostles but who were not. How was this done?

28. How could you "test" a man who claims to be an apostle today?

29. Would asking a faith healer for a demonstration today be testing God?

30. Objection: "You are just a sign seeker."

31. Objection: "Forbid not to speak in tongues."

32. Were the guidelines different for how the gift of tongues was used when in the assembly?

33. How many "spiritual gifts" are mentioned in the New Testament?

34. Does 1 Corinthians chapter 14 give us an idea of what the difference was between the gift of speaking in tongues and the gift of prophecy?

35. In addition to the "baptism of the Holy Spirit," how many other baptisms are mentioned in the New Testament?

36. Does a man have to have faith in order to receive a miracle?

37. Was Jesus unable to perform a miracle when someone did not have faith?

38. Can a Pentecostal member today pick up a serpent or drink poison and not get injured?

39. Can modern-day Pentecostals move mountains?

40. Can modern-day Pentecostals do greater works than Jesus?

41. Didn't Paul say that speaking in tongues would continue until Jesus comes back?

42. In 1 Corinthians 12:8 it mentions the gift of "the word of knowledge." Since some are saying that chapter 13 teaches that those gifts would end, are they saying that "knowledge" will end?

43. What is the significance of the time-table in the beginning of the book of Acts?

44. Is it true as several faith healers have claimed that if a man was faithful to God, he would never get sick, and that if he does get sick it is because of sin?

45. Do modern-day Pentecostals claim to be baptized with the Holy Spirit and with fire?

46. If Jesus is "the same today, yesterday and forever," doesn't that mean that we will always have miracles while on this earth?

47. Does Satan give false teachers the power to work miracles?

48. How do modern-day Pentecostal churches' claimed miracles compare to the New Testament?

49. If modern-day Pentecostal churches are not working real miracles, then how do you explain what is happening?

50. Do modern-day Pentecostals have to study?

Most of the topics covered in these questions have already been addressed in the previous chapters. But what will follow here will be shorter and more concise answers that the reader can use in Bible discussions.

ANSWERS

1. *What is the Bible definition of a miracle?*

The way the word was used in the New Testament was different than how many use it today. People today seem to use the word "miracle" in a way that is much looser and in an outright different manner than in the Bible. Anything that "beats the odds" is quickly labeled as a miracle, such as a baseball player who hits a home run that wins the World Series, a person who survives a bad car wreck but with injuries, or a person who is receiving cancer treatment and recovers, all are called miracles. But in the Bible, it was different.

In the Bible, a miracle is when God sets aside natural laws to cause an event to occur; therefore, it goes contrary to the laws of nature. When the laws of nature are suspended, we refer to it as "supernatural." Such an event is above ("super") or outside of the realm of the natural. We would then be forced to conclude that God was responsible for the event taking place since it was impossible for it to have happened naturally or in nature. When we hear an atheist say that the Bible is not true because it contains stories of miracles, and miracles are impossible, we answer, "Yes, they are." They are absolutely impossible by natural means. That is why we call them "supernatural." They are beyond the normal possibilities of nature. The atheist is only willing to consider the natural. He refuses to admit the possibility of the supernatural. That is what the definition of a miracle is, when that which is normally impossible happens. The miracle then points to God as the source. Some Bible examples in the Old Testament are the sun standing still (Joshua 10), the destruction of Jericho (Joshua 5:10–6:26) and the parting of the Red Sea (Exodus 14:15). Some Bible examples in the New Testament are the water turned to wine (John 2), Jesus walking on the water (John 6:19), feeding the multitude with five loaves and two fishes (John 6:9–10), and raising the dead (Acts 9:36–41).

In all of the events listed above, the laws of nature were suspended, and the events were contrary to nature. That which is impossible by natural means happened. We would look at any of those Bible events and say that they could not happen, that they are impossible. And yet:

Matthew 19:26

But Jesus looked at them and said to them, "With men this is impossible, but with God all things are possible.

Can you see the point? From man's standpoint, these things are impossible. But not with God. God does what is otherwise impossible.

So, by definition, what is impossible by natural means cannot happen unless God intervenes. It is then no longer natural but *supernatural*. The word "miracle" is a synonym for "a supernatural act or event." (See chapter two for additional information.)

2. ### What was the purpose of a miracle in the New Testament?

Mark 16:20

And they went forth, and preached everywhere, the Lord working with them, and **confirming the word with signs following**.

This passage tells us that the purpose of those miracles was to "confirm the word." It was "confirmed" to those unbelievers who were hearing the message. When a preacher made the claim that God had given him a message that men must follow, how would someone know for certain that the claim was true, since many false teachers were also making the same claim? Well, they would know when that man making the claim also was able to work a miracle as proof. If he was able to do "the impossible," which is what a miracle is, then the message must indeed be from God. New revelation and the confirmation of it went hand in hand. Since new revelation is not being given today because the Bible is complete, there is no need for any additional "confirmation." It would appear that all miracles in the New Testament were either for the purpose of giving new revelation, or of confirming revelation. To reveal and confirm! Those are the twin purposes of New Testament miracles. The miracles, signs, and wonders that Jesus performed before men confirmed that "He was a teacher sent from God." That is precisely what Nicodemus said of Jesus in John 3:2. In John 2:23, we are told, "...many believed in His name when they saw the signs which He did." When Jesus turned water to wine at the wedding feast in Cana, the text says, "This beginning of signs Jesus did in Cana of Galilee, and manifested His glory; and His disciples believed in Him." Note that His disciples believed in Him because of the signs. In John 14:11, Jesus said to His disciples, "...believe Me for the sake of the works themselves." All of these passages show the purposes of the miracles Jesus worked.

As noted earlier in Mark 16:20, when the disciples went forth and preached everywhere, the Lord worked with them by confirming their message with signs and wonders. This is consistent with what Hebrews 2:3-4 says. "...how shall we escape if we neglect so great a salvation, which at the first began to be spoken by the Lord, and was confirmed to us by those who heard Him, God also bearing witness both with signs and wonders, with various miracles, and gifts of the Holy Spirit, according to His own will?" The message was revealed miraculously by the Holy Spirit as He worked through these men. And the message was also confirmed to be true in a supernatural way through miracles, signs, and wonders. To reveal and confirm! Those are the twin purposes of New Testament miracles. (See chapter two for additional information.)

3. *Isn't it a miracle anytime God takes action on the earth?*

No, not in all cases. God many times works not in the supernatural but within the laws of nature to accomplish His ends. This is usually referred to as "the providence of God." It comes from a compound

Latin word "pro-video." "Pro" means before, "video" means to see, thus "to see before." In these cases, God, knowing the future, sees a need and "provides" for the desired outcome that He has in mind. But this will take place within the laws of nature and not through a miracle. There are numerous examples in the Bible of events in which God caused certain things to happen. In some of them He used miracles. In others He caused the very same thing to happen through natural means rather than a miracle (**Figure 10**).

Examples of Miracles and Providence

Miracle	Event	Providence
1. Tower of Babel confused languages (Genesis 11:7–9)	← scattered people →	through persecution (Acts 1:8; 8:1–4)
2. Three Hebrew boys (Daniel 3:16–18)	← delivered →	Paul from mob (2 Cor 1:8–10; Acts 19:31–41)
3. Jesus calmed the sea (Mark 4:37–41)	← delivered from death in storm →	Paul in shipwreck (Acts 27:21–44)
4. Sodom and Gomorrah (Genesis 19:23–25)	← cities destroyed →	Jerusalem (Matthew 24)
5. Lame man at gate (Acts 3:2; 4:22)	← sickness healed →	Hezekiah's boil (2 Kings 20:1–7) Put on lump of figs

Figure 10.

Example 1

These are cases of God scattering people. The people were scattered at the tower of Babel by God miraculously confusing their language, whereas God caused the gospel to go to all the world by allowing the disciples to be scattered as a result of persecution. A clear miracle was worked in scattering the people at the tower of Babel, yet no miracle was worked in God providentially scattering the people in Acts.

Example 2

These are cases of God delivering someone from death. The three Hebrew boys were miraculously delivered from death in the fiery furnace whereas God caused Paul to be delivered from death at the hands of the mob with the help of the town clerk. In Paul's case God worked in a non-miraculous way. No laws of nature were suspended. No miracle was worked. Nothing supernatural happened. Yet, God "provided" for Paul's deliverance!

Example 3

These are cases of people being delivered from death in a stormy sea. In the first case, Jesus calmed the storm by speaking to it, which was obviously a miracle. But in the case of Paul, they were not only caught in a fierce storm, but were actually shipwrecked. The people on the ship thought they were going to drown, yet in the face of certain death, they were all spared. They "just happened" to be in just the right place when the ship wrecked so that none drowned. Paul was the only one who knew that they would be saved because an angel had appeared to him and told him so. God then delivered them in a non-miraculous way! But consider this: If it was not for the angel telling Paul (and ultimately us) that it was God's providence that caused them to be spared, there would be no way to know for sure. God controlled and directed the forces of nature without a miracle. In this case, we are told that God saved the lives of all aboard the ship! God saved their lives, but no miracle was involved. Please note that some people think that the only way God can act is through a miracle. They have too small a view of God. They cannot see that the God who created the world supernaturally can now control that world through natural means. They would limit God to only acting in a miraculous way.

Example 4

These are cases of God destroying cities and the people in them. God miraculously destroyed Sodom and Gomorrah by raining fire from heaven. But in the case of the destruction of Jerusalem in A.D. 70, no miracle was worked. No laws of nature were suspended, and no fire rained down from heaven. Yet it was God who brought it all about!

Here, God decided to destroy the city of Jerusalem and the people of the city, but He accomplished it through natural means. He brought this judgment upon the Jews because they had rejected Christ and crucified Him. And God carried out this judgment by allowing the Roman army, led by General Titus, to completely destroy the city and the people in it. And if it were not for the fact that the scriptures tell us this, we could not even know God had caused this event to happen! God destroyed Sodom and Gomorrah miraculously and yet destroyed the city of Jerusalem non-miraculously. Consider also the Old Testament cases of judgment where God used invading armies to destroy cities and nations. When Jerusalem fell to the Babylonians in 605 B.C., no miracle was involved in the Old Testament judgment upon that city. Read 2 Chronicles 36:15–21 as God declares that He brought the Chaldeans (Babylonians) against Judah. God did it, but no miracle was involved!

Example 5

These are cases of people being healed. Peter heals the lame man in Acts 3. It is called a miracle in Acts 4:22. And yet in 2 Kings 20:1–7 a very interesting case of healing is found. Hezekiah is said to have been "sick unto death." He was told by God through the prophet Isaiah that he was going to die. After praying to God and asking Him to spare his life, God told him that He would grant his petition. He then instructed Hezekiah, again through Isaiah, to put a "lump of figs" on the boil and after doing so he recovered. We are specifically told in the account that it was God who healed him. Without that information, we might just attribute it to wise medical advice from Isaiah. But we know that it was God who healed him—and He did so through natural means. A clear miracle was worked in the healing of the lame man, yet no miracle was worked in God healing Hezekiah.

So, to answer the question of "Isn't it a miracle anytime God takes action on the earth?" No, not in all cases. It is up to God to determine how He takes some action on the earth. Based on these Bible examples, sometimes He uses miracles and sometimes He works within the natural realm. (See chapter 10 on Providence for additional information.)

4. *Did all of the 120 in Acts 1 receive the baptism of the Holy Spirit?*

Acts 1:15

> And in those days Peter stood up in the midst of the disciples (altogether the number of names was **about a hundred and twenty**)...

On the day of Pentecost, the baptism of the Holy Spirit came upon the apostles in Acts 2:1-4. But, the modern-day Pentecostal view is that on the day of Pentecost, the 120 people mentioned in Acts 1:15 all received the baptism of the Holy Spirit. Pentecostalism further says that the 3,000 converted on that day (Acts 2:41) also received the same miraculous outpouring of the Holy Spirit. The Pentecostals argue that this outpouring continued with every convert through the book of Acts and on through history up to today. Thus, this view says that everyone who is converted today should receive the baptism of the Holy Spirit. If, on the other hand, it could be proven that all of the 120 did *not* receive the baptism of the Holy Spirit, then that would be a fatal blow to modern-day Pentecostal doctrine. If all of the converts did not receive the baptism of the Holy Spirit in the first century, then perhaps we could see that it may not be for everyone today either. In fact, upon completing this material, we will have proven that *no one* receives the baptism of the Holy Spirit today! While that might seem like an extreme statement to make, it is considered extreme only because the majority of the religious world fails to understand what the baptism of the Holy Spirit was.

The confusion in the modern-day Pentecostal churches on this topic is a result of the wording of Acts 2:4 where Luke says that "they were *all* filled with the Holy Spirit and began to speak with other tongues, as the Spirit gave them utterance." The Pentecostals then conclude that Luke must have been referring to the 120 mentioned in the previous chapter. But let's examine it further.

Acts chapter one is Luke's account written to Theophilus detailing to him the events that took place by the apostles after Jesus had ascended back to heaven. It is critically important that we carefully follow Luke's narrative. He leaves no doubt about who received Holy Spirit baptism.

Acts 1

> [1] The former account I made, O Theophilus, of all that Jesus began both to do and teach,

> [2] until the day in which He was taken up, after He through the Holy Spirit had given **commandments to the apostles** whom He had chosen.

Specifically notice that verse two says that these *commands* were given to "the apostles"! These commands that had already been recorded in Luke 24:45–53 are repeated in Acts 1:4–5.

Acts 1

> [4] And being assembled together with **them**, He **commanded them not to depart from Jerusalem, but to wait for the Promise of the Father**, "which," He said, "**you** have heard from Me;

> [5] for John truly baptized with water, but **you** shall be baptized with the Holy Spirit not many days from now.

Luke repeats those commands that Jesus gave the apostles. First, He said to go back to Jerusalem. Then wait for the promise of the Father, which was a reference to the baptism of the Holy Spirit. It should be pointed out that the publishers of the various versions of the New Testament usually give this book the title, *The Acts of the Apostles*. Though it is not on the oldest manuscripts, it is a fitting title. Luke's first letter to Theophilus told of the life of Christ. This second letter begins with Jesus giving commands to the apostles. The remainder of the letter is a detailed account of how the apostles "acted" on those commands. Thus, *"The Acts of the Apostles."* After the ascension they went back to Jerusalem returning to the same upper room "where they were staying."

These all continued with one accord in prayer and supplication, with the women, and Mary the mother of Jesus, and with his brethren (Acts 1:14).

First of all, the phrase "these all" refers back to the previous verse where a list of the 11 apostles was given. "These all" does not refer to anyone else who might have been with the apostles because Luke says "these all *continued with*…" He then lists all the others that were accompanying the apostles there in the upper room. He makes a distinction between the apostles who were in that upper room and the rest of the group in the upper room. The reason for doing that will become apparent in the following few verses.

Acts 1:15

And in those days Peter stood up in the midst of the disciples, and said, (the number of names together were **about an hundred and twenty**)…

We have finally reached the passage of controversy. The question now that must be asked is this, is there some significance to the number 120? Of course not! It doesn't even say that there were 120, but rather that there were "about" 120! Luke is just giving us this bit of incidental information so that we might have a mental picture of what was going on. Not only is this the first and last place that "the 120" is mentioned, but it is the only place it is mentioned! Nowhere in the remainder of the book of Acts will the group be mentioned again. It will not be mentioned in any of the other books of the New Testament. This would be rather odd if, as the Pentecostals contend, all of the 120 received the same outpouring of the Holy Spirit as the apostles. As we are about to see, that is not at all what happened; the 120 did not receive Holy Spirit baptism.

Acts 1

16 Men and brethren, this Scripture had to be fulfilled, which the Holy Spirit spoke before by the mouth of David concerning Judas, who became a guide to those who arrested Jesus;

17 "for he was **numbered with us** and obtained a part in **this ministry.**

It is interesting that just after others (the 120) are introduced into the context, the context immediately focuses back onto the apostles in verse 17. Peter says that Judas "was numbered with us." Was Judas ever numbered with the 120? Certainly not! He had killed himself prior to the 120 assembling in that upper room. He was, however, numbered with the 12 apostles! Peter also said that Judas had obtained a part of "this ministry." What ministry had Judas been a part of? Certainly, it was that of the apostles. The 120 did not even have a "ministry!"

Acts 1:20

"For it is written in the book of Psalms: 'Let his dwelling place be desolate, And let no one live in it'; and, 'Let another take **his office**.'"

What office is Peter referring to? Certainly, it is not "the 120" since they had no office. It was simply a reference back to the office of an apostle. Why is Peter discussing this "office" from which Judas had fallen? Because, as a result of his death, there were only eleven apostles, and it was God's will that there be twelve. Peter then begins the process of choosing a replacement for Judas. Look at how chapter one concludes and how it transitions into chapter two.

Acts 1:26

And **they** gave forth **their** lots; and the lot fell upon Matthias; and he was **numbered with the eleven apostles**.

Acts 2

¹ When the Day of Pentecost had fully come, **they** were all with one accord in one place.

² And suddenly there came a sound from heaven, as of a rushing mighty wind, and it filled the whole house where **they** were sitting.

³ Then there appeared to **them** divided tongues, as of fire, and one sat upon **each of them**.

> ⁴ And **they** were all filled with the Holy Spirit and began to speak with other tongues, as the Spirit gave **them** utterance.

Keep in mind that the chapter break was not in the original Greek manuscript. And this has caused problems for some Bible students. If we read right into chapter two from chapter one, it will readily be seen who the pronouns "they" and "them" refer to. The last noun for those pronouns to modify was "apostles." Therefore "they" and "them" refer to the twelve apostles, not the 120! And as a result, we can easily see then that the 120 mentioned in Acts chapter one did not receive the baptism of the Holy Spirit as some today contend.

In this brief discussion we have tried to follow the pronouns from the beginning of chapter one through the opening of chapter two. We would recommend that you read this entire section aloud. When you read Acts 1:2, you will see the "apostles" directly mentioned. As you continue the reading, each time you come across the pronouns that point back to them, call out the phrase "the apostles." As an example, read Acts 1:3–5…

> To whom (**the apostles**) He also presented Himself alive after His suffering by many infallible proofs, being seen by them (**the apostles**) during forty days and speaking of the things pertaining to the kingdom of God. And being assembled with them (**the apostles**), He commanded them (**the apostles**) not to depart from Jerusalem, but to wait for the Promise of the Father, "which," He said, "you (**the apostles**) have heard from Me: for John truly baptized with water, but you (**the apostles**) shall be baptized with the Holy Spirit not many days from now…' "

Read the text all the way through to Acts 2:4. It will be abundantly clear who received Holy Spirit baptism. It was the apostles, not the 120. (See chapter four for additional information.)

5. *Does the phrase Holy Spirit always*
   mean the Baptism of the Holy Spirit?

No, it does not. This relates to one of the most common mistakes made by present day Pentecostals. It seems that every time they come across the word "spirit" they automatically make it "Holy Spirit." They then assume that it means the "baptism of the Holy Spirit." They also make a similar mistake in not distinguishing between the phrases "filled with" or "full of" the Holy Spirit and having the miraculous gifts of the Holy Spirit. Notice the following:

- Luke 1:15—John the Baptist was "*filled* with the Holy Spirit."

- Luke 1:41—His mother, Elizabeth, was "*filled* with the Holy Spirit."

- Luke 1:67—His father, Zacharias, was "*filled* with the Holy Spirit."

And yet:

We read in John 7:39 that "the Holy Spirit" had not yet been given. This had to do with the giving of the Holy Spirit in a unique way that had not happened before. This could include the baptism of the Holy Spirit (as in Acts 2:1–4), and also what is described in Acts 8:14–19, when those disciples at Samaria "received the Holy Spirit." This case involved the transmitting of miraculous gifts of the Holy Spirit; this was accomplished by the laying on of the hands of the apostles.

Acts 8:15

> who, when they had come down, prayed for them that they might **receive the Holy Spirit**.

The point to be understood here is that John the Baptist, his father Zacharias, and his mother Elizabeth were all said to be "filled with the Holy Spirit" *before* the "Holy Spirit was given." Therefore, those two phrases ("filled with the Holy Spirit" and "baptism of the Holy Spirit") are not necessarily equal. Those references above with the phrase "filled with the Holy Spirit" carry the idea of being under the influence of the Holy Spirit in some way. But those passages are not about the baptism of the Holy Spirit. Once we understand that, it will help us to understand some of the references in the later books of the New Testament. (See chapter four for additional information.)

6. *Can we be "witnesses" today as in Acts 1:8?*

No, we cannot.

Acts 1:8

> But you shall receive power when the Holy Spirit has come upon you; and **you shall be witnesses** to Me in Jerusalem, and in all Judea and Samaria, and to the end of the earth.

Jesus, in speaking to the apostles, told them just prior to His ascension to heaven, that they would "be witnesses" to Him. Later in the chapter when a replacement for Judas was being selected, we read:

Acts 1

> [21] Therefore, of these men who have accompanied us all the time that the Lord Jesus went in and out among us,
>
> [22] "beginning from the baptism of John to that day when He was taken up from us, one of these must become **a witness with us of His resurrection.**

The "us" is a reference to Peter and the other ten apostles who were present. Peter claims that all of the apostles were to be "witnesses of the resurrection." He said that they had accompanied Jesus from the beginning of His ministry, "beginning from the baptism of John." Peter also said they had followed Jesus "unto that same day that he was taken up from us," which is a reference to the ascension after His death and resurrection. Peter then stated that the replacement for Judas had to have been a witness of the resurrection like all of the other apostles. There are numerous references throughout the New Testament to the apostles being witnesses of the resurrection. (See Acts 2:32; 3:15; 4:33, and 10:39-41 as examples.) But what about today? We have seen many modern-day Pentecostal churches with Acts 1:8 posted behind the pulpit admonishing the members to "be witnesses" today. So, there is obviously a misunderstanding among many as to what being "a witness" means. Most simply equate it with telling someone how their life has changed since following Jesus. They call it "witnessing." And although that is admirable, that is not what being "a witness" means.

Let us give an illustration to clarify. Think for just a minute about a car accident that your friend saw. He was an eyewitness. What if he told you every single detail of that accident? You would then know as much about it as he knew, even though you did not see it. Now suppose that both of you were called on to testify at a hearing about the accident. You may be asked to get up and tell what you know to have happened. However, as soon as it becomes apparent that you were not personally an eyewitness, your testimony will be ruled second hand, or hearsay. But your friend who was there would then be called on to testify as to what he had personally seen, as an eyewitness. Though you could have given a correct account, you still were not an eyewitness, and your testimony would not be as convincing as his. Our courts today recognize the importance of that kind of evidence. It can constitute *proof*, considering the reliability of the witness. Since the apostles were told in Acts 1:8 that they would be the ones to first begin the preaching of the gospel, it would be important that they be able to answer the skeptics by saying, "We are eyewitnesses!" That, in essence, is what they claimed in Acts 2:32. They could then further produce proof by *confirming* their words with miracles! Nobody today then is a *witness* in the sense that it is used in the New Testament. (See **Chapter Seven** for additional information.)

7. *What is the significance of the writer telling us in Acts chapter two that on the day of Pentecost all who spoke in tongues were "Galileans"?*

Acts 2

⁶ Now when this was noised abroad, the multitude came together, and were confounded, because that every man heard **them** speak in his own language."

⁷ "And they were all amazed and marvelled, saying one to another, Behold, **are not all these which speak Galileans**?

Who were the Galileans? Notice Acts chapter 1:

Acts 1

⁹ Now when He had spoken these things, while they watched, He was taken up, and a cloud received Him out of their sight.

¹⁰ And while they looked steadfastly toward heaven as He went up, behold, two men stood by them in white apparel,

¹¹ who also said, "**Men of Galilee**, why do you stand gazing up into heaven? This same Jesus, who was taken up from you into heaven, will so come in like manner as you saw Him go into heaven."

Notice that the angels said, "men of Galilee." Who were these Galileans? If you will go back and read Matthew 4:25, it tells of the areas from which the disciples came. The very first ones were from Galilee, then from Decapolis, then from Jerusalem, from Judea, and then beyond Jordan. The reason the first ones were from Galilee was because that was where Jesus was from. It was from that area that the very first followers came, those who would later become the apostles. Since the context up to Acts 1:9 was dealing with the apostles, it is no coincidence that the angels addressed these men as "Galileans!"

If there is any question about who received the outpouring of the Holy Spirit on the day of Pentecost, it can be answered by just asking who the Galileans were. We have already shown that the apostles were the ones being referred to as Galileans! And this fits perfectly well with the context. It is interesting that those Jews present recognized that those men speaking were from the area of Galilee. There is a verse in Matthew 26 that may shed some light on this:

Matthew 26:69, 73

> Now Peter sat outside in the courtyard. And a servant girl came to him, saying, "You also were with Jesus **of Galilee**." ... "Surely you also are one of them, for **your speech betrays you**."

Apparently, there was a recognizable dialect for those who were from the area of Galilee, much like we can recognize someone from New York City today, as distinguished from someone from Birmingham, Alabama. Those Jews who gathered in Jerusalem in Acts chapter two were from all parts of the world as is seen in verses 8–11. Yet they readily perceived that those men speaking were from Galilee.

As an interesting and important point, it should also be noted that in John 11:1 it mentions Mary, Martha, and Lazarus as being from Bethany. Therefore, they were not Galileans. This is an important point simply because after Jesus raised Lazarus from the dead, those three are mentioned over and over again as being with the group following Jesus throughout the rest of His ministry. It is difficult to believe that after following Him throughout the country right up to the time of the crucifixion, they would then be strangely absent from that same group of followers after the ascension. It seems as though if anyone would have been there in Acts chapter one, in addition to the apostles, it would have been Mary, Martha, and Lazarus. Yet they were not Galileans, and all those who received the baptism of the Holy Spirit and spoke in tongues were Galileans!

Another interesting and important point, is that Judas Iscariot was not from Galilee, as the other apostles were. Instead, he was from the town of Kerioth located south of Jerusalem in Judea. Had Judas still been alive and in the group of apostles, those angels would not have likely referred to the group of apostles as "Galileans." But Judas, having died, was not present, and so the reference was accurate in referring to the rest of the apostles as Galileans.

Lastly, notice that Peter did not stand up with the "120" as he spoke.

Acts 2:14

But Peter, **standing up with the eleven**, raised his voice and said to them...

Instead of standing up with the 120, he stood up with the other apostles—all Galileans—and defended them since it was those apostles who were accused of being drunk. Why do you think they were the ones being accused? Simply because they were the ones who had spoken in tongues! The men of Galilee!

8. *What is speaking in tongues in the New Testament?*

The first reference to speaking in tongues in the New Testament record was given by Jesus in Mark chapter sixteen in what is generally referred to as "The Great Commission."

Mark 16

[15] And He said to them, "Go into all the world and preach the gospel to every creature.

[16] "He who believes and is baptized will be saved; but he who does not believe will be condemned.

[17] "And **these signs** will follow those who believe: In My name they will cast out demons; **they will speak with new tongues;**

> [18] "they will take up serpents; and if they drink anything deadly, it will by no means hurt them; they will lay hands on the sick, and they will recover."
>
> [20] And they went out and preached everywhere, the Lord working with them and **confirming the word through the accompanying signs**."

Jesus said that "speaking with new tongues" was one of the signs that His followers would use to "confirm" the word that they were preaching. We then have the apostles doing just that in Acts chapter two.

Acts 2

> [4] And they were all filled with the Holy Spirit and **began to speak with other tongues**, as the Spirit gave them utterance.
>
> [8] "And how is it that we hear, each **in our own language** in which we were born?
>
> [9] "Parthians and Medes and Elamites, those dwelling in Mesopotamia, Judea and Cappadocia, Pontus and Asia,
>
> [10] "Phrygia and Pamphylia, Egypt and the parts of Libya adjoining Cyrene, visitors from Rome, both Jews and proselytes,
>
> [11] "Cretans and Arabs—**we hear them speaking in our own tongues** the wonderful works of God."

Just as Jesus had said, the apostles went out preaching the new message to unbelievers. A central piece of that message was that they had each seen Jesus alive after He had been crucified. When that claim was met with skepticism, those men could work a miracle by speaking to those hearers in the hearer's local and unique language. And it was a language that was clearly evident to be "unknown" to the speaker. That was what gave it such a tremendous impact. The apostles were able to speak languages that they had never learned. How could they do that? This could only be done if God was behind those men and was confirming their message to be from Him. And this procedure worked to perfection just as Jesus had said. In the Acts chapter two account, it says that they spoke with other tongues "as the Spirit gave them utterance" (v. 4). It was the Holy Spirit who gave the words to those men in a language that they did not know. It was a miracle. And that was the conclusion that the hearers made that day. It says that they were at first "confounded" (v. 6) and they were "amazed and marveled" (v. 7). They realized that those men speaking were "Galileans" and yet were able, as a group, to each speak in the various languages of those foreigners who had assembled in Jerusalem for the Day of Pentecost. Modern-day Pentecostals simply cannot do this. (See chapter six for additional information.)

9. *When "speaking in tongues," was the miracle at the mouth of the speaker or at the ear of the hearer?*

Acts 2 (KJV)

> **6** Now when this was noised abroad, the multitude came together, and were confounded, because that **every man heard them speak in his own language**.

> **7** And they were all amazed and marvelled, saying one to another, Behold, are not all these which speak Galileans?

> **8** And **how hear we every man in our own tongue**, wherein we were born?

When a man spoke in tongues in the New Testament, what is meant when it says that they each heard in their own language? The question that is usually asked is. "Was the miracle at the mouth of the speaker or at the ear of the hearer?" First of all, the simple answer is that the miracle was at the mouth of the speaker. Those twelve apostles had just received the baptism of the Holy Spirit in Acts 2:1–4. It was then that they began to speak in tongues to those who were gathered from the other nations. And they actually spoke in the various languages of those foreign lands:

Acts 2

> [8] And how is it that **we hear, each in our own language in which we were born**?
>
> [9] Parthians, and Medes, and Elamites, and the dwellers in Mesopotamia, and in Judaea, and Cappadocia, in Pontus, and Asia,
>
> [10] Phrygia, and Pamphylia, in Egypt, and in the parts of Libya about Cyrene, and strangers of Rome, Jews and proselytes,
>
> [11] Cretes and Arabians...

There was no need for an interpreter because they spoke directly to those groups, each in their own different language. Yet, when this was done among believers in a church assembly, they were told not to speak unless there was an interpreter present.

1 Corinthians 14

> [23] Therefore **if the whole church comes together in one place**, and all speak with tongues, and there come in those who are uninformed or unbelievers, will they not say that you are out of your mind?
>
> [27] If anyone speaks in a tongue, let there be two or at the most three, each in turn, and let one interpret.
>
> [28] But **if there is no interpreter, let him keep silent** in church, and let him speak to himself and to God.

Therefore, we know of a certainty that the one speaking in tongues was speaking an actual language that he had not known, but that in some cases the hearer did know and could understand. On the other hand, if the miracle was at the ear of the hearer where the speaker was using some miraculous language that anyone would understand, then there would never be a need for an interpreter. So, when the miracle of Acts chapter two of the speaking in tongues says that they each heard in their own language, it meant just exactly that. They heard the very words that the apostles spoke. There was no miracle at the ear of the hearer. Can modern-day Pentecostals do this today? No, they cannot. (See chapter six for additional information.)

10. *In the New Testament, didn't all the saved speak in tongues?*

No, they did not. Notice the following:

1 Corinthians 12

> [28] And God has appointed these in the church: first apostles, second prophets, third teachers, after that miracles, then gifts of healings, helps, administrations, varieties of tongues.
>
> [29] Are all apostles? Are all prophets? Are all teachers? Are all workers of miracles?
>
> [30] Do all have gifts of healings? **Do all speak with tongues?** Do all interpret?
>
> [31] But earnestly desire the best gifts. And yet I show you a more excellent way.

Paul, through the Holy Spirit, asks rhetorical questions directly related to this topic. One of those questions was "Do all speak with tongues?" The answer to all of those questions is "No." All were not apostles. All were not prophets. All were not teachers. All were not workers of miracles. All did not have the gift of healings. And, all the saved in the first century did *not* speak in tongues. (See chapter six for additional information.)

11. *Is "speaking in tongues" and "the gift of tongues" the same thing?*

Yes, they are. However, many modern-day Pentecostals will tell you that these two are not the same thing. They do this in order to get around the guidelines given in First Corinthians chapter fourteen for "speaking in tongues."

1 Corinthians 14

²⁷ If anyone **speaks in a tongue**, let there be two or at the most three, each in turn, and let one interpret.

²⁸ But if there is no interpreter, let him keep silent in church, and let him speak to himself and to God.

In this passage, Paul commands those who might speak in tongues in the assembly to determine first, before they speak, whether there is an "interpreter" present. If not, then they are to "keep silent." Since it is a rare thing to see any such interpretation given in a modern-day Pentecostal church when claiming to speak in tongues, they are in violation of this prohibition. And so, their answer usually is to say that they were not "speaking in tongues" but that they instead had the "gift of tongues" which they will say is different.

1 Corinthians 12

¹ Now concerning **spiritual gifts**, brethren, I do not want you to be ignorant:

² You know that you were Gentiles, carried away to these dumb idols, however you were led.

³ Therefore I make known to you that no one speaking by the Spirit of God calls Jesus accursed, and no one can say that Jesus is Lord except by the Holy Spirit.

⁴ There are **diversities of gifts**, but the same Spirit.

⁵ There are differences of ministries, but the same Lord.

⁶ And there are diversities of activities, but it is the same God who works all in all.

⁷ But the manifestation of the Spirit is given to each one for the profit of all:

⁸ for to one is given the word of wisdom through the Spirit, to another the word of knowledge through the same Spirit,

⁹ to another faith by the same Spirit, to another gifts of healings by the same Spirit,

¹⁰ to another the working of miracles, to another prophecy, to
another discerning of spirits, to another **different kinds of
tongues**, to another the interpretation of tongues.

In order for them to get away with not giving an interpretation, they
must find a way to make their "tongues" different. And they do so by
arbitrarily making a distinction between the two. But the fact of the
matter is that "speaking in tongues" and the "gift of tongues" both refer
to the same thing. Those "spiritual gifts" mentioned in 1 Corinthians
12:1 are called "gifts" because they are given by God to certain men.
One of those gifts was the ability to speak in a language that the
man had not learned, "speaking in tongues." The "gift of tongues"
and "speaking in tongues" are one and the same. And if modern-day
Pentecostals want to make the claim that they have that gift today,
then they need to tell us what language is being spoken and then
have an interpretation given, rather than make excuses for why an
interpretation was not given. We actually know why an interpretation was not given. Because it was not a real language that could be
interpreted. (See chapter six for additional information.)

12. *When modern-day Pentecostals claim to
"speak in tongues" is it a real language?*

No, it is not. It is something else. Today, those claiming to have tongues,
do not even claim to have had apostles lay hands on them to transmit
that gift like in the New Testament (See Acts 8:14-19). For the most part,
and what we have seen after visiting many services, is that modern-
day "tongue speakers" just have it come on them. And in many cases,
they are actually taught how to do it. Or they may simply watch others
and imitate what they see them doing. And in many of those cases
you can hear several people speaking the same unintelligible words.
But, in all of those cases, no real languages are spoken. If you tried to
make up a fake language by simply speaking gibberish, then it would
sound exactly the same as what they are doing in those churches.

One of the interesting things that we have done over the years is to simply ask one of the Pentecostals to speak in tongues. Most of the time they will say that they cannot do it at will but only as the Spirit comes over them. In other words, they say that they do not have *control* of the "gift of tongues," (as if they actually had the gift). This is a convenient way for them to get out of having to give a demonstration and be tested. Also, this is unlike in the New Testament where they did have control over when they would use the gift. In fact, if you think about the guidelines given in First Corinthians chapter fourteen of how "tongues" was to be used in the church assemblies, they were told not to speak when there was no interpreter present, but that they could speak when one was present. In other words, it was up to the Christian who had the gift of tongues, to decide whether to use the gift or not. That is totally different than what you will see today if you visit a modern-day Pentecostal church. Not only do they say they have no control over its use, which we do not believe, but you will see several men speaking at the same time, and you will see men and women speaking when no interpretation is given. This simply causes confusion which goes against the very point being made in First Corinthians chapter fourteen. In the first century, when "speaking in tongues" to other believers in a church assembly, they apparently were giving new revelation in the absence of the written word. By giving it in tongues would guarantee to all who were present that it was from God and not just made up. Is this what is happening today? No, it is not.

Let us make a suggestion. Go visit a modern-day Pentecostal church and when you hear them claim to be "speaking in tongues," use your phone and record the episode. Then ask for an interpretation and if they are willing to give you one, record that as well. Next, take the recording of the speaking in tongues to a different modern-day Pentecostal church, play it to the pastor and ask for an interpretation, but do not let him hear the recording of the interpretation. If he is willing to give an interpretation, you will be surprised to hear something entirely different than what the initial interpretation was. And you will get a different one each additional time you ask some other modern-day Pentecostal to listen to the recording and give an interpretation. That of itself should answer the question of whether modern-day Pentecostal "speaking in tongues" is a real language! They are not real languages. And the interpretations that are sometimes offered are unreal as well.

And then lastly, modern-day "tongues" does not confirm anything at all. And which of the different Pentecostal groups are we to believe has the real tongues, if any? One group is teaching that God is confirming that there are three persons in the Godhead while another group is teaching that God is confirming that there is only one. And what about the charismatic Catholics? What are they confirming? And what are the Mormons confirming with their tongues? Can you see the confusion here? Remember, that the primary purpose of the gift of tongues was to confirm the message of the speaker. (Mark 16:17, 20). When we compare the alleged "tongues" in all of the modern-day Pentecostal groups, they all appear and sound the same. None are any different than the others. They are not real languages and cannot be interpreted. But when we compare them to what happened in the New Testament, we can see the real difference. There, they miraculously spoke real languages that they had not learned, and that is different than what we see today. (See chapter six for additional information.)

13. *Are modern-day Pentecostals speaking in "the tongues of angels"?*

In trying to defend the charge that their tongues are not real languages (as those were in Acts chapter two), Pentecostals often go to 1 Corinthians 13:1, and claim that they are speaking in the "tongues of angels." But, notice the word "though." Paul is obviously using a figure of speech called hyperbole which is when an exaggeration is used in order to make a point. We know this is the case since Paul did not give his body to be burned in verse three. He said *"though* I give my body to be burned" and have not love. *"Though* I understand all mysteries" and have not love. *"Though* I speak with the tongues of Angels" and have not love. He is just using this figure of speech to show the importance of love. In the Bible, when an angel spoke to a man, it was always done in the man's language. So, when modern-day Pentecostals claim that they cannot give an interpretation of their "tongues" because it is the language of angels, they are just looking for an excuse to get out of giving a demonstration which they know will fail, if compared to the Bible. (See chapter six for additional information.)

14. *Are modern-day Pentecostals speaking a heavenly language?*

In an additional attempt to defend the charge that their tongues are not real languages, like in Acts chapter two, they often go to First Corinthians chapter fourteen, and claim that they are speaking in a "heavenly language." Notice these passages:

1 Corinthians 14

> ² For he who speaks in a tongue **does not speak to men but to God**, for no one understands him; however, in the spirit **he speaks mysteries.**

> ²⁸ But if there is no interpreter, let him keep silent in church, and **let him speak to himself and to God.**

Modern-day Pentecostals will use these two passages in an attempt to deflect the accurate charge that their "speaking in tongues" are not real languages and thus cannot be interpreted. They will say that they are "speaking to God" and that He understands. However, this is not exactly what is stated in those passages. We must take them in the context of the entire chapter. The context is talking about speaking in tongues, in the assembly.

Context = in the assembly

- Verse 4—The gift of prophecy edifies the church.

- Verse 5—Tongues edifies the church only when there is an interpretation.

- Verse 12—Spiritual gifts edify the church.

- Verse 19—yet in the church, (a reference to the assembly)

- Verse 23—if the whole church be come together

- Verse 26—when you come together

- Verse 28—in the church

- Verse 30—The effect on someone "who sits by.

- Verse 33—in all the churches

- Verse 34—in the churches

- Verse 35—in the church

Guidelines for speaking in tongues in the assembly:

- Verse 27—Must only be two or at most three speakers.

- Verse 28—If no interpreter is present, he must keep silent.

But what happens when there is no interpreter present to help the audience understand? It is that situation that is under consideration when the passage says that the "tongues" speaker is "not speaking to men" since they cannot understand the message, but rather, he is simply speaking to "himself and to God," rather than to the church. Without an interpreter, he "speaks mysteries" to those other Christians who are present in that assembly. And that is the reason why the "tongue" speakers are told to "keep silent" when no interpreter is present. It is interesting how Paul describes that situation when the "tongue" speaker goes ahead and speaks without an interpreter.

1 Corinthians 14:9

So likewise you, unless you utter by the tongue words easy to understand, how will it be known what is spoken? For **you will be speaking into the air.**

There could not be a better and more accurate description than that. When there is no interpreter, the speaker is simply "speaking into the air" and it is serving no purpose to the hearers. And since we know that modern-day Pentecostals do not understand that the word translated "tongues" in the King James Version of the New Testament meant "languages" back in 1611, then we can understand the problem they are having in trying to make an application of these passages to their modern assemblies. (See chapter six for additional information.)

15. *Did Cornelius, in Acts chapter ten, speak in tongues before he was saved?*

Yes, he did. At the conversion of Cornelius in Acts chapters ten and eleven we see that he was given the gift to speak in tongues before he was saved as a sign to those Christians who were present that the gospel was to be preached to the Gentiles.

Acts 10

44 While Peter was still speaking these words, the Holy Spirit fell upon all those who heard the word.

45 And those of the circumcision who believed were astonished, as many as came with Peter, because the gift of the Holy Spirit had been poured out on the Gentiles also.

46 For they heard them **speak with tongues** and magnify God. Then Peter answered,

47 "Can anyone forbid water, that these should not be baptized who have received the Holy Spirit just as we have?"

48 And he commanded them to be baptized in the name of the Lord.

Acts 11

15 "And **as I began to speak**, the Holy Spirit fell upon them, as upon us at the beginning.

16 Then I remembered the word of the Lord, how He said, 'John indeed baptized with water, but you shall be baptized with the Holy Spirit.' "

¹⁷ If therefore God gave them the same gift as He gave us when we believed on the Lord Jesus Christ, who was I that I could withstand God?

¹⁸ When they heard these things they became silent; and they glorified God, saying, "Then God has also granted to the Gentiles repentance to life.

We are told by Luke, the author of Acts, that Peter gave a chronological account to the church at Jerusalem about what had happened, "Peter explained it to them **in order from the beginning**, saying..." (Acts 11:4). In this chapter, Peter goes on to say, "**As I began to speak**, the Holy Spirit fell upon them..." (Acts 11:15). The Holy Spirit caused Cornelius to speak in tongues at the beginning of Peter's teaching, not at the end. So, we can see that after Peter arrives at the house of Cornelius, he planned on teaching him the gospel. But before he had a chance to do that in any detail, Cornelius began to speak in tongues. This confirmed to Peter and later to the rest of the Christians at Jerusalem that the gospel was not just restricted to the Jews, but was also to be preached to the Gentiles.

Therefore, we can conclude that, in the New Testament, all the saved did not speak in tongues. And here we have in the example of Cornelius, a man speaking in tongues before he is even converted! The unknown "tongues" that we see today in many Pentecostal churches is not the same as in the New Testament. Today, they are not even real languages. They do not confirm anything to unbelievers and they do not give any new revelation to believers. Therefore, they serve no purpose. But what they actually do is to show us how Pentecostals have misunderstood the scriptures. (See chapter nine for additional information.)

16. *When someone received the gift of "speaking in tongues" in the New Testament, could they use it at their discretion, and did they have control over it when they used it?*

Unlike those in modern-day Pentecostal churches today who say that they have no control over when they speak, in the New Testament period they did have control over when they used it.

1 Corinthians 14

> **27** If anyone speaks in a tongue, let there be two or at the most three, each in turn, and let one interpret.

> **28** But if there is no interpreter, **let him keep silent** in church, and let him speak to himself and to God.

It is quite obvious that in order for a Christian to obey those guidelines given in First Corinthians chapter fourteen regarding when they were permitted to speak in tongues and when they were to "keep silent," they had to have control over the use of that gift. In fact, that is precisely what Paul later said.

1 Corinthians 14

> **32** And the spirits of the prophets are subject to the prophets.

> **33** For God is not the author of confusion but of peace, as in all the churches of the saints.

When he said that "the spirits of the prophets are subject to the prophets," that simply meant that the man or woman who had the gift was in control of its use. They decided when to use it and when not to use it. If the man did not have such control, then the resulting confusion that was happening at the church at Corinth was the fault of God. But we know that is not the case and is why we see in verse thirty-three the statement, "For God is not the author of confusion but of peace, as in all the churches of the saints." The person with the gift had control over when to use it and Paul gave guidelines on how that was to be done. Is this what we see in modern-day Pentecostal churches as they profess to speak in tongues? No, it is not. (See chapter six for additional information.)

17. *When modern-day Pentecostals claim to be "speaking in tongues," why are the interpretations given in Old English?*

For the most part, when someone visits a modern-day Pentecostal church, they will hear them give what is claimed to be "speaking in tongues." Most of the time, no attempt at giving an interpretation is made. But in those few cases when one is given, it will invariably be in the Old English style of speaking like in the King James Version of the Bible. That was the style of English spoken in England in the 1600s when that translation was made. Is this done today in an attempt to make it sound like scripture or is this just done out of ignorance? You will see the same thing done when the pastor claims to be giving some alleged revelation from God. They give it in the King James style of English! When God did give new revelation, whether it be in the Old Testament or New, He always gave it in the particular dialect of the man receiving the revelation. Why would God give a man today a new revelation and yet give it in a dialect of English that he does not speak? It would be like if God gave a new revelation to someone who has a Texas accent, yet gives it with a New York accent. It not only would not make sense, but would leave suspicions on the one making the claim. And that is exactly what happens when a modern-day Pentecostal gives an alleged interpretation and it comes in the form of Old English. We can accurately conclude that it did not come from God. (See chapter six for additional information.)

18. *How were the spiritual gifts transmitted in the first century?*

In the first century the spiritual gifts were transmitted through the laying on of apostles' hands.

Acts 6:3–8

> ³ Therefore, brethren, seek out from among you seven men of good reputation, full of the Holy Spirit and wisdom, whom we may appoint over this business;
>
> ⁴ "but we will give ourselves continually to prayer and to the ministry of the word."
>
> ⁵ And the saying pleased the whole multitude. And they chose **Stephen**, a man full of faith and the Holy Spirit, and **Philip**, Prochorus, Nicanor, Timon, Parmenas, and Nicolas, a proselyte from Antioch,
>
> ⁶ whom they set before the apostles; and when they had prayed, **they laid hands on them.**
>
> ⁷ Then the word of God spread, and the number of the disciples multiplied greatly in Jerusalem, and a great many of the priests were obedient to the faith.
>
> ⁸ And **Stephen**, full of faith and power, **did great wonders and signs** among the people.

In Acts 6:8 we see the first case of a non-apostle working a miracle in the book of Acts. Notice though, what happened just prior to Stephen working miracles. The apostles "laid their hands on" him. This was the act of imparting to Stephen, and the other six men, the supernatural spiritual gifts mentioned in First Corinthians chapter twelve.

Notice what happened to Philip, one of the other men mentioned as having the apostles lay their hands on him. Acts 8:5 says that Philip went down to Samaria to preach. Remember that back in Acts 1:8 Jesus told them that they were to first begin the preaching in Jerusalem, then go to Judea, then from there go to Samaria, and from there to the rest of the world. The gospel has now reached Samaria as a result of the efforts of the preacher, Philip. Notice what happened there:

Acts 8:5–8

⁵ Then **Philip** went down to the city of Samaria and preached Christ to them.

⁶ And the multitudes with one accord heeded the things spoken by Philip, **hearing and seeing the miracles which he did**.

⁷ For unclean spirits, crying with a loud voice, came out of many who were possessed; and many who were paralyzed and lame were healed.

⁸ And there was great joy in that city.

Notice how Philip used those miracles to "confirm" the word that he was preaching. Luke says that as a result of "hearing and seeing" those miracles done by Philip, that the people "gave heed" to those things which he said. This is exactly what Jesus said was going to happen back in Mark 16:15-20, that the miracles would be used to confirm the word. Now notice further what happened in Samaria as a result of Philip's preaching:

Acts 8:12–21

¹² But when they believed **Philip** as he preached the things concerning the kingdom of God and the name of Jesus Christ, both men and women were baptized.

¹³ Then Simon himself also believed; and when he was baptized he continued with Philip, and was amazed, seeing the miracles and signs which were done.

¹⁴ Now when the apostles who were at Jerusalem heard that Samaria had received the word of God, they sent Peter and John to them,

¹⁵ who, when they had come down, prayed for them that they might receive the Holy Spirit.

¹⁶ For as yet He had fallen upon none of them. They had only been baptized in the name of the Lord Jesus.

¹⁷ Then **they laid hands on them, and they received the Holy Spirit.**

¹⁸ And when Simon saw that through the laying on of the apostles' hands the Holy Spirit was given, he offered them money,

¹⁹ saying, **"Give me this power also, that anyone on whom I lay hands may receive the Holy Spirit."**

²⁰ But Peter said to him, "Your money perish with you, because you thought that the gift of God could be purchased with money!

²¹ "You have neither part nor portion in **this matter**, for your heart is not right in the sight of God.

When Samaria began to have conversions to Christ as a result of the preaching of Philip, these new disciples did not automatically receive the spiritual gifts that Philip had. Nor could Philip transmit those gifts to the new converts himself. What happened was that the apostles back at Jerusalem sent Peter and John, two apostles, to Samaria. Verses 17 and 18 tell us that it was through the "laying on of apostles' hands" that those new converts received the spiritual gifts. In verse 19 Simon asked for "this power," referring not to the spiritual gifts themselves, but rather, to the power Peter and John had to transmit those gifts to others. Peter replied that Simon did not have "part nor lot in this matter." This referred to the fact that the ability to transmit spiritual gifts was a part of the office and work of an apostle. That was why Peter and John came all the way from Jerusalem to Samaria. Had those disciples been able to receive the spiritual gifts another way, it would have been unnecessary for the apostles to make that journey. Notice these additional examples of an apostle's hands being used.

Acts 19:6

And when **Paul had laid hands on them,** the Holy Spirit came upon them, and they spoke with tongues and prophesied.

2 Timothy 1:6

Therefore I (the Apostle Paul) remind you to stir up **the gift of God** which is in you **through the laying on of my hands**.

It is not revealed to us which of the spiritual gifts Timothy had been given. However, we are told specifically how he received that gift, by the putting on of the Apostle Paul's hands!

There can be no doubt, as the scriptures are very clear, that the spiritual gifts were transmitted by the laying on of an apostle's hands. This stands in stark contrast to the claims made by modern-day Pentecostals. (See chapter five for additional information.)

19. *When a person received one of the gifts from an apostle in the New Testament, could he then in turn transmit it to someone else?*

No, he could not. Notice again the episode concerning Philip the evangelist:

Acts 8:14–15

¹⁴ Now when the apostles who were at Jerusalem heard that Samaria had received the word of God, they sent Peter and John to them,

¹⁵ who, when they had come down, prayed for them that they might receive the Holy Spirit.

¹⁶ For as yet He had fallen upon none of them. They had only been baptized in the name of the Lord Jesus.

¹⁷ Then they laid hands on them, and they received the Holy Spirit.

¹⁸ And when Simon saw that through the laying on of the apostles' hands the Holy Spirit was given, he offered them money,

¹⁹ saying, "Give me this power also, that anyone on whom I lay hands may receive the Holy Spirit."

Notice in this account that when Philip had converted those new Christians in Samaria, the apostles back at Jerusalem sent Peter and John. It was those two apostles who then laid their hands on them and they "received the Holy Spirit." If Philip, who had the apostles lay hands on him back in Acts chapter six, could have then in turn laid his hands on those Samaritan converts, he would have. But he did not do that because he did not have that power. Only the apostles were granted that power. (See chapter five for additional information.)

20. *Could a man with a gift personally and actually work a miracle?*

One of the ways that modern-day Pentecostals try to get out of giving a demonstration is by saying that nobody in the New Testament actually had the power to work a miracle themselves anyway. But notice:

Matthew 10:1

And when He had called His twelve disciples to Him, **He gave them power** over unclean spirits, to cast them out, and to heal all kinds of sickness and all kinds of disease.

Luke 24:49

Behold, I send the Promise of My Father upon you; but tarry in the city of Jerusalem until **you are endued with power** from on high.

Acts 1:8

But **you shall receive power** when the Holy Spirit has come upon you...

Acts 8:6

And the multitudes with one accord heeded the things spoken by Philip, hearing and seeing **the miracles which he did**.

Jesus actually gave the disciples the power to work miracles. That is why it is referred to as a "gift." Once He gave it to them, it was theirs to use as they had been directed. Certainly, it was God who was the actual source of the miracles, and God worked through these men whom He had given this power. They had power to perform miracles, and they used it!

So, if modern-day Pentecostals really had the power to work miracles today like in the New Testament, then when asked for a demonstration, they should be able to simply go to any hospital or cemetery and work a miracle for all to see. But they will not even attempt that since they know that it would fail.

21. *How many apostles were there in the New Testament?*

There originally were twelve.

Matthew 10

² Now the names of **the twelve apostles** are these: first, Simon, who is called Peter, and Andrew his brother; James the son of Zebedee, and John his brother;

³ Philip and Bartholomew; Thomas and Matthew the tax collector; James the son of Alphaeus, and Lebbaeus, whose surname was Thaddaeus;

⁴ Simon the Canaanite, and Judas Iscariot, who also betrayed Him.

After Judas killed himself, a replacement was chosen in Acts 1:

Acts 1

¹⁶ Men and brethren, this Scripture had to be fulfilled, which the Holy Spirit spoke before by the mouth of David concerning **Judas**, who became a guide to those who arrested Jesus;

> [17] "for he was numbered with us and obtained a part in this ministry."
>
> [20] "For it is written in the book of Psalms: 'Let his dwelling place be desolate, And let no one live in it'; and, **'Let another take his office.'** "
>
> [24] And they prayed and said, "You, O Lord, who know the hearts of all, show which of these two you have chosen
>
> [25] "to take part in this ministry and apostleship from which Judas by transgression fell, that he might go to his own place."
>
> [26] And they cast their lots, and the lot fell on **Matthias**. And he was numbered with the eleven apostles.

It says that Matthias was "numbered with the eleven apostles" which brings the total back to twelve again. That means that up to this point there have been a total of thirteen apostles. Next, we see in Acts chapter nine that Jesus appeared to Paul on the road to Damascus to make him "a chosen vessel" (v. 15).

2 Timothy 1:11

> to which I was appointed a preacher, an apostle, and a teacher of the Gentiles.

So, after Paul was appointed to be an apostle to the Gentiles, it brought the total number of men who either were or had been apostles to fourteen.

22. *What were the qualifications to be an apostle in the New Testament?*

We can see what those qualifications were by looking at the episode in Acts chapter one where the replacement for Judas was made.

Acts 1 (KJV)

²¹ Wherefore of these men which have companied with us all the time that the Lord Jesus went in and out among us,

²² Beginning from the baptism of John, unto that same day that he was taken up from us, **must one be ordained to be a witness with us of his resurrection**.

²³ And they appointed two, Joseph called Barsabas, who was surnamed Justus, and Matthias.

When the replacement was chosen for Judas, who had killed himself, Peter said it would have to be someone first, who had been with Jesus during His ministry, and second, one who was a "witness of the resurrection." This meant he had to have seen Jesus alive after He had been crucified. When Paul was chosen to be an apostle to the Gentiles in Acts chapter nine, Jesus appeared to him on the road to Damascus, which made Paul a witness as well. See Acts 26:16, when Jesus spoke to Paul He said, "I have appeared to you for this purpose, to make you a minister and a witness of the things which you have seen…"

23. *Was Barnabas one of the apostles?*

No, he was not. Modern-day Pentecostal groups, in an attempt to validate with scriptures their claim of having miraculous gifts and apostles today, will try to show that there were more apostles than just the twelve. They will point to Acts 14:14 and say that Barnabas was later added as one of the apostles. And that this office continued all the way up to today. They think the case of Barnabas validates their claim of having apostles in our time.

Acts 14:14

Which when the **apostles, Barnabas and Paul**, heard of, they rent their clothes, and ran in among the people, crying out.

Modern-day Pentecostals have misunderstood the use of this Greek word. Though Barnabas was referred to as an "apostle" in the passage above, he did not hold the "office" referred to in Acts 1:20 and 26. Rather he was "sent" which is the basic meaning of the Greek word ἀπόστολος (apostolos, Vine's, p. 63). Barnabas was an apostle of the church because he "was sent" from the church at Antioch. But, he is to be distinguished from those personally chosen and sent by Christ.

The primary usage of "apostle" in the New Testament is in reference to the office of the twelve who were personally "sent" by Jesus Himself to preach to the Jews and of Paul who was also personally "sent" by Jesus Himself to preach to the Gentiles. However, since the word literally means "one sent," it can also have a secondary usage as well. In Acts 11:22 Barnabas was "sent out" by the church eat Jerusalem to go to Antioch. The word for "sent out" in that text is the same as the root word for apostle. In that secondary sense, Barnabas was an apostle. He was an apostle of the Jerusalem church as they sent him out. In that sense only, he was an apostle. He was not an apostle in the primary sense as were James, John, Peter, or Paul. This designation did *not* involve some kind of office for Barnabas as is referred to when a replacement was chosen for Judas in Acts 1;20, "Let another take *his office.*" We see the same thing again in Acts 13:1-3, 14:14 where the brethren at Antioch "sent" Paul and Barnabas on their preaching trip.

There are numerous other passages where the word is used in this secondary sense. Remember though, to be an apostle in the primary sense, referring to those men personally sent by Jesus Himself, certain qualifications were set down because it involved an office. That office involved the transmission of spiritual gifts through the laying on of their hands. Barnabas did not hold that office.

24. *Are there apostles in the primary sense today?*

No, there are not.

1 Corinthians 12

[28] And God has appointed these in the church: **first apostles**, second prophets, third teachers, after that miracles, then gifts of healings, helps, administrations, varieties of tongues.

[29] **Are all apostles?** Are all prophets? Are all teachers? Are all workers of miracles?

[30] Do all have gifts of healings? Do all speak with tongues? Do all interpret?

Also note this passage in Ephesians:

Ephesians 4:11

And He Himself gave **some to be apostles**, some prophets, some evangelists, and some pastors and teachers

Both of the above passages show that only some were apostles even in the New Testament period. And none of those men are still alive today. The office of apostle served its purpose in the establishing of the church, and corresponded to the time when new revelation was being given, resulting in the New Testament scriptures.

25. *What were the "signs of an apostle"?*

2 Corinthians 12:12

Truly **the signs of an apostle** were wrought among you in all patience, in signs, and wonders, and mighty deeds.

Whatever "the signs" referred to, it must have been something unique to the apostles. There only appears to be one thing that fits this category and that is the transmission of the miraculous spiritual gifts through the laying on of the apostles' hands.

Acts 8

¹⁴ Now when the apostles who were at Jerusalem heard that Samaria had received the word of God, they sent **Peter and John** to them,

¹⁵ who, when they had come down, prayed for them that they might receive the Holy Spirit.

¹⁶ For as yet He had fallen upon none of them. They had only been baptized in the name of the Lord Jesus.

¹⁷ **Then they laid hands on them, and they received the Holy Spirit.**

¹⁸ And **when Simon saw that through the laying on of the apostles' hands the Holy Spirit was given,** he offered them money,

¹⁹ saying, "**Give me this power also, that anyone on whom I lay hands may receive the Holy Spirit.**"

²⁰ But Peter said to him, "Your money perish with you, because you thought that the gift of God could be purchased with money!

²¹ "You have neither part nor portion in **this matter**, for your heart is not right in the sight of God.

Not everyone in the early church was an apostle. They had a very important role in the beginning stages of the church.

Ephesians 4

¹¹ And He Himself gave **some to be apostles**, some prophets, some evangelists, and some pastors and teachers,

¹² **for the equipping of the saints** for the work of ministry, for the edifying of the body of Christ

The apostles had a very special role in the beginning of the church, even before any New Testament scriptures had been written. In that time, new revelation was given by the Holy Spirit through miraculous gifts, such gifts as speaking in tongues and prophecy. And the way that a non-apostle would receive those gifts was through the laying on of the apostles' hands. Since this was something that was unique to the apostles, then that very likely is what is referred to as "the signs of an apostle." Regardless of the claims made by modern-day Pentecostals, nobody today is able to perform the "signs of an apostle."

26. *How could a person get a miraculous spiritual gift after the apostles had died?*

He couldn't. In the New Testament record, the only way a non-apostle would receive a miraculous spiritual gift was through the laying on of an apostle's hands (Acts 6:3–8; 8:12–21; 19:6; 2 Timothy 1:6; Romans 1:11). Therefore, after all the apostles died, there would no longer be a way for anyone to receive those spiritual gifts. And in fact, those gifts would have served their purpose and would no longer be needed. Those gifts "passed away" just as Paul had taught.

1 Corinthians 13

> ⁸ Love never fails. But whether there are prophecies, **they will fail**; whether there are tongues, **they will cease**; whether there is knowledge, **it will vanish away**.

> ⁹ For we know in part and we prophesy in part.

> ¹⁰ But when that which is perfect has come, then that which is in part **will be done away**.

Those spiritual gifts were never intended to be a permanent fixture in the church; they were only temporary. The ability to transmit those gifts ended when the last apostle died. But that was also at about the same time as when the New Testament Scriptures were completed, and so those gifts were no longer needed.

27. *The New Testament speaks of "trying" or "testing" men claiming to be apostles but who were not. How was this done?*

2 Corinthians 12:12

> Truly the signs of an apostle were accomplished among you with all perseverance, in signs and wonders and mighty deeds.

1 John 4:1

> Beloved, do not believe every spirit, but **test the spirits**, whether they are of God; because many false prophets have gone out into the world.

Revelation 2:2

> I know your works, your labor, your patience, and that you cannot bear those who are evil. And you have **tested** those who say they are apostles and are not, and have found them liars

In 1 John 4:1, the early church was warned that since "false prophets" were in the world, the church was commanded to "test" them in order to expose them. We then read in Revelation 2:2 that the congregation at Ephesus had done just that and did indeed find some to be false apostles! How might they have tested them? Since the passage in 2 Corinthians 12:12 speaks of "the signs of an apostle" and since the apostles had the unique power to transmit the spiritual gifts through the laying on of their hands, that would have been one way to try a man if there was a question about his apostleship. Paul had clearly demonstrated to the Corinthians that he was an apostle; he had done so by demonstrating that he had the signs of an apostle. Also, one of the miraculous spiritual gifts was the gift of discernment or as it is referred to in 1 Corinthians 12:10, the "discerning of spirits." There is the case of this gift being used in Acts chapter five when Ananias and Sapphira lied to Peter concerning their giving of money. In that case Peter was able to "discern" what was really in their hearts. So, it seems that either of these two features could have been utilized to "try" any man who was claiming to be an apostle when there was a question about his credentials.

28. *How could you "test" a man who claims to be an apostle today?*

1 John 4:1

> Beloved, do not believe every spirit, but **test the spirits**, whether they are of God; because many false prophets have gone out into the world.

A man claiming to be a present-day apostle would be "tested" in the same way that they were in the New Testament period (see question 27 above). Since nobody today has the "gift of discernment" as they did in the first century, then we simply should ask him two questions.

Question 1: Does he meet the qualifications to be an apostle set out in Acts 1:21–22, having seen Jesus alive after His death on the cross?

Question 2: Does he have the power to transmit miraculous spiritual gifts today like was done in the first century through the laying on of his hands?

Paul showed himself to be an apostle of Christ "in signs and wonders and mighty deeds." We would ask the same of any man today who claims to be an apostle of Jesus Christ. Since we know that there are no apostles today, then we also know that any man who makes the claim of being an apostle, would fail when tested.

29. *Would asking a faith healer for a demonstration today be testing God?*

No, it would not be testing God. When asked for a demonstration or proof that Pentecostals have miraculous powers, they often balk and accuse us of testing God. But it is not testing God. It is testing the faith healer! In fact, it would be obeying God when doing such a test since we are commanded to do so.

1 John 4:1

> Beloved, do not believe every spirit, but **test the spirits**, whether they are of God; because many false prophets have gone out into the world.

If a man truly had miraculous spiritual gifts, then he would welcome such a test because it would give him the opportunity to prove his claim. The only one who does not want to be tested is someone who is making a false claim about having those gifts. In the numerous times when we have visited one of those faith healing services and tested a man, the reaction would almost always be the same: anger. They would then point you to someone in their group who would testify that they had seen the healer work some miracle in the past. They would also question you for even asking.

Let me give you a simple illustration of this problem. Let's say that you met a man who claimed that he could fly like superman. When you showed skepticism, would you simply accept the testimony of others who said that they had seen him fly? Of course not. Instead, you would expect him to just stretch out his arms and start flying, if he could indeed fly!

The modern-day Pentecostals will point us to Mark 16:17, "these signs shall follow them that believe" and ask us why these signs are not following us if we are believers. Well, first of all those spiritual gifts ceased according to Paul in First Corinthians chapter thirteen. But also, this question is being asked of the wrong group, for it is not us who are claiming to have those gifts. To modern-day Pentecostals, we ask, "Are those signs following you?" If so, then give us a demonstration! How about we use Mark 16:17-18 for a test. It speaks of casting out demons, speaking in tongues, taking up serpents, drinking poison and healing the sick. Some of our Pentecostal friends might agree to be tested if it involves them casting out demons, speaking in tongues or healing the sick. But when we mention those other two items in that verse, taking up serpents and drinking poison, they quickly will say that "they do not want to test God."

Pentecostals may tell you that...

- Casting out demons is *not* testing God. (Because they claim to be able to do that.)

- Speaking in tongues is *not* testing God. (Because they claim to be able to do that.)

- Healing the sick is *not* testing God. (Because they claim to be able to do that.)

Yet, they will also tell you that...

- Taking up serpents *is* testing God! (Because they refuse to do that.)

- Drinking poison *is* testing God! (Because they refuse to do that.)

These five powers are all in the same passage (Mark 16:17–18). Could it be that the danger is what makes it testing God or not in their minds! If a man or woman today claims to have one of the miraculous spiritual gifts, then they know that the New Testament commands us to test them. So, they should simply use the gift for all to see, if indeed they have it. If they refuse to give a demonstration, then they have failed the test and have proven to us not only that they do not have the gift, but that they are also false teachers.

Please allow us to comment further on the three things above that Pentecostals claim to do.

- Casting out demons is *not* testing God. Before a demon can be cast out, it must first be proven that the person is actually possessed by a demon—which they cannot do! It is interesting to hear Pentecostals talk about what kinds of demons they profess to cast out. We have heard them claim to cast out "alcohol demons, drug demons, lusting demons, and blasphemy demons." That is very different from what is found in Scripture. In the Bible sinful practices were never attributed to demon possession. If they were, then the individual would not be responsible for his sinful conduct.

Furthermore, in Scripture, demons were never seen to blaspheme. Instead, they had the utmost respect and fear toward Jesus. See the case in Mark 5:1-10. It was often the case that demon possession manifested itself in doing harm to the one who was possessed. Jesus and His apostles could cast out real demons. Men today cast out imaginary demons!

- Speaking in tongues is *not* testing God. Once again, they must demonstrate that they can speak actual foreign languages that they have not learned—which they cannot do.

- Healing the sick is *not* testing God. What Pentecostals actually believe on this is that God answers prayer. Most of them do not believe they have the actual power to heal; they cannot do what the apostles of Jesus did. Yet, some people appear to actually benefit from the prayers of the faith healer. How could that be if the faith healer has no power from God? Let us give an example: If a person has a psychosomatic illness—that is, an imagined illness—if they believe the faith healer can heal them, then they might truly be helped. They are helped only because their mind has been changed about their imagined illness. While the physical illness was not real, neither is the healing—because there was nothing wrong with the person's body to begin with. And so, people "are healed" of imaginary illnesses. On the other hand, people who go to the faith healer sometimes imagine that they are healed from real illnesses. We have seen numerous cases of sick people who were convinced in an emotional moment that they were actually healed—only to suffer even more when they came down from their emotional high. People healed from imaginary illnesses, and people who imagine they are healed from real illnesses. Very sad. And in both cases, faith healers make merchandise of them.

30. *Objection: "You are just a sign seeker."*

When we have asked for a demonstration to prove their claims, modern-day Pentecostals many times will respond, that we are no different than those in the first century who wanted Jesus to perform a sign or wonder and they will say that He refused to give a demonstration. Here are the passages that they will offer:

Matthew 12

38 Then some of the scribes and Pharisees answered, saying, "Teacher, we want to see a sign from You.

39 But He answered and said to them, "An evil and adulterous generation **seeks after a sign**, and **no sign will be given** to it **except the sign of the prophet Jonah**.

Matthew 16:4

A wicked and adulterous generation seeks after a sign, and **no sign shall be given** to it **except the sign of the prophet Jonah**.

John 4:48

Then Jesus said to him, "Unless you people see signs and wonders, you will by no means believe.

This is their way of getting out of being put to the test and being exposed. However, these passages cannot be used to defend the fact that they do not want to give a demonstration. In John 4:46–54 Jesus did heal the boy in question! In Matthew 12 Jesus did not say that no sign would be given, but that no sign would be given **except** for the sign of the prophet Jonah! This was a reference to His being raised from the dead! When those Jews asked to see another sign, Jesus in essence was saying that instead of demonstrating a miracle similar to the ones He had been doing, He would do the ultimate miracle. He would allow Himself to be put to death and then come back to life! No Pentecostal would be willing to offer a challenge like that today.

The point is, Jesus did not refuse to give them a sign. He would give them the ultimate sign—that of being raised from the dead. It was that sign that caused so many to believe in Him as the Son of God. What sign will modern Pentecostals give us?

31. *Objection: "Forbid not to speak in tongues."*

We have been accused of violating 1 Corinthians 14:39, "Forbid not to speak in tongues" when we have questioned modern-day Pentecostals. Is this accusation valid? No, it is not.

In this passage Paul is speaking to a church in the first century that did in fact have people with that gift. In that context, they were not to forbid them to speak under the conditions enumerated in 1 Corinthians 14:39. Nobody has that gift today.

But, if someone claims to have the gift of tongues, we are not "forbidding them to speak." On the contrary, we encourage them to give us a demonstration so that we might put them to the test, as we are commanded in 1 John 4:1! If they truly have this gift as is claimed, then they should not be offended when we put them to the test.

32. *Were the guidelines different for how the gift of tongues was used when in the assembly?*

Yes, they were. When the apostles in Acts chapter 2 spoke in tongues on the day of Pentecost, they spoke in the language of those many different travelers who were present that day. There was no need for an interpreter in that case. Why not? Because those present who spoke those languages needed no interpreter; they heard and understood because the apostles were speaking in the native languages of those present—people from many nations. But when the Christians spoke in tongues in one of their assemblies, they would be speaking in languages that were not only "unknown" to the speaker, but were also unknown to the entire audience. That is why those guidelines were given.

1 Corinthians 14

> [27] If anyone speaks in a tongue, **let there be two** or **at the most three**, each **in turn**, and **let one interpret**.

28 But if there is no interpreter, let him keep silent in church, and let him speak to himself and to God.

In the church assemblies the member who was about to speak to the church "in tongues" was not to speak over someone else, but rather to speak "in turn." That assembly was not to have more than three speakers and even then only if there was an interpreter present. We have been to many modern-day Pentecostal churches that claim to have those spiritual gifts in operation, yet they are not following those guidelines. The truth is though, that they are not really "speaking in tongues" anyway but are making sounds that they think are "tongues."

33. *How many "spiritual gifts" are mentioned in the New Testament?*

Lists of miraculous spiritual gifts are mentioned in two different sections:

Mark 16

17 And these signs will follow those who believe: In My name they will (1) cast out demons; they will (2) speak with new tongues;

18 they will (3) take up serpents; and (4) if they drink anything deadly, it will by no means hurt them; they will (5) lay hands on the sick, and they will recover.

1 Corinthians 12:

8 for to one is given (1) the word of wisdom through the Spirit, to another the (2) word of knowledge through the same Spirit,

9 to another (3) faith by the same Spirit, to another gifts of (4) healings by the same Spirit,

10 to another the (5) working of miracles, to another (6) prophecy, to another (7) discerning of spirits, to another different kinds of (8) tongues, to another the (9) interpretation of tongues.

Here are the two lists side by side (**Figure 11**):

Comparison of Lists of Spiritual Gifts in Mark 16:17–18 and 1 Corinthians 12:8–10

Mark 16:17–18	1 Corinthians 12:8–10
1. Cast out demons	1. Word of wisdom
2. Speak in tongues	2. Word of knowledge
3. Take up serpents	3. Faith
4. Can drink poison	4. Healing
5. Healing	5. Miracles
	6. Prophecy
	7. Discernment
	8. Speak in tongues
	9. Interpretation of tongues

Figure 11.

Five spiritual gifts are listed by Jesus in Mark 16 and nine are listed by the Apostle Paul in 1 Corinthians 12. Neither of these lists are meant to be taken as complete, but rather as an example of the type of miracles or "signs" (Mark 16:20) that would be used to "confirm" the word being taught. You might notice that "tongues" and "healings" are in both lists. So, if we total up the gifts mentioned in those two lists there are twelve. However, some Bible students classify "taking up serpents" and "drinking poison" without being hurt as falling under the general classification of "miracles" found in First Corinthians chapter twelve. In any case, we do know that "special miracles," were sometimes done through the apostles. See the case of Paul in Acts 19:11–12.

Whatever the total number of miraculous spiritual gifts might be—and however those gifts might be manifested—no one has those special powers today.

Let us add a couple more comments on this subject. We need to be pragmatic when it comes to the topic of miraculous spiritual gifts. If we have drawn improper conclusions from our study on this topic, there is a very simple way to prove that we are wrong: Just work the miracles. Let the charismatics and Pentecostals actually give a demonstration that they have power from God. Go ahead and perform the same signs that the apostles performed. No one is stopping them. The fact that they cannot perform the same signs and wonders that Jesus and His apostles performed tells us a lot, doesn't it?

When it is clear that the Pentecostals cannot perform the signs, they will still try to prove that they have them. How will they do that? By appealing to the Scriptures. They will try to confirm from the Bible that signs are available today and that they have them. Pay careful attention to what they are trying to do. They are trying to confirm that they have signs by appealing to the Bible message. And they have it backwards in trying to do that. In the book of Acts, the apostles confirmed that their message was true by the signs they performed. Modern Pentecostals try to confirm their signs by the message. Pentecostals appeal to the message to confirm that signs are available. The apostles appealed to the signs to confirm their message. In any case, if anyone today actually has the signs, then they should go ahead and demonstrate them. The signs should speak for themselves.

34. *Does 1 Corinthians 14 give us an idea of what the difference was between the gift of speaking in tongues and the gift of prophecy?*

Yes, it does.

1 Corinthians 14:22

Therefore **tongues** are for a sign, not to those who believe but **to unbelievers**; but **prophesying** is not for unbelievers but **for those who believe.**

This passage tells us that the gift of "tongues" was for the benefit of unbelievers and the gift of "prophecy" was for the benefit of believers. We also know that all of the gifts were for "the equipping of the saints" (Ephesians 4:12) and to help the church become complete (verse 13). It appears that these two gifts mentioned in verse 22 above are very similar. They both involved the giving of new revelation by the Holy Spirit. In regard to "tongues," since the new revelation was for unbelievers, that revelation was given in a language unknown to the speaker in order to confirm the message to those hearers who were unbelievers. But, with "prophecy," since the new revelation was for believers, it was simply given in the speaker's regular language since those hearing understood the language and already knew that the message was coming from God. Again, in both cases it was a message from God, but the messages were to two different groups, either to believers or unbelievers, and that would dictate which gift was needed, tongues or prophecy.

35. *In addition to the "baptism of the Holy Spirit," how many other baptisms are mentioned in the New Testament?*

Hebrews 6

¹ Therefore, leaving the discussion of **the elementary principles** of Christ, let us go on to perfection, not laying again the foundation of repentance from dead works and of faith toward God,

² "Of the **doctrine of baptisms**, and of laying on of hands, and of resurrection of the dead, and of eternal judgment.

In this passage, "the doctrine of *baptisms*" is plural. But notice what was said earlier in verse one. The passage contains teaching to those Hebrew Christians that they needed to leave "the elementary principles of Christ." They needed to "go on to perfection." And they needed to no longer "lay again the foundation of repentance from dead works and of faith toward God."

He ties in the "doctrine of baptisms" to the "elementary principles" that were used in laying the foundation of the faith. He said that they needed to "go on to perfection" or the idea of completion or maturity of the church. So, what were some of these baptisms to which he was referring? Here is a list of some baptisms noted in the New Testament:

1. Baptism of John (Matthew 21:25)

2. Baptism with fire (Matthew 3:11)

3. Baptism of suffering (Matthew 20:22)

4. Baptism into Moses (1 Corinthians 10:2)

5. Baptism for the dead (1 Corinthians 15:29)

6. Baptism of the Holy Spirit (Matthew 3:11)

7. Baptism in water in the name of Christ (Acts 8:38)

The (1) baptism of John was valid only up to the time of the cross. The (2) baptism with fire was simply a reference to judgment using symbolism to describe those who were lost. The (3) baptism of suffering is Jesus using symbolism to refer to the time of His death. The (4) baptism into Moses is referring to the time when the Jews walked through the Red Sea. The (5) baptism of the dead is simply Paul making a rhetorical argument that if there was no resurrection of the dead, then baptism was a futile practice. The (6) baptism of the Holy Spirit is found in only two cases in the Bible record—in Acts chapters two and ten. It never applied to all Christians and was not practiced throughout the first century. And the (7) baptism in water in the name of Christ refers to baptism into Christ, that to which the sinner submits in becoming a Christian (Acts 2:38). So, in the New Testament, the word baptism is used to refer to seven different things. Yet, when the book of Ephesians was later written (around A.D. 60–62), we are told by Paul in chapter four that at that time there was only one baptism.

Ephesians 4

⁴ There is one body, and one Spirit, even as ye are called in one hope of your calling;

⁵ One Lord, one faith, **one baptism,**

⁶ One God and Father of all

The fact that Paul speaks of "one baptism" does not contradict Hebrews 6:2. The solution to this apparent dilemma is simple. When we read in Hebrews 6:1–2 of the plurality of "baptisms" it is referring to the various times and circumstances when these other baptisms applied or were valid. And yet, when the book of Ephesians was written in approximately A.D. 62, almost 30 years after the church was established, Paul tells us that only one baptism was authorized by God and administered by the disciples by that time. And that would have to be the water baptism that all lost sinners must submit to as part of their conversion. Water baptism, the baptism of the Great Commission, which puts us into Christ, was to last till the end of the world (Matthew 28:19–20). The other baptisms, to which Hebrews 6:2 referred, did not last until the end of the world.

36. *Does a man have to have faith in order to receive a miracle?*

No. In fact, the miracles of the New Testament were done in order to produce faith in unbelievers! Yet, in modern-day Pentecostalism, this is something that is often said—that one must have faith in order for God to work a miracle. This is often used as an excuse to explain why attempts at healing or some other miracle did not work. They will say that the person who needed to be healed did not have enough faith and that was why the healing failed. They never say that it was because of a lack of faith on the part of the healer. They will also twist some of the Scriptures in an attempt to prove their point. See the next question.

37. *Was Jesus unable to perform a miracle when someone did not have faith?*

When asked to give a demonstration to prove the claims made by modern-day Pentecostals or to explain why the healings did not happen, they will many times point to Matthew chapter thirteen and say that even Jesus had times when he could not work miracles.

Matthew 13:58

Now He did not do many mighty works there **because of their unbelief.**

They will use this passage as an excuse for their failures. But notice the matching passage in Mark chapter six:

Mark 6:5

Now He could do no mighty work there, **except that** He laid His hands on a few sick people and healed them.

Go back and re-read the passage. It starts by telling us that Jesus had gone back to His "own country."

Mark 6

¹ Then He went out from there and came to **His own country**, and His disciples followed Him.

² And when the Sabbath had come, He began to teach in the synagogue. And many hearing Him were astonished, saying, "Where did this Man get these things? And what wisdom is this which is given to Him, that such **mighty works are performed by His hands!**

³ "**Is this not the carpenter**, the Son of Mary, and brother of James, Joses, Judas, and Simon? And are not His sisters here with us?" And they were offended at Him.

⁴ But Jesus said to them, "A prophet is not without honor except in his own country, among his own relatives, and in his own house.

⁵ **Now He could do no mighty work there, except that He laid His hands on a few sick people and healed them.**

⁶ And **He marveled because of their unbelief**. Then He went about the villages in a circuit, teaching."

Jesus had gone back to where He grew up and, when those people recognized who He was, they questioned how He was able to do those things. But verse two shows that He did indeed work miracles there. And verse six shows that the unbelief of those people could not stop Jesus from working miracles. When it says that "He could do **no mighty work there**, except that He laid His hands on a few sick people and healed them," it simply means that Jesus did not see the large crowds come out to meet him as had been done in the other cities. When the people heard who He was, many did not want to see Him. But, those who did come to Him did receive healing from Him. The unbelief of those others in that city did not prevent Jesus from still working miracles on those who did come to Him. So, this argument made by modern-day Pentecostals is faulty and does not exempt them from giving a demonstration when asked.

38. *Can a Pentecostal person today pick up a serpent or drink poison and not get injured?*

No, they cannot. If they try, they will be severely injured or even killed. But why is that? They are the ones who tell us that they have the same power as the disciples did in the New Testament period.

Mark 16:18

> They shall **take up serpents**; and if they **drink any deadly thing**, it shall not hurt them; they shall lay hands on the sick, and they shall recover.

We have several videos and anybody can watch similar ones online that show modern-day Pentecostals trying to either take up a poisonous snake or trying to drink poison. And in every case, without exception, they receive harm. It is interesting to us that they read this passage to mean that if they take up a snake or drink poison, *and live*, then they have fulfilled what the passage says. But notice that it does not say that when they do one of those things that they may get injured but will survive. Instead, it says that "it will not hurt them." Modern-day Pentecostals cannot take up a serpent or drink poison without seeing the exact same results you and I would have if we were to do it.

39. *Can modern-day Pentecostals move mountains?*

Matthew 17:20

> And Jesus said unto them, Because of your unbelief: for verily I say unto you, If ye have faith as a grain of mustard seed, ye shall **say unto this mountain**, Remove hence to yonder place; and **it shall remove**; and nothing shall be impossible unto you.

No. But, remember that it is the modern-day Pentecostals who are making the claim that they have the same power today to work miracles as they had in the New Testament. Well, if that is true, then we want to see some mountains moved! But we all know that there will not even be an attempt, only claims.

40. *Can modern-day Pentecostals do greater works than Jesus?*

No, they cannot. However, in their attempt to offer scriptural proof that they have miracles today, they will often offer the following passage:

John 14:12

> Most assuredly, I say to you, he who believes in Me, the works that I do he will do also; and **greater works than these he will do**, because I go to My Father.

Modern-day Pentecostals simply do not understand the context of that passage. It is not saying that in the future, disciples will be able to do greater miracles than what Jesus had done. That would not even be possible. How could anyone do a greater miracle than calming the stormy sea or raising the dead? But instead, the passage is referring to the beginning of the church that was only a short period of time away. And with the beginning of the church, those disciples would be teaching the lost what they needed to do to be saved. And that is the "work" that Jesus had in mind when He spoke of "greater works."

It is important to note that no miracle ever saved a soul. In the scriptures we read about miracles that calmed the seas, healed the sick, caused the blind to see, and raised the dead. All of those miracles confirmed the gospel message. But it was the message that saved. Jesus gave his disciples the mission of preaching the gospel to the whole world (Matthew 28:18–20). Proclamation of that message leads to the salvation of countless numbers of souls. That was indeed the "greater work" of which Jesus spoke.

41. *Didn't Paul say that speaking in tongues would continue until Jesus comes back?*

1 Corinthians 13

> [8] Love never fails. But whether there are prophecies, they will fail; whether there are tongues, they will cease; whether there is knowledge, it will vanish away.

> [9] For we know in part and we prophesy in part.

> [10] But when **that which is perfect** has come, then that which is in part will be done away.

Modern-day Pentecostals will refer you to verse 10 and say "that which is perfect" is a reference to Jesus. And, therefore, the meaning of the passage is that those miraculous gifts will be on the earth until Jesus comes back. However, that is not what it says. It says "that" which is perfect, not "he" who is perfect. The Greek word translated "perfect" simply means "complete" or "mature." The sense of the text is about something that is imperfect (or incomplete) now, but is coming to completion. It is referring to the completion of God's revelation through those spiritual gifts in the beginning of the church. And that they would "cease" since they would no longer be needed once the written word was finished or completed.

42. *In 1 Corinthians 12:8 it mentions the gift of "the word of knowledge." Since you are saying that chapter thirteen teaches that the gifts would end, are you saying that "knowledge" will end?*

No. Ordinary knowledge will not end, but the word of knowledge did indeed end. See the passage again:

1 Corinthians 13

[8] Love never fails. But whether there are prophecies, they will fail; whether there are tongues, they will cease; whether there is **knowledge, it will vanish away**.

[9] For **we know in part** and we prophesy in part.

[10] But when that which is perfect has come, then that which is in part will be done away.

This is a reference back to the previous chapter where a longer list was given.

1 Corinthians 12

[4] There are diversities of **gifts**, but the same Spirit.

[5] There are differences of ministries, but the same Lord.

[6] And there are diversities of activities, but it is the same God who works all in all.

[7] But the manifestation of the Spirit is given to each one for the profit of all:

[8] for to one is given the word of wisdom through the Spirit, to another **the word of knowledge** through the same Spirit

The "word of knowledge" was one of the miraculous gifts that had been mentioned in chapter twelve and then in chapter thirteen is mentioned again. And in chapter thirteen it shortens the phrase from "word of knowledge" down to simply "knowledge," but it is the word of knowledge that is under consideration—a spiritual gift. The gift of the "word of knowledge" was a reference to a miraculous "knowledge" that the Holy Spirit was giving to those men as the church was in the process of being established and built up in various cities. So, what is referred to in chapter thirteen as that which would "vanish away" was not the normal type of knowledge that everyone has, but the miraculous gift of "knowledge."

Pentecostals make a serious error when they try to make "knowledge" in 1 Corinthians 13:8 to mean ordinary knowledge (that is, to know anything—the common knowledge that all people to some degree possess). Why is that a serious error? It is because they believe that everything in verse eight will last until the coming of Jesus; but when Jesus comes, these things will be done away. If one holds to that view, then it would mean that when Jesus returns, no one will know anything—all common knowledge will vanish away. The truth is, the word "knowledge" when used in the context of spiritual gifts, means "the word of knowledge." That miraculous spiritual gift, along with all others, ceased when God's revelation was complete.

43. What is the significance of the time reference given in the beginning of the book of Acts?

After many Bible studies over the years with Pentecostals, it seems that one of the reasons for their misunderstanding of who received the baptism of the Holy Spirit in Acts chapter two is related to where the chapter break falls at the end of chapter one (Acts 1:26). Keep in mind that the chapter breaks were not in the original manuscript authored by Luke. Sometimes chapter breaks occur in places that give the appearance of a change in context when in fact there was none. That is the case at the end of Acts chapter one and the beginning of chapter two. When reading through this section, it will become clear as you carefully observe the pronouns, that it is the apostles who are being referred to in Acts chapter two.

Acts 2:4

And **they** were all filled with the Holy Spirit and began to speak with other tongues, as the Spirit gave **them** utterance.

It appears that there is a reason though, why the chapter break (which is credited to the work of Stephen Langton, A.D. 1205) falls where it does. It is likely because of the potential time gap between the casting of lots at the end of chapter one and the day of Pentecost at the beginning of chapter two.

In establishing the correct time-line we must first go back to the end of the book of Luke.

Luke 24

50 And He led them out as far as Bethany, and He lifted up His hands and blessed them.

51 Now it came to pass, while He blessed them, that He was parted from them and carried up into heaven.

52 And they worshiped Him, and returned to Jerusalem with great joy,

53 and were continually in the temple **praising and blessing God**. Amen.

Luke tells us that after Jesus ascended back to heaven, the disciples "returned to Jerusalem" as they had been told by Jesus (Acts 1:2–4). Luke further tells us that when the disciples returned to Jerusalem that they "were continually in the temple." We can then calculate approximately how many days elapsed between Jesus' ascension to Heaven in Acts 1:9 and the outpouring of the Holy Spirit at the beginning of Acts chapter two. It would have been about ten days.

The Passover (Nissan 14, on Friday, though some say Thursday) would at least have been two days before the day of Jesus' Sunday resurrection. The fifty days was figured from the day after the Passover Sabbath. Here is Leviticus 23:15–16…

> And you shall **count** for yourselves **from the day after the Sabbath,** from the day that you brought the sheaf of the wave offering: seven Sabbaths shall be completed. **Count fifty days to the day after the seventh Sabbath**; then you shall offer a new grain offering to the LORD.

The counting was done from a Sunday (the day after the Sabbath) and would also end on a Sunday (the day after the seventh Sabbath). Let's see if we can add up some of the events that took place during this period (**Figure 12**).

Counting the Days from Passover to Pentecost

Days	Description
	Start with the Sunday after the Passover (when Jesus was raised from the dead.)
+ 40 days	The amount of time Jesus was with the apostles from the resurrection to the ascension (Acts 1:3, 12).
+ 10 days	The amount of time from their return to Jerusalem to the day of Pentecost.
= 50 days	The total amount of time from the day after the Passover Sabbath to the day after the seventh Sabbath, Pentecost (Acts 2:1).

Figure 12.

So, depending on how it is counted, there were about ten days that elapsed from the time Jesus ascended back to Heaven and the Day of Pentecost (50 – 40 = 10). It was during those ten days that the disciples were going back and forth to the temple (Luke 24:52–53), waiting to receive what they had been promised, "the power of the Holy Spirit" (Acts 1:8). And it was at the end of the ten days that the outpouring of the Holy Spirit took place in Acts 2:4.

Whether replacing Judas with Matthias happened at the beginning, middle or end of the ten days, we cannot say for certain. Luke had recorded that event in chapter one beginning in verse twelve by saying that the disciples "returned to Jerusalem…they went up into the upper room…in those days Peter stood up in the midst of the disciples." Luke then gives the account of the replacement of Judas. So, it appears that this took place at the beginning of the ten-day period just after they had returned back to Jerusalem. That would then be over a week between Acts chapters one and two.

And so that may be why the chapter break takes place at the end of Acts 1:26, and a new chapter begins with Acts 2:1. Again, the placement of the chapter break has caused confusion to some in leading them to falsely conclude that the 120 received the baptism of the Holy Spirit, when in fact it was just the twelve apostles.

44. *Is it true as several faith healers have claimed that if a man was faithful to God he would never get sick, and that if he does get sick it is because of sin?*

We have heard this claim made several times in modern-day Pentecostal churches. But, the fact is that we all know it is not true. Whether a man is faithful or not, he can become infected with some illness or disease. And faith healers themselves can catch the various diseases such as COVID-19 just like the rest of us. We saw a video online of one of the televangelists making just such a claim and then a few weeks later, him stating that he had just tested positive for Covid. Such a claim was never made by those who lived in the New Testament period.

2 Corinthians 12

> 7 And lest I should be exalted above measure by the abundance of the revelations, **a thorn in the flesh** was given to me, a messenger of Satan to buffet me, lest I be exalted above measure.

⁸ Concerning this thing I pleaded with the Lord three times that it might depart from me.

⁹ And He said to me, "My grace is sufficient for you, for My strength is made perfect in weakness." Therefore most gladly I will rather boast in **my infirmities**, that the power of Christ may rest upon me.

¹⁰ Therefore I take pleasure in **infirmities**, in reproaches, in needs, in persecutions, in distresses, for Christ's sake. For when I am weak, then I am strong.

Though Paul did not tell us what exactly the "thorn in the flesh" was. He did call it an "infirmity." So, the Apostle Paul, who was a faithful man of God, was stricken with some type of physical infirmity.

The doctrine that physical illness is related to a man's sin is addressed in the New Testament. Notice the following:

John 9

¹ Now as Jesus passed by, He saw a man who was blind from birth.

² And His disciples asked Him, saying, "Rabbi, **who sinned, this man or his parents, that he was born blind?**"

³ Jesus answered, "**Neither this man nor his parents sinned**, but that the works of God should be revealed in him.

They asked Jesus if the man's blindness was a result of either his sin or that of his parents. Jesus answered that his illness was related to "neither." So, for a faith healer to claim that he would never get sick again because he does not sin is false in two ways. First, if he catches Covid it is not a result of some sin on his part but the result of him being exposed to someone who had Covid and was contagious. And second, he is claiming that he no longer has any sin. We know that is not true either.

1 John 1

⁸ If we say that we have no sin, we deceive ourselves, and the truth is not in us.

⁹ If we confess our sins, He is faithful and just to forgive us our sins and to cleanse us from all unrighteousness.

¹⁰ If we say that we have not sinned, we make Him a liar, and His word is not in us.

So, this is just another false claim made by modern-day Pentecostals.

45. *Do modern-day Pentecostals claim to be baptized with the Holy Spirit and with fire?*

Yes, they make that claim. They get that language from Matthew chapter 3.

Matthew 3:11

I indeed baptize you with water unto repentance, but He who is coming after me is mightier than I, whose sandals I am not worthy to carry. **He will baptize you with the Holy Spirit** and fire.

They use this passage to teach that Jesus said they would be baptized with two things, (1) with the Holy Spirit and (2) with fire. They then tie this passage with Acts chapter 2:

Acts 2

¹ When the Day of Pentecost had fully come, they were all with one accord in one place.

² And suddenly there came a sound from heaven, as of a rushing mighty wind, and it filled the whole house where they were sitting.

**³ Then there appeared to them divided tongues, as of
fire, and one sat upon each of them.**

⁴ And they were all filled with the Holy Spirit and began to
speak with other tongues, as the Spirit gave them utterance.

But a careful study of these two passages will show that, though
they are definitely related, there is a point in each that modern-day
Pentecostals are missing. First, let us re-read the Matthew 3 passage
in its full context.

Matthew 3

¹ In those days John the Baptist came preaching in the wilderness of Judea,

² and saying, "Repent, for the kingdom of heaven is at hand!"

**⁷ But when he saw many of the Pharisees and Sadducees
coming to his baptism, he said to them, "Brood of vipers!
Who warned you to flee from the wrath to come?**

⁸ "Therefore bear fruits worthy of repentance,

⁹ "and do not think to say to yourselves, 'We have Abraham as
our father.' For I say to you that God is able to raise up children
to Abraham from these stones.

**¹⁰ "And even now the ax is laid to the root of the trees.
Therefore every tree which does not bear good fruit is
cut down and thrown into the fire.**

¹¹ "I indeed baptize you with water unto repentance, but He
who is coming after me is mightier than I, whose sandals I
am not worthy to carry. **He will baptize you with the Holy
Spirit and fire.**

¹² "His winnowing fan is in His hand, and He will thoroughly
clean out His threshing floor, and gather His wheat into the
barn; **but He will burn up the chaff with unquenchable
fire."**

John the Baptist was teaching in the wilderness of Judea. In the crowd around him he saw two distinct groups. There were those who would believe the gospel, and those who would reject it. Some of those who would believe it would later receive the baptism of the Holy Spirit. And some of those present would later be punished by God, "baptized with fire." This is stated three times. First in verse ten, "thrown into the fire." Second in verse eleven, "and fire." And third in verse twelve, "He will burn up the chaff with unquenchable fire." The reference in Acts 2:3, "there appeared to them divided tongues, as of fire," is a reference to the apostles being baptized with the Holy Spirit, but not with them being "baptized with fire" as they were not being punished. The reference to "tongues as of fire" is just a description by Luke as to what it looked like.

So, what our modern-day Pentecostal friends are saying when they claim to be baptized with the Holy Spirit and with fire is not what the passage in Matthew chapter three even means. Surely, they do not want to be "baptized with fire" in the context of John's statement. John's statement is about the fires of judgment, not about some spiritual blessing that would come from God. We have seen people actually pray for the baptism of fire to come upon them, being totally ignorant of what John was talking about.

There is another lesson to be drawn from the words of John the Baptist. It is clear from the text that John was comparing himself to Jesus. John said that he was not worthy to carry Jesus' sandals. Jesus is greater than John. John also made it clear that Jesus was mightier than he was. John said, "He who is coming is mightier than I." John could only baptize with water. The one who was coming had far greater power than John. He could baptize with the Holy Spirit and with fire. John could do no such thing. John is making a contrast between himself and Jesus. John did this so that people would understand the greatness of Jesus.

46. *If Jesus is "the same today, yesterday and forever," doesn't that mean that miraculous spiritual gifts will always be here on earth?*

Hebrews 13:8

> Jesus Christ is the same yesterday, today, and forever.

Their argument is that if Jesus is "the same yesterday, today and forever," and since there were miracles in the Old and New Testaments, then there must also be miracles today. What may have been done in either testament does not really prove anything about what is happening today. In the Old Testament God commanded Noah to build an ark out of gopher wood (Genesis 6:14). Is anyone building an ark today? God commanded animal sacrifices in the Old Testament, but there is no such command today. Just because something was found in the Old Testament does not mean it applies today. The same thing is true with respect to the New Testament. Just because something is found in the New Testament does not mean it applies to us today.

We must always respect the context. Context is your best friend when it comes to studying the Bible. We must ask questions like, "Who is speaking" and "Who is spoken to?" Notice the following:

Acts 1

> **4** And being assembled together with them, **He commanded them not to depart from Jerusalem, but to wait** for the Promise of the Father, "which," He said, "you have heard from Me;
>
> **5** "for John truly baptized with water, but you shall be baptized with the Holy Spirit not many days from now."

Just before He ascended into heaven, Jesus commanded the *apostles* to go back to *Jerusalem* and "wait" for the promised baptism of the Holy Spirit. Are we supposed to go to that city and also "wait?" Of course not. We have to look at the context of those statements and those commands and see who was being spoken to. That text does not apply to us.

The language in Hebrews 13:8 is about the fact that Jesus does not change (as some false teachers might have claimed); Jesus is the same as He was yesterday; He is the same today; He will always be the same. That passage has nothing whatever to do with miraculous spiritual gifts being present today! It does not mean that we will have miracles today.

Pentecostals use Hebrews 13:8 to oppose Paul's teaching in 1 Corinthians 13:8, where the Holy Spirit instructed Paul to say that the miraculous gifts would cease. When they do that, they are committing the error of pitting one scripture against another. By their improper use of Hebrews 13:8, they are trying to say that the gifts will not cease because Jesus never changes. That text has nothing to do with the miraculous gifts. They need a passage that says spiritual gifts will always be here—which is what they are trying to do with the text from Hebrews.

But there is another problem with their view. They try to argue from Hebrews 13:8 that since "spiritual gifts were here yesterday; spiritual gifts are here today." But why stop there, the text says "forever." But that conflicts with their view on First Corinthians chapter thirteen, where they believe the gifts will cease when Jesus comes back. But the gifts cannot cease when Jesus returns and still be "forever." In a debate I (Max) had with a Pentecostal preacher named Billy Stanley, the preacher never brought up Hebrews 13:8 to prove the gifts would continue in our time. Why not? Because he knew the "forever" part of that verse would get him in trouble. A Pentecostal woman in the audience thought he had forgotten Hebrews 13:8, so she made up a sign with that verse on it and stood in the back of the room waving that sign to her preacher. But he never used it; he knew better than to bring it up in debate, though he brought it up all the time in his home church.

Yes, Jesus is the same, but we have been given very specific teaching in the New Testament that those miraculous gifts were only temporary and would "cease" when the revelation was complete. The New Testament said the gifts would cease, and indeed they did. Remarkably, Pentecostals will typically agree with that truth. Nearly all informed Pentecostals will acknowledge that the gifts ceased at about the end of the first century. But they claim that the gifts have now been restored and are available today.

47. Does Satan give false teachers the power to work miracles?

There is no indication in the Bible of that being the case. Miracles were given by God to confirm the word of His teachers of the truth. But, if God also were to allow Satan to use real miracles then that would nullify the confirmation of the truth. For men would not be able to know which teachers were teaching the truth and which were teaching error, because both truth and error would be accompanied with confirming signs. God, through the Holy Spirit, is not confirming error as truth. Instead, He wants to expose the error. Since those false teachers are only using deception rather than real miracles, then through close scrutiny the truth will rise above the error, and it will become apparent which teachers are from God and which are not.

Please note 2 Thessalonians 2:9, as it says, "The coming of the lawless one is according to the working of Satan, with all power, signs, and *lying wonders…*" (NKJV). The English Standard Version (ESV) is worded a bit differently: "The coming of the lawless one is by the activity of Satan with all power and *false signs* and wonders…" As noted earlier, false teachers use deception. They do not have genuine miracles.

48. How do modern-day Pentecostals claims to miracles compare to the New Testament miracles?

We have attended many modern-day Pentecostal church services and encourage each of you to do the same to see for yourself what is really happening there. Are real miracles taking place as they claim? We predict that when the service ends, you will leave right along with those being pushed out in the same wheelchairs that they used when they came in. And while the preacher claimed that miracles were done, you will leave knowing that you actually saw no such thing. However, if you had lived in the first century that would not have been the case. During that time when real miracles were being performed, even the enemies of the gospel admitted that miracles were in fact being done.

John 11

45 Then many of the Jews who had come to Mary, and had seen the things Jesus did, believed in Him.

46 But some of them went away to the Pharisees and told them the things Jesus did.

47 Then the chief priests and the Pharisees gathered a council and said, "**What shall we do? For this Man works many signs.**

Acts 4

14 And seeing the man who had been healed standing with them, **they could say nothing against it**.

15 But when they had commanded them to go aside out of the council, they conferred among themselves,

16 saying, "What shall we do to these men? For, indeed, that **a notable miracle has been done through them** is evident to all who dwell in Jerusalem, and we cannot deny it."

Though many of the Jews rejected Jesus, in the New Testament even the enemies of Jesus and of the church conceded that miracles were really being performed. They could not deny that fact. Sadly, that is not the case today. After having visited numerous modern-day Pentecostal churches and after listening to their claims and carefully watching what is being done, we have not seen a single verifiable miracle. We have heard many of their members claim that they were sick and then healed. But in those cases, nothing was visible to view and verify. And that is different than in the New Testament.

49. *If modern-day Pentecostal churches are not working real miracles, then how do you explain what is happening?*

We have attended many modern-day Pentecostal services and person-ally witnessed what goes on and what is said. We have specifically seen claimed speaking in tongues, claimed casting out demons, claimed discernment, claimed prophecy and claimed healings. But in every single case, we actually saw nothing that is like in the New Testament stories and nothing that was not suspicious.

With regards to the claimed gift of speaking in tongues, what is being done in modern-day Pentecostal churches are not real languages. It cannot be interpreted. In fact, the next time you hear someone speak in their type of "tongues" ask them what language it was and what did they say? They cannot tell you—and no one can tell you—because they are not real languages.

With respect to the claimed gift of casting out demons, what is being done in modern-day Pentecostal churches is not real. We have seen multiple cases where it was done, yet in none of those cases was it like those cases in the New Testament. You saw nothing that would prove to you that their claim was true.

With regards to the claimed gift of healings, what is being done in modern-day Pentecostal churches is different than what you read about in the New Testament. In the Bible, you had people with veri-fiable illnesses where a healing could readily be seen by all. That is not the case today. You have to take the word of the one about to be healed that they really have something wrong with them since it is not visible and then you have to take their word that they have been healed. You do not see missing limbs grown back, sight restored, or the dead raised.

With regards to the claimed gift of discernment, we have seen in many of these modern churches someone give a "discernment" where we knew in fact that it was false. We remember going to a healing service in the Beaumont Civic Center where we took a small group to see the televangelist, Peter Popoff. At one point in the service, he began to claim to be using the gift of discernment to receive from God information about some of the members in the audience. He then walked down the aisle, raised his hand and pointed to one of the members of our group and said, "Brother, the Lord has told me that you are about to do a great work in His kingdom." Little did Popoff know that this "brother" had come to the service to expose him!

With regards to the claimed gift of prophecy, we have seen many attempts to give prophecy in modern-day Pentecostal churches. But it is not the same as in the Bible. What you will always hear today is some vague, broad statement that anyone could easily make and it come true. We heard someone say one time that there were going to be some severe tornadoes in Kansas later that year. But wait a minute. There are tornadoes in Kansas almost every year! Again, what is seen in these modern churches does not match up to the New Testament. Though, both the Old and New Testaments have something to say on this subject that seems to apply very well:

Jeremiah 5

30 An astonishing and horrible thing Has been committed in the land:

31 **The prophets prophesy falsely**, And the priests rule by their own power; And **My people love to have it so**. But what will you do in the end?

2 Thessalonians 2

9 The coming of the lawless one is according to the working of Satan, with all power, signs, and **lying wonders**,

10 and with all unrighteous **deception** among those who perish, because they did not receive the love of the truth, that they might be saved.

11 And for this reason God will send them **strong delusion**, that they should believe the lie,

12 that they all may be condemned who did not believe the truth but **had pleasure in unrighteousness**.

Notice that in describing those "false prophets," Paul said through the Holy Spirit that they were using "lying wonders" and "deception" and that God would allow "strong delusion" to be sent because those people "had pleasure" in it. The members of these modern-day Pentecostal churches are clearly either innocently mistaken, have been deceived or some likely are dishonest. But the verifiable fact is that they do not have any of those real gifts mentioned and used in the New Testament. In no case does what they do "confirm the word" as instructed in Mark 16:20.

50. *Do modern-day Pentecostals have to study?*

Of course they do. If the Pentecostals today want to claim to have the same powers possessed by those in the first century, then they don't have to study to acquire their knowledge. In the first century, during the period before the New Testament was written, they could not study what had not yet been written. This is why there was a need for the spiritual gifts during that period. They received direct revelation from God.

Matthew 10

> ¹⁹ But when they deliver you up, do not worry about how or what you should speak. **For it will be given to you in that hour what you should speak;**
>
> ²⁰ "for it is **not you who speak, but the Spirit of your Father** who speaks in you.

John 14:26

> But the Helper, the Holy Spirit, whom the Father will send in My name, **He will teach you all things, and bring to your remembrance all things that I said to you.**

Luke 21

> ¹⁴ Therefore settle it in your hearts **not to meditate beforehand on what you will answer;**

[15] "for I will give you a mouth and wisdom which all your adversaries will not be able to contradict or resist.

Galatians 1

[11] But I make known to you, brethren, that the gospel which was preached by me is not according to man.

[12] For **I neither received it from man, nor was I taught it**, but it came through the revelation of Jesus Christ.

Can Pentecostals today do as Jesus said? Do they have a miraculous remembrance of all that Jesus taught? Obviously not! They must study just like everyone else.

On one occasion, on our radio program, "Searching the Scriptures," a listener called in to try to refute something we had said on the air. He claimed to have the Holy Spirit speaking to him, just as in the passages above. At one point during his call, he was searching for a particular verse that he thought would prove his point. He could quote part of the verse, but could not remember where it was. I (Max) quoted the rest of the verse to him and told him where it was. He thanked me for that. But then, I asked him, "Why did I have to help you find the verse? If you claim the Holy Spirit is guiding you in a supernatural way, why did He not remind you where the verse was?" The Holy Spirit was not guiding him at all. But maybe the most remarkable thing was that he called the radio program to try to prove to me that I did not have the Holy Spirit guiding me! I had to study in order to know where that verse was. He did not have the Holy Spirit guiding him; and he had not studied enough to know where the verse was.

Pentecostals and Charismatics are just like everyone else. They have to study in order to know God's will. When they don't study, they don't know. The Holy Spirit is not supernaturally guiding them.

15

Noteworthy Pentecostal Encounters

Over the years we have had a practice of visiting as many local Pentecostal churches and healing services as possible. As a result, we have developed a deep and accurate knowledge of what is actually taking place in those services. What will follow is an account of some of the more noteworthy encounters that we have had. It is hoped that after reading the details of these encounters, you will have a better understanding of this very important subject.

Encounter 1 — Call-in to 700 Club

I (Curtis) was watching the *700 Club* one time and they started discussing how "the 120" in Acts chapter one had received the baptism of the Holy Spirit. They also gave out a phone number and encouraged anyone with a question to call in. I could not resist. When I called, I was surprised to hear the assistant host himself, Ben Kinchlow answer. I told him that I had a question for him. The question was:

> "Why are you saying that all of the 120 received the baptism of the Holy Spirit in Acts chapter one? This could not be correct because we know that some of the 120 were not from Galilee. We see in John 11:1 that Mary, Martha and Lazarus were from Bethany and not from Galilee. But Acts 2:7 says that all those who spoke in tongues were from Galilee. Therefore, not all of the 120 received the baptism of the Holy Spirit as you have said."

Mr. Kinchlow responded that he thought it was a good question and he did not know the answer, but that he would have a letter sent to me with the answer. A few weeks later I got that letter. It simply restated what he had said on the phone, that he was "not sure all spoke in tongues." He then said that he hoped that his answer was helpful.

Encounter 2 — Snake Box Story

Though we were not present in this case, we have been able to confirm the following account as accurate. A local preacher from a church of Christ, David Harkrider, had an ongoing discussion with a Pentecostal preacher concerning whether he had the gift of working miracles today. They were specifically discussing Mark chapter 16 where it says that they would "take up of serpents."

Mark 16

> [16] "He who believes and is baptized will be saved; but he who does not believe will be condemned.
>
> [17] And **these signs will follow those who believe**: In My name they will cast out demons; they will speak with new tongues;
>
> [18] **they will take up serpents; and if they drink anything deadly, it will by no means hurt them; they will lay hands on the sick, and they will recover."**
>
> [19] So then, after the Lord had spoken to them, He was received up into heaven, and sat down at the right hand of God.
>
> [20] And they went out and preached everywhere, the Lord working with them and confirming the word through the accompanying signs."

The Pentecostal preacher was challenged to a public debate and he accepted. On the first night of the debate, the preacher from the church of Christ made a point to come in late and had two assistants carry a large box with poles resembling what the Ark of the Covenant had in the Old Testament. The audience could not see what was in the box as it was covered with a cloth. As they entered the auditorium, he asked that everyone remain calm and quiet for the next few minutes as they slowly walked with the box from the back of the auditorium to the front. They then proceeded to the pulpit and carefully and gently set the box next to it. The preacher then repeated the request that all be calm and quiet because what was in the box would prove that the Pentecostal preacher had no such power as he claimed to be able to take up a serpent. As the cloth covering was slowly removed, the audience and the Pentecostal preacher could see that the wooden box had several small openings covered with screen and a small door with a pad lock, but they were unable to see inside. They were also able to see a large label on each side of the box that said, "Miracle Whip." The preacher then began to unlock the door giving the warning again and repeating that what was inside would prove his side of the debate. The audience also began to notice that the Pentecostal preacher was getting very nervous and began sweating profusely. As the box was slowly opened, the preacher from the church of Christ slowly and carefully reached his arm into the box, taking a moment to properly grab its contents. He then slowly pulled out what the audience began to realize was simply his debate notes. He held them up for all to see and exclaimed, "These notes will prove that my opponent does not have the power that he claims!"

Encounter 3 — Gospel Assembly Church National Convention

We had been studying with a Pentecostal group from Port Arthur, Texas and they invited us to a service over in Houston. They assured Max that if we attended that service, he would be permitted to speak to the assembly. So we went, Max, Curtis, and two other men who were preachers from churches of Christ who all had been involved in the previous study. We were under the impression that this was going to be some small church with a special service and that we may or may not be permitted to speak. That was certainly not the case. When we arrived at the location, it was a very large church with a large parking lot. Even though we arrived before the service was supposed to start, the parking lot was full with cars parking on the street. After we parked and walked to the entrance, we immediately realized that this was no ordinary church service. Something was different. The large auditorium which appeared to hold perhaps as many as a couple of thousand people was completely full with standing room only.

Something unusual happened at this point. Max and I (Curtis) were standing next to each other just inside the door and both were wearing suits with a tie. A man who apparently was an usher, mistakenly thought we were two of the guest speakers for the event and he said, "Follow me." He then led us up to the large pulpit area which had chairs set up for approximately twenty people. He pointed to that area and said, "You can sit wherever you want." So, we took two seats just behind the podium and began scoping out the scene trying to figure out where we were. After a few minutes all of the podium area seats were full. At that point, one of the elderly men on the stage got up and walked to the podium as the audience got quiet. They welcomed everyone to what he called the National Convention of the Gospel Assembly Church. Max and I looked at each other in disbelief as to what we had stumbled into. The speaker spoke briefly and said that when they have the yearly convention, it is not set up with any organized format nor are there any assigned speakers. Rather, he said that any man who "is moved by the Holy Spirit to speak" is permitted to do so. Without even looking at Max, I knew that he was about to be "moved" to speak!

As the older man sat down, another man close to the podium went forward and began speaking generally about the church there. When he was finished and sat down, another close by immediately followed him. Even though the introductory speaker had said that there was no planned format for the speakers, it appeared to us that they did in fact have assigned speakers. Every time one would finish, another would quickly get up before Max was able. After about four speakers and about an hour into the service, Max leaned in to me and confidently and quietly said, "I am going next." And he did.

When the speaker finished, Max quickly jumped up and was standing at the podium. I thought within myself that this is going to be exciting, to say the least. After introducing himself, he started his speech with positive thoughts and much thanks for all who were present and for them letting him speak to them. He thanked God for the opportunity, as well. He then began a short talk on how a man is saved according to the Bible as contrasted to what many churches are teaching today. As he proceeded into this talk, I was carefully watching the audience as well as the other men on the stage. It did not take long for what I will describe as "a wave" to go across the group as they began to realize that Max was not teaching what they would normally hear. In fact, it was contradictory to much of what would normally be taught at a Pentecostal church. Max spoke for about twenty minutes and after thanking them again, he returned to his seat. I noticed that three or four of the men who were seated by the elderly man who gave the introduction were huddling together and occasionally looking back over towards Max.

At that point the elderly man approached the podium again and after a long pause, turned to Max and said, "We do not normally discuss doctrine at the convention. But since brother Dawson has done so, I hope he is prepared to answer some questions." My impression was that this was being done in an attempt to intimidate Max. What they did not realize was that Max had been doing a call-in talk radio show five days a week for many years and in that show regularly deals with difficult questions and callers attempting to trip him up. So, this was in no way going to end up the way they thought. In fact, at that point, Max spoke up and loudly said "Brother Dawson would willingly take any such questions from the other speakers or even from the audience." At this point, the elderly man stepped back from the podium and the small group quietly huddled up again. After a few minutes, he returned to the podium a third time and shocked everyone by thanking them for coming and simply dismissed the service. At that point it seemed as though everyone present came forward to speak further with Max.

As I sat on the stage and watched it all end, I thought in my mind that this was no doubt the first time that a preacher from a church of Christ had spoken at their national convention and would probably be the last! And whether Max's opportunity to speak to this large group was him being "moved by the Holy Spirit," you be the judge.

Encounter 4 — The Prophetess

We attended a healing service in Beaumont advertised as having a "Prophetess" present. After arriving, we witnessed a woman dressed in an outfit similar to what a high school student would wear to their graduation ceremony. It had emblazoned on the front the word "Prophetess." After about thirty minutes of introduction telling of the many healings she had done in the past and another thirty minutes of loud music, she began the healings. Several members of the audience went forward to be healed. In none of them were there any visible ailments that could be used to confirm that a real miracle had been done. Rather, all spoke of illnesses and injuries that could not be seen, such as a shoulder problem and a leg problem. Each was pronounced healed. Yet, we could see several members of the audience with visible ailments such as someone in a wheelchair where there was no attempt made to heal them.

At that point Max went forward. He walked down the center aisle, with Bible in hand and directly approached the so-called Prophetess. As surprising as it was, she leaned into him with the microphone and allowed him to speak. Max, with a stern expression on his face looked intently at her as he opened his Bible. He then informed all present that he was reading from 1 Corinthians 14:37, written by the Apostle Paul through the inspiration of the Holy Spirit. He read:

> If any man think himself to be a prophet, or spiritual, let him acknowledge that the things that I write unto you are the commandments of the Lord.

He then asked the woman if she, thinking herself to be a "Prophetess" will acknowledge that the things Paul wrote were "the commandments of the Lord." She responded "Yes, I do." Max then said in the same chapter and just three verses earlier Paul had also written the following:

> Let your women keep silence in the churches: for it is not permitted unto them to speak; but they are commanded to be under obedience, as also saith the law (1 Corinthians 14:34).

The Prophetess, for the first time that night, was speechless! Max calmly walked back to the bench where he had been sitting. The service ended shortly thereafter with numerous attendees gathered around our small group wanting additional information and having questions. We are not aware of the Prophetess ever coming to our area again.

Encounter 5 — Modern-Day Apostle

Several of us attended an event at the Beaumont City Auditorium. It had been advertised on TV as a healing service by a man claiming to be a modern-day apostle. We arrived early, as usual. But it was a rainy day and attendance was very low. We sat in the back and noticed a small group also in the back. As the "apostle" began the service, numerous audience members went forward to receive a healing. In each case we watched very carefully and saw that there was nothing visibly wrong in order to confirm a healing. Instead, it was always something inside like a back pain that they were claiming as a healing. But when a woman in the back started forward, it was obvious that she was limping. When she reached the stage, the healer laid his hands on her and pronounced her leg healed by the power of God. He danced around the stage a bit whooping and singing. He then extended the microphone to the lady he had supposedly just healed and asked her if there was anything she would like to say. She slowly took the microphone in her hand and looked at him intently and said, "It is not my leg, it is my uterus, I have uterus cancer." She turned and limped off the stage as the healer tried to change the subject and talk about something else.

Encounter 6 — Attempted Leprosy Healing

We went to an advertised "healing" service in Vidor, Texas. The advertisement said to bring anyone who was sick and they would receive miraculous healing. Along with us that night was another preacher from the church of Christ, Rick Lanning. Rick had an ailment since childhood that caused large swollen rashes on both of his arms. We were told that it was a modern-day form of leprosy, but that he was able to manage it with medication. Since he was having a flair up at the time, we thought it would be good to have him attend.

Max and I, as was our custom, sat at the front in order to see clearly what was happening and make it easier if the opportunity arose for him to go to the pulpit. Rick sat by himself in the back.

As the healer began the service, he began a short sermon on how, as he taught it, that all illnesses and diseases are a result of man's sin. And that when a man is converted and as he grows in his faith, he will reach a point where he will never get sick again. The healer stated confidently that he had indeed reached that point himself and that he would not ever again be sick. After reading passages about healings in the New Testament, the faith healer asked for anyone who had come to be healed to come forward.

A long line in the center began to form and we noticed that Rick was the last one. All of those in the line, except for Rick, had no visible signs of any ailment but said that they had a problem with internal things such as a back pain, knee pain, etc. After embracing each one who came forward, the healer proclaimed them to be healed. Most would raise their arms in the air with joy as they returned to their seat. Rick was now face-to-face with the healer as he spread his arms out in front of him revealing the large, red, swollen patches with oozing pus.

The healer stared at Rick's arms before touching him. He then took hold of Rick's hands and asked, "What is wrong my son?" It was at that point that Max said, "Be careful! He has leprosy!" At that point a very alarmed demeanor came on the healer's face. He was shocked and scared. Then, in a quiet and soft voice he asked Rick, "Is it contagious?" At that point Max and I, who were seated only a few feet from them, were unable to contain our laughter and it further shocked the healer. He was careful not to touch the rashes on his arms and began to pray, and then pronounced Rick healed. We could readily see that no healing had taken place as his arms were still red and swollen. So, Rick slowly and deliberately turned to the audience and lifted up his arms for all to see and said, "They are not healed, but are still the same." He then turned back to the healer extending his arms towards him and exclaimed for all to hear, "Maybe you need to try again!" The healer appeared confounded and thought for a few seconds before saying, "Let me anoint you with oil." He then went to the back of the stage and returned with a small vial of oil. After rubbing some on Rick's forehead as he prayed, he again pronounced Rick healed. For the second time Rick slowly turned to the audience and held up his arms and said, "They are still not healed." He turned back to the healer and held out his arms one more time. This time he was simply asked to leave, and the healer ended the service. Everyone in attendance seemed shocked at the abrupt ending and many gathered around our small group to ask questions. We are not aware that the healer ever came back to our area again.

Encounter 7 — Professional Boxer Claimed Healing

The following incident took place at my (Max) office at our old church building on Lucas Drive in Beaumont. It involved Billy Stanley (a Pentecostal preacher with whom I had several public discussions and interactions) and a man who said he used to be a professional boxer. As I recall, the man's first name was Louis. Several months prior to this incident, the man had a stroke that left him with a speech impediment and a limp. The man had been a member of a Baptist church on the Southside of Beaumont.

Billy Stanley called in on our radio program and insisted that this man had been healed at his (Billy's) Pentecostal church. This was not uncommon; Billy often tried to prove he had God's power to heal by testifying about incidents that had taken place in his church. Billy gave me a little bit of background about Louis and wanted to bring him to my office as proof of his power to heal. He told me of Louis' background in the Baptist church, and that he had been a member of the South Park Baptist church at the time of his stroke.

To confirm that Louis was actually a stroke victim, I called the pastor of that church and set up an appointment with him. The man was cordial to me and confirmed that Louis was a stroke victim. The stroke had taken place several months earlier, just as Billy had said. The pastor also told me that Louis had been making a normal recovery for a stroke victim. While he was still attending the Baptist church, Louis was able to walk without a cane and was even able to walk up and down the stairs in the Baptist building. The pastor also confirmed that Louis had a speech impediment, with his face slightly drawn to one side.

It is important to know that Billy Stanley claimed a complete healing of Louis' body. Billy said, "Now that Louis was healed, he was attending the Pentecostal church and had left the Baptists." If indeed Louis was completely healed, there should have been no limp and no speech problem.

When Billy Stanley brought Louis to my office, I saw that Louis was in exactly the same condition as the Baptist pastor had described. I told Billy and Louis that I had been to the Baptist pastor and that he told me that Louis was making a normal recovery from his stroke. I explained that he told me of the continuing symptoms that Louis had—the exact same symptoms that he had when he came into my office! There was no miracle. I don't know how Billy Stanley thought he was going to prove anything by bringing this man to me. But that was not the end of the story.

Billy said to me, "Are you trying to deny that this man is a walking miracle?" My reply was that there was no evidence of a miracle in Louis' case. At that point, Louis became angry and agitated. He said, "Are you trying to take away my a-miracle?" Louis spoke as many recovering stroke victims speak. He had a definite impediment and had trouble saying the word "miracle."

I told Louis that I was happy that he was recovering from his stroke. I further explained that I was not trying to take anything away from him. I wished him well, but there was no evidence that anything miraculous had taken place. At that point, Louis said, "If you say that one more time, I am going to knock you through that wall. You can't take away my a-miracle." He was getting more agitated, and it became increasingly difficult for him to speak clearly.

Maybe he could have knocked me through the wall with his good arm. The other arm still showed that he was a recovering stroke victim. I don't know why Billy Stanley thought this man would be a proof of his power from God. Billy had no such power and I told him so. I also told Billy that if he had miraculous power from God, then he could use it on me as Paul did to the man in Acts 13:8-11. If Billy had spoken the word and struck me blind, that would be sufficient to me that he had such power. Billy never attempted that.

Encounter 8 — Richard Roberts Healing Service

We saw an advertisement for a faith healing service in Beaumont, Texas at the Julie Rogers Theater in downtown Beaumont. The "healer" was the famous televangelist, Richard Roberts, son of Oral Roberts. We assembled a small group of six members from our congregation including Larry Berard. Let me tell you about Larry. He had been severely injured in an auto accident years earlier when he was a teenager. That accident left him unable to walk or stand and he had to use a wheelchair. The accident also left him unable to speak well. This will end up being very important as the events unfolded. Larry had in the past volunteered to come with us to these "healing services" in order to test them since he had a visible malady. In this case, we wanted to present the "healer" with a case of someone really being ill or injured as a candidate to be healed. When we arrived, the auditorium, which appeared to seat nearly two thousand, was completely full and there were no seats left. An usher who saw us setting up our camera in the lobby told us that they did not permit anyone but their own team to record the event. I (Curtis) had already informed everyone in our small group that if we were not permitted to record, then we would do so anyway and we would videotape us being escorted out. The usher, seeing us continue to put together the camera (this was back in the '80s and the camera was rather large), simply said, "OK, you can record it if you follow me and stay in the area that I show you." He then led us down a side hall past a number of rooms full of people and through a door at the right of the auditorium, which was near the stage. The usher said that if we stood at the doorway, we should be able to get some good shots of the stage. He was right. In fact, the close proximity that we had to the stage would prove to be very important for us to see and record the events that were about to unfold.

Since it was still a few minutes before the starting time, I accompanied a member of our group who was holding the camera, Phil Cavender, back down the hall and into several of the rooms to see what those people were doing. After a few conversations we realized that those rooms were where the ushers were directing any visitor who had come to be healed, specifically if they were in a wheelchair or in some cases had been brought in on stretchers. We met several people who had brought their family members who were obviously very ill or had been severely injured and who were waiting for the healing part of the service to begin. They had been told that if they would wait in one of those rooms, Roberts would personally minister to them. As an important note, we did not see any evidence of this later happening.

When the service did begin, Richard Roberts gave his standard healing service speech that we had heard before on television. He told of the many healings that had taken place in the preceding weeks and months at other such services. He had several people come forward and give testimonies. He sang several songs. Then he gave a short talk tying the collection to whether someone would receive a healing. He said you had to "give in order to receive." He said you had to "release your faith" and then gave examples of people giving money. After that he took up a collection. Next, in setting the tone for the healing part of the service, Roberts spoke of how each one would have to "have faith" to receive the miracle. And that without such faith on the part of the recipient, no miracle could take place. This appeared to me to be his way of explaining away any healing failures as he would simply say that they did not have enough faith. It would not be his fault but the fault of the person who came forward.

Next, he said that he was receiving information from the Holy Spirit concerning certain ones that were present in the audience that had ailments. He then proceeded to name virtually every body part that there is, such as someone with a shoulder problem, someone with a hip problem, someone with a knee problem and someone who was having a pain in their side. When he was finished, I thought to myself that he essentially had covered every body part that there is! If anyone in the audience had a pain, it did not matter where that pain was, Roberts had just called it out and claimed that the Holy Spirit told him about it. It would be difficult for him to miss with that blanket approach. He then told the audience that if anyone felt that he was speaking of them, that they were to stand up and tell one of the ushers nearby before coming forward to the stage to be healed. We then watched as several audience members who were close by spoke to an usher. In some cases, the usher would tell them to go on up to the stage and in other cases the usher would simply show compassion to them and tell them that prayer will be offered for them but for them to stay in their seat. What was actually happening was those ushers were screening those who stood up to see who might be a good candidate to allow them to go to the stage.

It was during this period that I heard a commotion coming from the right end of the stage. Roberts, after looking over to that area, paused and then said that Satan had gotten hold of someone and that he was ordering the demon to come out. After a period of time the commotion stopped and Roberts continued the service by speaking to a man on the far-left side of the auditorium. As a note, I had switched out with Phil and was now shouldering the somewhat large camera. I was unable to see the man that Roberts was speaking to and so inched my way over to the middle aisle near the front of the auditorium and directly in front of Roberts. As I videotaped this man giving his testimony, I heard a voice come from behind me that I recognized as my wife. She said, "Curtis, come quickly, it is Larry!" She then surprised me by quickly ascending up the steps directly in front of Roberts and ran across the stage to the right side. I followed with the camera on my shoulder and recording as I went. I followed her back past the right end of the stage and into a small room to the rear where I was shocked to see Larry on the floor being assaulted by a man with approximately three others watching. This man, as he hit Larry was saying, "Satan come out of him." I demanded that he stop hitting him and asked why he was doing so and his response was "Oh, I was not hurting him, I was just trying to get the demon to come out of him." At that moment, another man in a suit came over, and seeing that I was holding a camera and recording this episode, he started trying to help Larry up. He later told me that he was the program director. He explained to me that Larry had somehow wheeled himself up on the stage at the right end and since he did not have permission to be there, they had tried to forcibly remove him. In doing so the program director said that his "tie got caught in the wheelchair" and that a sort of tug of war ensued.

At this point it all came together for me. The earlier commotion at the right end of the stage had been Larry and the program director. Roberts had mistakenly concluded when seeing the struggle that someone was demon possessed; and then further thought that when he heard Larry mumbling, being unable to speak well in his condition. Roberts claimed to "cast out the demon" from a man who did not have a demon but who was, in fact, simply disabled. Next, those other men who were following Robert's incorrect diagnosis, very roughly forced Larry into the small room to the rear of the stage where another man took it on himself to further the attempt at casting out what he now thought was a demon. Had I not entered that room with the camera, who knows how it would have ended.

At that point I had my wife wheel Larry out of the building. The only ones left in the room at that point were myself and the man who had told me that he was the program director who said that he had witnessed the whole episode. After explaining to him that Larry had been injured in an auto accident resulting in his disability and that he did not have a demon, I looked sternly into the eyes of the man and demanded to know what was going on. He apologetically said he knew that some things were not done entirely as they should be and offered to help Larry if there was any further need. We left.

Keep in mind that this event was advertised as a "healing service." And yet, Larry was not only *not* healed of his real and visible ailment, but was further injured by the beating, leaving the service with bruises on his arms and face. As an important final note, we still have the entire episode recorded and saved and have watched it many times since then, still in disbelief.

There was another element of that service that I (Max) would like to comment on. I had stationed myself in the hallway on the south side of the Julie Rogers Theater. There were a number of people with serious ailments in that hallway. They were kept out of the main auditorium because their serious ailments were obvious to any observer. Roberts, and other faith healers do not like for people like that to be seen in their gatherings. Why not? Because the question can be raised, "Why are you not trying to heal these people who have observable and obvious ailments?" There is a reason why they do not bring these people up on their stage. A good reason.

Among those that I saw in the hallway was a man on a wheeled stretcher. He was a stroke victim. He was an older man of about 70 years. He could not speak or move his limbs. It was a pitiful heart-rending sight. They had brought him to the venue in an ambulance. I watched as they brought him into the building through a back door. His family wanted to take him into the auditorium. The ushers said that was not possible. They told the family that if they would keep him in this out-of-the-way area that Roberts would pray for him when the event was over. But, why not now? If Roberts had any power from God, this man would have been a prime candidate for healing in the presence of all who were in the auditorium. Why not now? The reason was obvious.

In that same hallway was another person who had an obvious ailment. It was a young boy of about ten years in age. He was in a wheelchair, but it was a reclining wheelchair, almost like a gurney. The boy had no control over his arms or legs. His eyes would not look at you or follow any movements you made. It was a pitiful case. I asked his mother about his ailment. She said the doctors had diagnosed him with a rare form of encephalitis that was caused by a mosquito bite. It left the boy totally incapacitated. The mother further informed me that she believed Richard Roberts had God's power working through him, and that she had brought her son to the event so he could be healed. She was very optimistic and obviously had faith that her boy could and would be healed by Roberts.

She and her son were kept in that same hallway with the man who was a stroke victim. From where we were, we could see the stage where Roberts was, but we were kept out of the view of the audience. The boy's mother wanted to get Roberts' attention, but the ushers prevented her from doing that. She was assured, however, that Roberts would pray for her son after the event was over.

There were several other people in that hallway, and several more in the rooms adjacent to it. They were all kept out of the view of the audience. Once more, the reason was obvious. Roberts had no power whatever from God. He could do nothing for such victims.

Encounter 9 — Snake Handling

We have an old video tape of several modern-day Pentecostal churches in the Kentucky and Tennessee areas. On this video you can watch as several different men take up snakes and drink poison. They believe that they are directed to do so based on a passage in the New Testament.

Mark 16:

> [17] And these signs will follow those who believe: In My name they will cast out demons; they will speak with new tongues;

> [18] **they will take up serpents; and if they drink anything deadly, it will by no means hurt them**; they will lay hands on the sick, and they will recover.

The men in the video point to this passage and are adamant that they are commanded to do those things. In the video, several of the men and women shown have severe injuries from past snake bites received at services, though they had survived. One of those in the interview was later killed from a snake bite. It also shows a man drinking poison. He later died as well.

One of the interesting aspects of this video is the reaction of those other members after the death. They said things like, "God must have decided to take him." But in none of the interviews did any of those members question whether they might be misunderstanding that passage in the book of Mark. Jesus did *not* say that "they will take up serpents" and if they are bitten they will survive. Nor did He say that "if they drink any deadly thing" they may get sick but they will survive. Rather, Jesus said that after doing those things, "it will by no means hurt them." In other words, in the first century when Jesus gave this command, He said that in order to "confirm the word" (verse 20), these two miracles would be done, taking up serpents and drinking poison. And when they did it no harm would come on them. It would be a miracle for all to see and it would confirm their claim to be true, that their message was from God and must be obeyed.

It seems that in modern-day Pentecostal churches, taking up snakes and drinking poison is not something that is common in the vast majority of those churches, but is only found in isolated locations. But this does raise an important question. Why not? They are making the claim that those "signs" and miracles that are recorded in the New Testament are also taking place in their churches today. But we all know that it is not the case. And in those few churches that do take up snakes and drink poison, at a minimum they are severely injured and, in some cases, have died. The fact that it is "hurting" them is different than what Jesus said, "it will by no means hurt them." So we can conclude with these two points: The modern-day Pentecostal churches that refuse to take up serpents and drink poison are dis-obeying Jesus and are showing a lack of faith, since they say those things are for today. And those modern-day Pentecostal churches that are taking up serpents and drinking poison are getting hurt, which obviously proves that those miraculous gifts were only for the new first century church and not for today.

Encounter 10 — Peter Popoff Healing Service

We saw an advertisement of a healing service at the Beaumont Civic Center by the televangelist Peter Popoff. We had watched him on TV many times and knew how his services would usually go. At this particular event, he spent a lot of time talking about making many trips to East Germany while the wall was still up, in order to deliver Bibles to those people. And that was his angle in asking for money that day. He needed money to send more Bibles to Germany. Several times he mentioned that he was using the Ambassador in West Germany to help with his project. He even mentioned how they had become close friends. At the end of the service, one of the members of our group, Jesse Eastep, and in front of many witnesses, told Popoff that his sister lived in West Germany. Jesse simply asked Popoff for the Ambassador's name that he had been using. He quickly changed the subject as it was very apparent that he did not know his name, as that was something that could easily be checked.

At that same service, Popoff came up to me (Max) and declared that I was to be a modern-day prophet, that I would be another David and would accomplish great things for God. Little did he know that on that very day I was exposing him on our radio call-in show for the fraud that he was.

I need to give you a little background on Peter Popoff and how he ran many of his services. People were amazed when they watched him on TV and saw him call out people in his audience, identifying where they lived and the ailments they had. How did he know all of that personal information about the folks in his audience? He claimed it was from the Holy Spirit, that the Spirit of God was miraculously giving him this information as he moved through his audience.

James Randi also wondered how he got this personal data about audience members. A little background on Randi will be helpful here. James Randi was a Canadian-American stage magician, author, and scientific skeptic who has extensively challenged paranormal claims, as well as the claims of faith healers. He was widely known as "The Amazing Randi." He appeared as a guest on the old Johnny Carson Tonight Show a number of times. We had him as a guest via telephone on our radio program in 1986. Randi told me the story of his encounter with Popoff.

He explained that he was watching Popoff's TV program on one occasion, and saw how the faith healer would call out information about audience members. But he also noticed that Popoff appeared to be wearing a hearing aid. Randi told me that he wondered why a man who claimed he could heal everything would have to wear a hearing aid? Maybe it was not a hearing aid? Could it be a radio receiver? That was Randi's question. He was going to investigate. (By the way, there are numerous videos on YouTube where Randi tells the story of his investigation. Just go to youtube.com and type in Randi-Popoff. It will bring up the Carson interviews as well as other videos where Randi exposed the charlatan.)

Randi explained to me that he chose to go to one of Popoff's Miracle Healing Crusades. He did not go inside the venue. Instead, he rented a truck that had all sorts of radio equipment in it; he stayed outside the venue and used the equipment to scan for a nearby radio signal. He got technical assistance from a crime scene analyst and electronics expert, Alexander Jason. With the scanner equipment, Jason was able to demonstrate that Popoff's wife, Elizabeth, was using a radio transmitter to broadcast information that she and her aides had culled from prayer request cards filled out by audience members. Popoff received the transmissions via a receiver and earpiece he was wearing and repeated the information to astonished audience members.

In May of 1986, Randi exposed the charlatan on the Johnny Carson show. The expose hurt Popoff's donations which had exceeded over half a million dollars monthly. In 1987, Popoff declared bankruptcy. Popoff made a comeback in the late 1990s and is still on TV today, running infomercials and promoting "Miracle Spring Water." The promotions depict individuals testifying that the blessed water has brought them financial gains from God.

Encounter 11 — Miracle of Man Who Could See With No Eyeball

One of the most unique cases that we have encountered over the years is the case of Ronald Coyne (pronounced like "coin"). Coyne traveled across the country with his performance for decades. The story is that when he was seven years old, he lost his right eye in a farming accident. His eye had been slashed with bailing wire. While doctors tried to save the eye, all attempts failed. The right eye was then surgically removed and a plastic eye was put in its place. Of course, he could not see from that empty eye socket. The eye was gone.

According to Coyne, at a revival service a couple of years later, God performed a miracle and enabled him to see with that plastic eye! With that testimony, Coyne has traveled across the land "demonstrating" how he can see from an empty eye-socket. An "empty eye-socket," because when Coyne does his performance, he removes the plastic eye!

A church in Bridge City, Texas, not far from where we live, advertised a healing service with Ronald Coyne. The advertisement was in our local newspapers. Several of us from our congregation (including Curtis and me—Max) decided to go to this multi-night event. It was billed as "the man who can see without an eye." While we believed that Coyne's show would be fraudulent, we wondered how he would pull off such a trick. I (Max) spoke to the famous stage magician, James Randi ("The Amazing Randi") and asked him how it was done. He explained that Coyne would cover his good left eye with a folded handkerchief; he would tape the handkerchief down using a lot of adhesive tape. But he would leave just enough space between the handkerchief and the left side of his nose, so he could peek down the left side of his nose and read things that were put in front of him. Magicians call this the "nose-peeker" trick.

I was doing a call-in radio program at that time. I announced that I was going to that service on that evening. When we got to the miracle healing revival that night, Coyne went through the standard spiel on miracles in the Bible, took up the collection (for people to prove their faith), and then went into his act, first removing the plastic eye—leaving an empty right eye socket. I quickly learned that I did not need the help of James Randi to understand how Coyne did his trick. It was apparent to any objective observer that Coyne was peeking down the left side of his nose. How could we tell? First, he had to scrunch up his face in order to widen that gap between the handkerchief and the left side of his nose. If he could see from an empty eye-socket, why did he have to distort his face? Second, he could only read what was placed in that line-of-sight that went down the left side of his nose. If he could see from an empty eye socket, then the things he read should have been placed directly in front of the socket where the eye was missing. Additionally, he should have been able to just "look" around the room and see anything that anyone might hold up in front of him. Third, because the sight from his good left eye was limited by that peek area down the side of his nose, he would read very slowly, and sometimes get only a few words at a time.

People brought him all sorts of things to read: driver's licenses, credit cards, or maybe they would write out part of a Bible verse on a paper.

He read them slowly, but reasonably well as he looked down the left side of his nose with his good eye.

I got in line with something for him to read. I had a note pad with me. When I got to the head of the line, I gave him the note I had written. He began to slowly read. "I…know…how…you…do…your…trick…and…I…" He stopped without reading aloud the rest of my note. When reading slowly, and struggling to see the words, he did not put together the entire sentence before reading it. He did not realize what he was reading until it was too late. The entirety of my note read, "I know how you do your trick, and I am going to expose you on the radio tomorrow."

Coyne was understandably angry with me. Fakers always get angry when they are exposed. He went on to say that if I even mentioned his name on the air, that he would sue me. I told him that I would see him in court. And, indeed, the next day I exposed him as a fraud, explaining to the radio audience how he did his trick.

We went back on the second night of that "Holy Ghost miracle revival." But this time we were not allowed to enter the building. The local pastor of that church had called the police. They would not allow us entrance to the building. That local pastor knew that I had exposed Coyne in front of his congregation. But he went right on with the charade, knowing people were being deceived! His actions convinced me that there was more than one faker in that church building that night. As to Coyne taking me to court, I am still waiting for the summons.

Encounter 12 — Miracle of Growing Longer Legs

After seeing advertisements for a healing service at one of the Pentecostal churches in Nederland Texas, we assembled a small group and went to visit. The healer was not from our area, but the sermon was the same as many we had heard before. After a lot of music and a sermon on healings in the New Testament, he asked for anyone who needed to be healed to come forward. The very first three in line were women. As the first one was asked what her physical problem was, she responded that she was experiencing back pain. The healer smiled and said, "I have seen this many times before and know exactly what it is." He had a chair brought up to the stage and asked her to be seated. He then grabbed both of her feet and asked the audience to look at them. He asked, "Do you all see how her legs are not the same length?" He had in reality simply partially pulled one of her shoes off from her heel a little bit to make it appear that one leg was longer than the other. After praying for her he proclaimed her healed. He then asked her how her back felt and she said that it seemed better.

The next woman in line was asked to come forward and she said that she was having a pain in her hip. After placing her in the chair, the healer again smiled and said, "You also have one leg that is shorter than the other and that is what is causing your pain." He held up her legs as he had done before and attempted to make them appear to be different lengths. Again, after praying for her, he proclaimed her healed and asked how she now felt. She also said that it seemed better.

Next, the third woman was asked to come forward, and yes, you guessed it, she had one leg that was shorter than the other. The same procedure was followed, and another healing was pronounced. In this case we did not have an opportunity to address the audience from the stage as in other cases but, after the event, we did have many discussions with those present. We pointed out how odd it was that so many of those who had come to be healed of various ailments ended up finding out that most of them had the same thing causing the problem, a short leg! Many of them had spoken about how they had been to doctors but did not receive any relief. Yet this healer was able to see the problem and quickly grow that short leg and make it longer!

Encounter 13 — Modern-Day Raising the Dead

There is a story that was related to us by an elderly sister in the church. She claimed to have witnessed the incident in the 1950s. It involved a preacher from the church of Christ who attended a faith healing revival in Port Arthur, Texas. At that service, he challenged the healer asserting that he was a fraud. He questioned before all those present why the healer had not raised any dead people. So, in response, the healer said that he indeed had raised the dead and would do so again for all to see. Another service was announced, but this time it would be in Houston and the claim was made that a dead person would be raised back to life. Upon arriving at the site in Houston, the gospel preacher saw that the building was full and there was a casket in the front with what appeared to be a dead body inside. The preacher had to take a seat in the back of the auditorium. Then, after a long introduction by the healer as to why they were there that day and after reading passages from the Bible of the dead being raised, he said that since there were those in the audience who were "unbelievers," he was going to let everyone present form a line and walk by the casket to see the body before it is brought back to life. Since the preacher from the church of Christ was sitting in the back, he ended up being the very last one in the line. He finally reached the casket and sure enough, there was a body inside. But being suspicious of fraud, he had a plan. Prior to walking up to the front of the auditorium, he borrowed a hat pin from a lady in the audience. He held that hat pin up for all to see and then jabbed it into the arm of the "deceased." It was at that point that modern history was made. It was the preacher from the church of Christ who ended up "raising the dead!" The fraud had been exposed, again.

Encounter 14 — Mormon Apostle with Gift of Discernment

We heard of an event that was going to take place in Vidor, Texas where the local Latter-Day Saints (Mormons) were having a guest speaker, and the general public was invited. The guest speaker was billed as "Apostle Russell Nelson." Since the Mormons are one of the groups that make the claim of having the spiritual gifts active in their church today, we wanted to attend. We took a group of about six who were witnesses to what happened and can verify the accuracy of what we are about to document. Apostle Nelson gave a talk on the LDS leadership and how they not only had all of the spiritual gifts mentioned in First Corinthians chapter twelve, but spent most of his talk discussing the particular "gift of discernment." Notice the following passage where the gifts are listed:

1 Corinthians 12

> [1] Now concerning **spiritual gifts**, brethren, I do not want you to be ignorant:
>
> [4] There are diversities of gifts, but the same Spirit.
>
> [5] There are differences of ministries, but the same Lord.
>
> [6] And there are diversities of activities, but it is the same God who works all in all.
>
> [7] But the manifestation of the Spirit is given to each one for the profit of all:
>
> [8] for to one is given the word of wisdom through the Spirit, to another the word of knowledge through the same Spirit,
>
> [9] to another faith by the same Spirit, to another gifts of healings by the same Spirit,
>
> [10] to another the working of miracles, to another prophecy, to another **discerning of spirits**, to another different kinds of tongues, to another the interpretation of tongues.

Apostle Nelson used for his illustration Acts chapter five and the events that ended with the death of Ananias and his wife, Sapphira. In that story, Ananias lied to the Apostle Peter about whether he and his wife had given all of the money to the church that they had acquired from the sale of some property—or whether they had kept some of that money back. Peter, being full of the power of the Holy Spirit, was able to detect that Ananias was lying to him about the transaction, apparently in an attempt to gain notoriety among the members of the church. Peter specifically accused them of "lying to the Holy Spirit" (verse 3). In that story, both Ananias and his wife were struck dead. Apostle Nelson's point in referencing this story was not that anyone was being struck dead today, but that the LDS leadership, like the New Testament Apostles, had the same gift of discernment today. And just like Peter was able to discern the mind and thoughts of Ananias and Sapphira, so are he and the other Mormon Apostles able to do the same.

When the service ended, a line formed down the center aisle to speak to the Apostle. Since our small group was sitting in the rear of the auditorium, we found ourselves at the end of this line. Along with Mr. Nelson were the local LDS leaders all gathered around listening to him discuss various points and questions from those in the line. I (Curtis) was at the front of our group and so was the first one to arrive in front of Nelson. But, as soon as I stepped forward and before I could say anything, a large smile came on his face and he asked me how I was doing. I responded, "Fine." He then said, "It has been a long time since I have seen you." I quickly detected that he incorrectly thought that I was someone else. And so, I decided to just stay silent in order to see if he would venture out with some information that he thought he knew about me, and he did.

He said, "I haven't seen you since we spoke back at that event several months ago." I kept silent and just stared at him. He raised his hand in the air as if trying to remember where that had been and again asked, "Now in what city was that where we met?" At this point, I had enough and simply responded, "Mr. Nelson, you and I have never met." He said back, "Aren't you a member of the local Ward here." I then informed him that, "No, I am not only not a member here, nor am I even a Mormon." Apostle Nelson seemed very perplexed at that point and looked at those others around him for assistance as to who I was. I then said in a voice loud enough for all around to hear, "Apostle Nelson, it does not appear that your gift of discernment that you have been discussing tonight is working very well!" A stern and agitated look then appeared on his face. At that point our small group was quickly escorted to the exit door nearby.

And that is a good example of how the modern-day Pentecostal "gift of discernment" works. It doesn't! Unlike when Ananias and Sapphira were immediately detected through the gift of discernment when they had given false information to Peter, LDS Apostle Nelson was unable to discern that I was not who he thought I was. I never lied to him like Ananias did to Peter. But he was unable to discern my thoughts as he claimed in his speech. As a note, Mr. Nelson is now (at the time of the writing of this book) the Prophet of their entire organization.

Encounter 15 — Tent Revival Healing Service

We heard an advertisement of a healing service in Beaumont that was billed as a "Tent Revival." We assembled a group of about ten of our church members and planned to attend. Upon arriving at the site that evening, they did in fact have a large tent, in the Beaumont summer heat. As a result, the healer continually had to wipe the sweat off his forehead during the service. He gave a standard "faith healer" type sermon using the miracles of the New Testament as examples of what he said we should see today. However, that was not the case. What we did see was the same as always. We saw people going forward claiming to have various maladies that were not visible but that were internal. Some had back problems. Some had neck problems. Some said they had been to the doctor for various reasons but to no avail. Yet, none had any visible issues that we could actually witness a healing like in the New Testament.

The healer clearly could see in the small audience that many of us in attendance were showing skepticism towards what was taking place. He even stated that, "We have doubters in the audience." Yes, that was certainly the case, and we were vocal in saying that we had not yet seen any real miracles and were still waiting. After about an hour of loud music, and reading Bible passages, the healer decided to end the service. After most had left the tent, I (Curtis) approached him and asked if we could speak further, privately. To my surprise he said, "Yes." He then led me and about three or four others of my group to his mobile home that was parked nearby.

As we entered the front door, he had a table and he and I sat opposite each other in silence for a while. I then simply stated to him that he should be ashamed of what he was doing in deceiving people in order to get a contribution from them. To my surprise, he took on the facial appearance of remorse and said that "Yes, I know that some things may not be right, but I am doing some good." I responded that deceiving people has no good in it and that he would someday have to face God in judgment and give an account of all of this. After a short discussion, he asked us to leave and, to my knowledge, has never come back to our city.

Encounter 16 — Elderly Couple Scammed At Healing Service

Several of us attended a healing revival back in 1985 at the Julie Rogers Theater in Beaumont. I don't recall the faith healer's name, as so many years have passed since then. But his name is unimportant, since there are so many like him. We certainly can't recall the names of all the men we have heard and observed. It can be said that "When you have heard one of these men, you have heard them all." Why is that so? It is because nearly all of them use the same techniques and have the same message.

As was my (Max) custom at such events, I got a seat down in front. In fact, I got a seat on the front row right next to an elderly couple. They were about 70 years old. The man was an amputee. He had lost one of his legs to diabetes. The lady was a stroke victim. She could not walk and had to use a wheelchair. They had come to the service that night expecting a miracle. As I sat there with them prior to the service, they told me their story.

When the service began, there was lots of loud music and shouts of "Praise the Lord." The elderly couple sitting next to me were excited and filled with anticipation. The message was one about miracle healing, and the claim was made that "God's power to heal is present tonight." The people were told to expect miracles.

But first, it was necessary to take up a collection. Ushers came down the aisles of the Julie Rogers Theater with large buckets similar to those that you see at Kentucky Fried Chicken. The faith healer told his audience that their donation would be a proof of their faith in the power of Jesus to heal. (Isn't it strange that when you read about the Lord Jesus healing people in the New Testament that He never took up a collection as proof of someone's faith?) The faith healer was very specific as to how much people should give. He told the audience, "I want everyone here tonight to give at least twenty dollars. If you give less than twenty dollars, I hope the transmission falls out of your car on the way home!" Those were his exact words. I was shocked at such a statement.

The couple sitting next to me wanted to come up with the twenty dollars. The man had only a few dollars in his billfold. The little lady was digging through her purse for change. I think they came up with about seventeen dollars. My heart was breaking for the two of them. They were poor, they were sick, and they were hurting. I told the little lady, "If God is going to heal you, He will do it without your giving your seventeen dollars." I urged her not to give the money, but she did it anyway. My heart hurt for her and her husband even more.

When the healer went into his act, he said things like, "There is someone here tonight who has a back problem. God is healing you right now! If that is you, hold up your hand." There were three or four in the audience who held up their hands. "There is someone in the audience who needs a hip replacement. God is giving you a new hip right now!" Again, a few in the audience claimed they were healed at that moment. The healer even allowed a few of them to come up on the stage. There was one woman who claimed she was healed of her hip problem who put her walker aside and pranced across the stage.

At about that time the healer said, "Aren't we having fun here tonight!" I could not take the deception any longer. I was angry, and I let my anger get the best of me. It was the only time at any of these kinds of services that I acted out of order. When he said, "Aren't we having fun here tonight," I shouted from my seat, "This lady is not having any fun. She has given all of her money to you, and you have not even looked her way!" The fake healer walked over to the edge of the stage, looked at me and said, "You shut your mouth, or I will come down there and shut it for you." I said nothing more. But he still paid no attention to the little lady.

When the service was over, we intended to talk to the healer. But it was an "Elvis has left the building" moment! The healer left the stage while the loud music continued. He was out the back door of the theater and into his black limousine before anyone had a chance to speak to him.

We hung around for a good while as people left the theater. Some of us talked to the little couple at length. They seemed bewildered and disappointed. They had taken a cab to get to the theater, since they owned no automobile. I asked the man, "How are you going to get home?" He replied, "I don't know. We gave all of our cab fare to that preacher. That was our money to get home." I told him not to worry, that we would get them home. While we were happy to give them a ride to their house, I was still angry about how that preacher had exploited the couple.

As some of us were going to our car that was parked across the street, we happened to come upon the woman who had pranced across the stage thinking God had given her a new hip. She was standing on the corner with her daughter as they waited for their ride to pick them up. She was back on her walker. She was crying. She was in terrible pain. She told me, "When I was up on that stage, I believed I was healed. I didn't feel any pain. But now the pain is worse than ever. I don't care if I am not healed. I just want the pain to go away." She sobbed as she spoke those words to me. Another elderly person exploited by a pretender!

When we got our car and drove to the pick-up point outside the theater, we helped the elderly couple get into our car. We drove them home. I explained to them that I had a radio program and that I was going to expose the healer on the air the next day. They gave me permission to use their story; I told them that I would not use their names on the air.

The next day, I told the radio audience what had happened at the Julie Rogers Theater. When I explained that the faith healer never even attempted to heal the little lady, a Pentecostal preacher called in and said that he could heal her! I took his name and phone number (off the air) and then I called the elderly couple. They were willing to have the Pentecostal preacher come to their house and try to perform a miracle. I told them that I did not approve of any of the Pentecostal preachers or their actions. I explained that I did not want anyone to take advantage of them. But the little lady was desperate; she was hurting and incapacitated. She was willing to try anything.

The next day, I met the Pentecostal preacher at their house. Interestingly, he did not ask for any money, like most faith healers do. If he had asked for money, I certainly would have tried to bring the meeting at their house to a halt. I would not let the couple be exploited any further.

I took a small portable cassette recorder with me. The Pentecostal preacher got loud as he prayed over the elderly woman. He spoke in "tongues," though it was only gibberish. He went on for a long time. Finally, he claimed she was healed even though there was no visible change in the lady. I told him that I was going to report his failure on the radio the next day. After he left, I asked the couple a few questions about what had just happened at their house. The elderly lady was happy to answer my questions, but she said, "I am not going to lie for you. I am not going to tell anyone that I am healed when I am not."

I appreciated her honesty, as well as that of her husband. I played the tape on the radio program the next day. To my surprise, the Pentecostal preacher called in again. He admitted that the lady had not been healed, but blamed his failure on me! He said, "God was prevented from working a miracle on the lady because of your unbelief!" He explained that God wanted to work a miracle at that house, and would have worked a miracle if I had only believed. I had heard that same thing from other Pentecostals. It was said that my unbelief prevented God from working a miracle!

I told the Pentecostal preacher that he was ascribing too much power to me. I have no power at all to stop God from working a miracle. It is amazing to see the lengths to which Pentecostals will go to explain their failures. I find it interesting that Pentecostal preachers always preach success in the beginning of their message, but always close with failures. When they see that no one is healed, they will often say, "We are not going to put a time limit on God. He will heal when He is ready." That is one of the ways they deal with their failures. Another way is to put the blame on someone—either the person who needed healing, or on a bystander like me.

Encounter 17 — Muscular Dystrophy Healing

We have a friend named Johnny who was a member of the congregation that we were attending in Beaumont. He knew that we had visited many Pentecostal churches and had many studies with their members. Johnny told me (Curtis) that he had a family member who had just joined a Pentecostal church in the area and he was concerned that she was being taken advantage of. He said that the church was going to have a healing service and asked if I would go with him. I responded that of course I would. I should also point out that Johnny was born with Muscular Dystrophy that had caused him to lose weight and he has much difficulty walking. When we arrived at the building it was rather small with seating for about 100 but with approximately 30-40 in attendance. We sat in the middle and waited for the service to begin. As it started, they played music that was so loud that it actually had many in attendance putting their fingers in their ears to soften the noise, myself included. After a short sermon on New Testament miracles the healer invited any in attendance to come forward and receive their healing. Johnny looked at me for encouragement and we both headed down the center aisle to the front. It was clear to any present that Johnny had a physical ailment that prevented him from walking very well. After arriving at the front, the healer asked him if he believed in Jesus and Johnny responded that he did. After a short prayer the healer placed his hands on Johnny's head and pronounced him healed. I did not see any difference and asked Johnny in front of all in attendance if he would try to walk. He did, but it was very obvious that he was still having difficulty doing so. At this point the healer appeared agitated but placed his hands on Johnny's head again and offered another short prayer. Johnny tried walking again, but with obvious unsteadiness still. At this point I turned to the audience and questioned whether the healer really had any such power, since this was clearly a failure on his part. The faith healer then motioned to a man of large stature in the back dressed in a white suit who appeared to be an usher. This man walked up to the front and told me I would have to leave. I decided at that point to do as Jesus had done on several occasions and simply say nothing. The man then used his large body, without grabbing me, to push me towards the back. Johnny and his wife slowly walked along side as well. This man pushed until we were at the entrance door, and he ordered me, "Don't come back."

THE FAITH HEALER'S SERMON NOTES

After attending many of these modern-day Pentecostal services, we began to notice a common feature. Almost all of the sermons that preceded the healing part of the service, were exactly the same in their approach and content. As a result, we have put together what we re-named as:

The (Fake) Healer's Sermon Notes

   I. Introduction: "You should have seen what happened last week."
- Tell several stories of past healings.

(He is trying to get the audience psyched up in order to believe what they are about to hear, but not see.)

   II. Segment with passages on "faith."
- **A.** All things are possible.
- **B.** Thy faith hath made thee whole.
- **C.** When you release your faith, you will receive a miracle.

(Many of the things he says that he attributes to Bible passages are not there but are just made up. He is covering himself for when it later becomes obvious, again, that people were not healed during the healing session.)

   III. Preparing for the Collection.
- **A.** Give and it shall be given to you.

(This will tie together the giving of money to the receiving of the miracle. The collection must always be taken before the healing session. Otherwise, the amount collected would likely be low.)

   IV. The healing session.
- **A.** The Lord is telling me that He is healing someone right now...
- **B.** There is someone with a back problem.
- **C.** There is someone with a knee problem.

(This is supposed to be the word of knowledge. The healer then names just about every body part that there is, and that someone in the audience has a problem with that body part. You must take a person's word that he or she is sick to begin with, and then take their word again that they have been healed, since you will see no difference in the person being healed.)

When it is over, unfortunately, everyone who came in a wheelchair will leave in one. And the healer will leave with money in his or her pocket.

16

Conclusion

We began the introduction of this book by presenting a dilemma. Modern-day Pentecostal churches make the claim that they have miraculous spiritual gifts today in the same way as in the New Testament. There are other churches that teach that those spiritual gifts were limited in their duration to the first century and to the time when new revelation was being given, resulting in the Bible being written. These churches teach that modern-day Pentecostal churches are not doing the same thing as was done in the first century, but something else. And even among those churches today claiming to have spiritual gifts, such as speaking in tongues, many of them teach conflicting doctrines. And yet, they each teach that their group is the one with the "real" spiritual gifts as contrasted to the others. Who is correct? That is the dilemma we have been discussing in this book. And we have attempted to solve this dilemma in two ways, (1) through an examination of related Bible passages and (2) by presenting what we have actually seen in Pentecostal churches, as eyewitnesses.

An important point to remember is that most of the modern-day Pentecostals do not actually teach that those supernatural spiritual gifts of the New Testament period have been in existence since the first century. Rather they teach that those gifts ended sometime around the end of the first century and were then later restored by God in 1906 at the Azusa Street Revival. So, the Pentecostal "scholars" and historians themselves admit that the gifts ceased at some point. In that regard, they agree with what Paul taught in 1 Corinthians 13:8–10. And, it should go without saying, in that regard they agree with the premise of this book. Virtually everyone acknowledges the truth that the miraculous spiritual gifts ceased at about the end of the first century. What we do not agree with is that the gifts were restored at some later date.

We also saw in a previous chapter that when the Christian Greek historian Eusebius (A.D. 260–339) wrote of those "miraculous events performed *of old*," He spoke of them in the past tense as they were not taking place in his time. So then, the controversy is whether those gifts were truly restored in our modern times. If so, then does that match what is taught in the Bible? And can it be verified through a demonstration? We have clearly shown that the answers to those two questions are "No" and "No." The Bible clearly teaches that those gifts were never intended to be a permanent fixture in the Lord's church, but were only temporary in the beginning stages as new revelation was being given. And if that is not enough, though it should be, then all one needs to do is test modern-day Pentecostals in their claims as we have done many times over the years. Anyone who takes our advice and asks the Pentecostals for a demonstration will quickly see them dodge and evade. In the event that someone actually tries to perform a modern-day miracle, you will see failures 100% of the time, just as we have.

Remember that we have been warned to watch out for "false Prophets" and commanded to "try" those making such claims.

1 John 4:1

> Beloved, believe not every spirit, but **try the spirits** whether they are of God: because many false prophets are gone out into the world

It is important to note, that most Bible students will at first take the Bible and then after studying it make various applications to what they see in life around them. And yet, the modern-day Pentecostals seem to have a similar but backward process. With respect to the question of miracles today and whether they exist or not, most Bible students would simply study to understand what the Bible says and then look at our modern-day society and clearly see that those Bible miracles are not happening today. Modern-day Pentecostals, on the other hand, look at what are clearly questionable and suspicious cases in their assemblies and use those incidents to interpret the Bible. They will use what they claim are true miracles today and then twist Bible passages to make them say what they want in order to fit their cases.

In addition, they will try to confirm from the Bible that signs are available today rather than use signs and miracles to confirm that the Bible revelation is true, which was the purpose of those miracles in Bible times. And they have it backwards in trying to do that. In the New Testament, the apostles used miracles to confirm that their message was really from God. But Pentecostals today, instead, use the Bible to try and confirm that they have miracles. Again, if anyone today actually had the ability to work miracles like in the Bible, then all they need to do is to simply go ahead and demonstrate them. We are pragmatists when it comes to miracles, signs and wonders. By that, we mean that if our study on the topic of spiritual gifts is in error, then it is a simple matter for the Pentecostals to prove that we are in error. Work the miracles and prove we are wrong! The signs should speak for themselves. But such signs do not exist today. Instead of producing the miracles, signs, and wonders the Pentecostals will charge us with "tempting God," or some such thing.

We have all heard it said that "seeing is believing." In other words, anybody can make a claim to have some power. But forgive us if we do not take their word for it, we want to see a demonstration just as the Apostle Paul said that he gave.

1 Corinthians 2:4

> And my speech and my preaching were not with persuasive words of human wisdom, **but in demonstration** of the Spirit and of power.

And that is all that we have been asking for all these years from the Pentecostals. We do not want to hear any more claims, but simply give a "demonstration" as Paul stated that he did.

CONCLUDING QUESTIONS TO BE ANSWERED

Concerning the "gift of healing" (1 Corinthians 12:9):

- When was the last time you saw a Pentecostal healer on the news because he was in the hospital emergency room healing everyone who was brought in?

- When was the last time you saw a Pentecostal healer on the news because they had cancelled the Telethon due to all the kids having been healed?

- When was the last time you saw a Pentecostal healer on the news because he had put up a website saying that you need not go to the doctor, but simply come see him and be healed?

Concerning the "gift of discernment" (1 Corinthians 12:10):

- When was the last time you saw a Pentecostal preacher on the news because he was being used by the local District Attorney's office to determine who was telling the truth in some case?

Concerning the "gift of tongues" (1 Corinthians 12:10):

- When was the last time you saw a Pentecostal preacher on the news because he was demonstrating how he could miraculously speak any language known to man?

Concerning the "gift of interpretation of tongues" (1 Corinthians 12:10):

- When was the last time you saw a Pentecostal preacher on the news because he was demonstrating how he could interpret any language known to man?

Concerning the "gift of prophecy" (1 Corinthians 12:10):

- When was the last time you saw a Pentecostal preacher on the news because he was telling the nation exactly what was about to happen in some important national security event?

Concerning the "gift of miracles" (1 Corinthians 12:10):

- When was the last time you saw a Pentecostal preacher on the news because he was at a cemetery raising the dead?

We all know the answer to these questions, "Never!" We have never seen any of that happen nor will we. Instead, all we "see" are their claims of past such signs and wonders. But we never actually see anything for ourselves. Instead, we have to take someone's word that a miracle has taken place. And this is the case with each one of the different Pentecostal groups. None is any different than the other in this regard.

On the other hand, if any of them were to really have those powers, everyone would know it because they would be using it just as it was used in the New Testament, to confirm the word.

Mark 16:20

> And they went out and preached everywhere, the Lord working with them and **confirming the word through the accompanying signs.**

But the modern-day Pentecostal preachers are not doing that. Instead, they only make claims. None of the claims are ever able to be "confirmed." When it gets down to it you never actually see anything at these Pentecostal services, but rather, must rely on testimonies. There are two words that we believe summarize the problem:

Objective — A person believes something because of the *evidence.*

- After evaluating the evidence, it produces a belief based on that evidence.

MODERN-DAY PENTECOSTALISM

Subjective — A person believes something because of *how they feel.*

- After evaluating the evidence, that evidence is different than how they feel and they hold on to a belief based on their feelings in spite of contradictory evidence.

The bottom line is that these Pentecostals cannot produce what they claim to have—miracles! Yet many of them continue to hold on to something that is nothing less than a make-believe sort of religion. They claim to have something that in reality they do not have and cannot be demonstrated. On our radio program that ran through much of the 1980s, Pentecostals often called in to the broadcast claiming they had miraculous spiritual gifts. But when they were put to the test, they could produce nothing. They have an empty religion that is full of claims but has no power. Many of those radio callers became frustrated and even angry that their preachers could not give an actual demonstration when tested. The Pentecostals made lots of claims but could produce nothing.

In the chapter on False Prophets, we saw that Paul said through the inspiration of the Holy Spirit that they were using "lying wonders" and "deception" and that God would allow "strong delusion" to be sent because those people "had pleasure" in it. The people of these modern-day Pentecostal churches fall into one of two categories. They are clearly either (1) innocently mistaken and have been deceived or (2) are simply dishonest. But the verifiable fact is that they do not have any of those real gifts mentioned and used in the New Testament. In no case does what they do today "confirm the word" as instructed in Mark 16:20. And so, that leaves us with the conclusion that what they are involved in is a "delusion" and, as a result, it could accurately be described as a religion of "make-believe" or "believing will make it so." If God will not give them miracles, they will make some for God as they describe incidents that are not miraculous and call them "miracles." They are claiming to have powers that they know in their heart that they do not have. And they think that if they believe strongly enough and claim to have miracles that somehow God will make it happen! Since they have assumed that this power is available to them in our present day (which it is not), they continue to make their claims hoping that someday something real will happen. Meanwhile, they continue in their delusion.

Since modern-day Pentecostalism is one of the fastest growing religious movements today, it only makes sense that we carefully analyze it to see if its claims are verifiable. If what someone believes to be truth cannot be analyzed and tested, then it is not really truth, but something else. And if those claims are true, then we should all be a part of it. But if those claims are false, then it should be exposed to all. It is our hope that the material presented in this book not only has opened your eyes to what is happening regarding this important topic of modern-day Pentecostalism, but that it also will encourage you to study the topic further. And in that study, we encourage you to visit with someone who is a member of one of the Pentecostal groups. We also encourage you to use the companion Modern-Day Pentecostalism Workbook as a study tool in a Bible class at the church that you attend. May God bless you in your effort.

John 8:32

"And you shall know **the truth**, and **the truth** shall make you free."

www.ingramcontent.com/pod-product-compliance
Lightning Source LLC
Chambersburg PA
CBHW071316090426
42738CB00012B/2709